Emily Dickinson's Approving God

Emily Dickinson's Approving God

Divine Design and the Problem of Suffering

For Carol & Paul,
In fond memory of our time
together in Wordsworth country.

Patrick J. Keane

University of Missouri Press

Columbia and London

Library of Congress Cataloging-in-Publication Data

Keane, Patrick J.
   Emily Dickinson's approving God : divine design and the problem of
suffering / Patrick J. Keane.
        p.   cm.
   Includes bibliographical references and index.
   Summary: "Focusing on Emily Dickinson's poem 'Apparently with no
surprise,' Keane explores the poet's embattled relationship with the deity of her
Calvinist tradition, reflecting on literature and religion, faith and skepticism,
theology and science in light of continuing confrontations between Darwinism
and design, science and literal conceptions of a divine Creator"—Provided by
publisher.
   ISBN 978-0-8262-1808-7 (alk. paper)
   1. Dickinson, Emily, 1830-1886—Criticism and interpretation.   2. Dickinson,
Emily, 1830-1886—Religion.   3. Dickinson, Emily, 1830–1886—Knowledge—
Calvinism.   4. Theology in literature.   5. Belief and doubt in literature.
6. Religion and literature—United States—History—19th century.   7. Science
and literature—United States—History—19th century.   I. Title.
   PS1541.Z5K36 2008
   811'.4—dc22

                                                                    2008020814

Designer: Jennifer Cropp
Typesetter: BookComp, Inc.
Printer and binder: Thomson-Shore, Inc.
Typefaces: Palatino, Cochin, and Aquinas

Contents

Dedicated to Michele Christy
and, in particularly loving memory,
to Kay Farquhar

Though nothing can bring back the hour

Of splendour in the grass, of glory in the flower,

We will grieve not, rather find

Strength in what remains behind;

In the primal sympathy

Which having been must ever be;

In the soothing thoughts that spring

Out of human suffering

The whole truth about Emily Dickinson will elude us always. She seems almost willfully to have seen to that.

—Richard Sewall, *The Life of Emily Dickinson*

God offers to every mind its choice between truth and repose. Take which you please,—you can never have both. Between these, as a pendulum, man oscillates. He in whom the love of repose dominates will accept the first creed, the first philosophy, the first political party he meets,—most likely his father's. He gets rest, commodity, and reputation; but he shuts the door to truth. He in whom the love of truth predominates will keep himself aloof from all moorings, and afloat. He will abstain from dogmatism, and recognize all the opposite negations, between which, as walls, his being is swung. He submits to the inconvenience of suspense and imperfect opinion, but he is a candidate for truth, as the other is not, and respects the highest law of his being.

—Ralph Waldo Emerson, "Intellect"

The question whether the universe and the place human beings have within it owe their origin to blind chance or to a supremely wise and good plan arouses us all.

—Christoph Cardinal Schönborn,
"Reasonable Science, Reasonable Faith"

A god who is all-knowing and all-powerful and who does not even make sure that his creatures understand his intention—could that be a god of goodness? Who allows countless doubts and dubieties to persist, for thousands of years, as though the salvation of mankind were unaffected by them, and who on the other hand holds out the prospect of frightful consequences if any mistake is made as to the nature of the truth? Would he not be a cruel god if he possessed the truth and could behold mankind miserably tormenting itself over the truth?

—Friedrich Nietzsche, *Daybreak*

If we love Flowers, are we not "born again" every day?

—Emily Dickinson, *Letters*

There is no new thing under the sun.

—Ecclesiastes

Acknowledgments

My thanks to the friends, especially Dennis and Sylvia O'Connor and Debbie Hutchison, who responded to my e-mailed request that they say a few words about Emily Dickinson's "Apparently with no surprise."

My friend Ann Ryan's American literature class provided, not for the first time and I hope not for the last, the occasion that became the stimulus to this project. I am grateful for the encouragement and conversation of several friends with whom I discussed these matters in the spring and summer of 2007. They include Dan Dowd, Robert and Vesna Moynihan, Warren and Susan Cheesman, Barron Boyd, Maureen Hanratty, Bruce Shefrin, Tom Parker, and, especially, Roger Lund and the two friends referred to in the Introduction, Jim Cerasoli and Paul Johnston. I am also in Paul's debt for sending me a CD of a fine lecture by Professor Jewel Brooker, "Literature and Theodicy," given in February 2006 at Eckerd College.

My thanks to Annie Smith and Laura Faul for their encouragement, and to Meredith Terretta and Jennifer Gurley, both of whom were subjected to my first awkward draft. However flawed it remains, the book is better because of their comments. I have benefited, too, from the insights of my friend Jonathan Schonsheck, a philosopher with whom I have had discussions and debates for more than a quarter century now, many of them having to do with two of the major subjects of this book: theology and neo-Darwinian evolutionary biology.

Finally, and most important, I am once again in the debt of Helen Vendler and Harold Bloom. On this occasion, the latter's guidance came in a form (in terms central to the Dickinson poem and to the book that follows) apparently "accidental" but serendipitous enough to seem "designed." In the course of a casual phone call, he asked me what I was working on. When I told him that I was, for the second time in the past few years, venturing well beyond my area of expertise, this time not only into the poetry of Emily Dickinson but also into theology and science, Harold said, "Make sure you read the fine book by my former colleague James McIntosh, *Agile Believing*." The memory even of Harold Bloom, famed for eidetic recall, was imperfect; the book is, of course, *Nimble Believing*. In any case, if Harold hadn't directed me to it, my own book would be a much poorer thing.

I am further in debt to Professor McIntosh, who, I only recently discovered, was one of the readers wisely chosen by the University of Missouri Press to evaluate my manuscript. Among many discerning suggestions, the most generous was that I winnow my praise of *Nimble Believing* on the grounds it might make my own book "appear more derivative than in fact it is." Though I occasionally differ with *Nimble Believing*, I have gladly accepted all of its author's recommendations— most reluctantly when it came to the winnowing suggestion.

Helen Vendler read an earlier and inferior version of the manuscript and I was encouraged by her positive response to that effort, especially her empathetic understanding of the *spirit* of the project, conceived less as a scholarly monograph than as a causerie, falling "into that informal category of a mind pursuing an interest in a conversational way." She saw that basing a whole book on a single short poem was only apparently "absurd," this being "only a pretext, as the reader soon perceives." I appreciated *her* appreciation of the range of theological and scientific reference, my casting of a wide contextual net in order to engage other minds struggling with the question confronting Dickinson: "the co-presence of God with unspeakable and unwarranted suffering."

A Note on Dickinson Texts

L (cited parenthetically) refers to *The Letters of Emily Dickinson,* ed. Thomas H. Johnson and Theodora Ward, 3 vols. (Harvard University Press, 1958). The pagination is continuous. In keeping with the general custom, Dickinson's poems are cited throughout (parenthetically) by poem rather than page number. My citations refer to the numbers assigned by Thomas H. Johnson, both in his three-volume *Poems of Emily Dickinson* (Harvard University Press, 1955) and in his one-volume *Complete Poems of Emily Dickinson* (Little, Brown and Company, 1957, and often reprinted).

Most Dickinson scholars now cite *The Poems of Emily Dickinson: Variorum Edition,* ed. R. W. Franklin, 3 vols. (Harvard University Press, 1998). Though Franklin assigns different numbers to the poems, his texts (also available in a one-volume Reader's Edition offering the latest version of each poem) are, for the most part, virtually identical to those in Johnson's edition. Since Johnson's is still the edition most familiar to general readers (the audience I have in mind here) I have stuck with it. But for the convenience of readers who happen to have the Franklin text, I include his numbers along with Johnson's in my Index of First Lines.

Though the annotations differ in the Johnson and Franklin editions, even here, at least for my limited purposes, which text we use makes little difference. That point is illustrated in the discussion, early in Chapter 1, of "I had some things that I called mine" (Johnson 116, Franklin 101), a whimsical garden-frost-God poem that foreshadows my main text, the 1884 "Apparently with no surprise," another poem in which a flower is assaulted by an unseasonable frost apparently sanctioned by "an Approving God."

Emily Dickinson's Approving God

Introduction

A Poem and Its Theological, Scientific, and Political Contexts

Though the United States is an overwhelmingly theistic nation, the debate between faith and skepticism, God and science, is more intense today than at any time since the original impact of Darwinism in the third quarter of the nineteenth century. Even so, contemplating a God-centered poem in the United States in 2007 turned out to have more ramifications than I anticipated.

My initial focus was on a specific Emily Dickinson lyric, the 1884 "Apparently with no surprise"—a poem epitomizing her lifelong wrestling with God and symbolically addressing the theological problem presented by violence and suffering. The interdisciplinary study that eventually emerged, though primarily a work of literary criticism, is also a personal reflection on literature and religion, faith and skepticism, theology and science. Its mixed genre reflects its genesis and evolution. What began with discussions in a classroom and with two old friends became, at first, an attempt to account for contrasting responses to the Dickinson poem by a range of contemporary readers—students and adults. But whatever my initial attention to those responses and, later, to Dickinson scholarship, the present book is essentially my own modest contribution to two much-explored subjects, both involving what the German polymath G. W. Leibniz termed "theodicy." The first has to do with Emily Dickinson's varying perspectives on God; the second, with the overarching question of the role played by God in a natural and human world marked by violence and pain: the great Problem of Suffering.

Why does an all-powerful, all-loving God permit so much unspeakable misery in the world—disease, natural disasters, war? Above all, why does he allow the innocent to suffer? That compelling, ultimately insoluble question has, of course, a long history, with many contradictory answers. Those answers have been orthodox and individual; biblical, philosophic, and literary—in the case of the Book of Job, all of these at once. As a consequence, my approach to Emily Dickinson's poems and letters is both intrinsic (much of the book consists of close reading of specific texts) and comparative, or contextual. Those contexts, mainly literary and theological, are also historical, philosophic, and scientific.

Emily Dickinson's creative life coincided with the momentous changes associated with Darwin and Nietzsche, and her poems and letters reflect Darwinian and other challenges to faith in an increasingly secular age. She rejected many of the tenets of her own faith, not least the doctrine of Original Sin; and she seldom shirked from confronting a God who often seemed indifferent to suffering. Most post-Enlightenment skeptics questioned God's existence. Emily Dickinson asserted in the opening line of a poem that ends in bitterness: "I know that He exists" (338). But if suffering did not preclude God's existence, it *did* raise the question of what *kind* of God he is and how we are to relate to him. Emily Dickinson remained preoccupied throughout her life with the role played in the natural and human world by a supreme being said to be not only omnipotent and omniscient but also all-loving. She had her doubts and was not afraid to express them, at least *privately*—in unpublished poems or in intimate letters. But to question is not to deny. To wrestle with God, even at times to denounce him, is still to have a relationship, however stormy.

Dickinson's ambivalent, often combative relationship with God resulted in "that religion / That doubts as fervently as it believes" (1144). It was precisely this tension—what W. B. Yeats would later term, in his poem of that title, "vacillation"—that generated the dramatic power of the often contradictory poems in which Emily Dickinson engages the divine. Given her Christian heritage, that engagement involved both the Father and the Son: the first in the form of the distant, often capricious, even cruel God of her Calvinist legacy; the second, in the more cherished, incarnate form of the crucified Jesus—suffering, potentially salvific, yet at times himself as remote and unresponsive as the Father.

In the chapter that follows, I discuss Genesis, Job, and Ecclesiastes as well as Shakespeare and Milton. But there is, of course, a more immediate context. In emphasizing Emily Dickinson's place in the nineteenth-century Romantic tradition, I am sometimes interested in direct influence, more often in analogy and mutual illumination. In stressing, for example, a Dickinson-Wordsworth "connection," I am not proposing Wordsworth (as one might Shakespeare or Milton) as a precursor. An isolated and bookish poet, Dickinson was not, except when it came to Scripture, an allusive one, and her direct references to and echoes of other poets, including Wordsworth, are few. Her subjects (nature and the imagination, death and immortality, innocence and experience) and themes (transience and the yearning for the infinite, loss and compensation, experience transformed by consciousness) locate her in the great Romantic tradition. Yet she only rarely refers in her letters to Keats and Wordsworth, and never to the other major British Romantics. Absence of evidence, however, is not evidence of absence. She is, as Harold Bloom has remarked, "recognizably a post-Wordsworthian poet," though, as with Emerson and Thoreau, Whitman and Melville, there is what Bloom calls "the American difference." In addition, Emily Dickinson was a woman and nothing if not an individual. Indeed, her very individualism and gender, one critic has argued, differentiated and often alienated her from the male British Romantics, making her interaction with them "necessarily subversive."[1]

Still, Dickinson's imagination *was* dialogic and transatlantic. "For Poets," she wrote T. W. Higginson in April 1862, "I have Keats—and Mr. and Mrs. Browning" (*L* 404). While a number of her poems interact directly with Elizabeth Barrett Browning's verse novel *Aurora Leigh*, Dickinson's response to Wordsworth, to whose poetry she was introduced by Benjamin Franklin Newton (*L* 282), may have been filtered in part through Keats as well as through American writers of the preceding generation directly and powerfully influenced by him. The fact remains that in Dickinson's as well as Emerson's America, Wordsworth was part of the transatlantic conversation; unsurprisingly, the four-volume Longman edition of his *Poetical Works* (1832) was in the Dickinson family library. He was a pervasive poetic and

---

1. Bloom, *Genius: A Mosaic of One Hundred Exemplary Creative Minds*, 345; Joanne Feit Diehl, *Dickinson and the Romantic Imagination*.

even *religious* presence; Elizabeth Barrett's description, in an 1842 sonnet, of Wordsworth taking "his rightful place as *poet-priest*" was by then a commonplace. His poems about nature and a divine or quasi-divine "presence"—"Tintern Abbey" and the Intimations Ode as well as parts of *The Prelude,* the "Prospectus" to *The Recluse,* and, on a religiously more orthodox level, *The Excursion*—made Wordsworth, in M. H. Abrams's word, a poetic "evangelist" to many American writers. It was on the basis of such poems that he emerged, philosopher Charles Taylor has recently observed, as "the paradigm poet for so many in the nineteenth century, across an ontological spectrum ranging from orthodox Christians to atheists."[2]

In addition to engaging Emily Dickinson's century, the book I have written begins and ends by reflecting its own moment: spring through autumn 2007. This was the immediate context—a time of increasingly angry theological and political debate in America—in which I was reading Dickinson's poems and letters on God, with my own writing essentially completed in November. Since it affected that reading, beginning with "Apparently with no surprise," this contemporary context—theological, scientific, political, and personal—should be fleshed out.

During March and April 2007, I visited with two friends of long standing. Aside from intellectual curiosity, they have nothing in common; or at least hadn't, until also visited by that indiscriminate democrat, cancer. With the first, Jim, a friend since Catholic elementary school, I had a conversation that was part of a continuing discussion that now stretches back more than half a century. "Does God exist and, if so, does he care?" It began, melodramatically enough, one stormy evening, when we were fourteen and walking through a wooded area in a then rural section of the Bronx. When I expressed religious doubts, Jim pointed toward a tree shaking in the wind. "Tell that tree you don't believe in God," he challenged. I found I couldn't. Now that we are

---

2. Abrams, *Natural Supernaturalism: Tradition and Revolution in Romantic Literature,* 134–40. The future Mrs. Browning's "On Mr. Haydon's Portrait of Mr. Wordsworth on Helvellyn" responds to B. R. Haydon's famous 1842 oil painting. Taylor, *A Secular Age,* 607. Though he rightly recognizes the centrality of Wordsworth, Taylor, a committed Catholic, most ardently identifies with Gerard Manley Hopkins, the poetic hero of his final chapter, significantly titled "Conversions."

both retired, and have both had bouts with cancer (his far more serious than mine), we still discuss the old question.

This time, the discussion included a number of current articles and a handful of recent much debated books by the so-called neo-atheists: Sam Harris, Richard Dawkins, Daniel C. Dennett, and Victor J. Stenger (Christopher Hitchens would weigh in the following month). We also found ourselves responding to the chapter "Einstein's God" in Walter Isaacson's new biography, *Einstein: His Life and Universe*. It was in the course of this conversation that I quoted "Apparently with no surprise," in which the beheading of a "happy Flower" by an unseasonable Frost, a "blonde Assassin," is overseen and sanctioned by "an Approving God." My friend's response reflected his religious position, and something of mine. By way of full disclosure, I should say that we have both "evolved" (if not progressed) from the Catholicism of our boyhood. I have become an agnostic. Jim, professionally an engineer, is really a scientist, conversant with the workings of quantum mechanics but also interested in biblical scholarship, The result is that he is, and has been for some time, an atheist: a conviction unaffected by the fact that he knows, though he is presently doing well, that he is dying of an incurable form of cancer, multiple myeloma.

The second friend with whom I had conversations in the spring of 2007 has also had a recent encounter with cancer. I met Paul in graduate school, and we have stayed in touch, exchanging visits over the past quarter century. While I was visiting him and his wife in March, he directed my attention to an article in the Catholic theoconservative publication *First Things*. It was by Christoph Cardinal Schönborn, general editor of the new Catholic *Catechism* and a prominent Church spokesman on issues involving creation, evolution, and design. I was aware of Schönborn as a result of an op-ed he had published in the *New York Times* in 2005: a piece that stirred so much controversy that I had been following some of his subsequent pronouncements, of which this essay seemed the most important.[3] Since I devote parts of two chapters to the commentaries of Cardinal Schönborn, I should explain

---

3. The essay is titled "Reasonable Science, Reasonable Faith." A related and supportive piece, "God and Evolution," by Avery Cardinal Dulles, appeared in the October 2007 issue of *First Things*. Schönborn's op-ed and subsequent lectures are incorporated and expanded on in his *Chance or Purpose: Creation, Evolution, and a Rational Faith*.

why, and just what the issues he engages have to do with Emily Dickinson's poem about Nature and God, and with an audience, especially an American audience, reading such a poem in 2007.

The immediate context of the cardinal's July 7, 2005, op-ed was the controversy over the teaching of Intelligent Design, with school boards, notably in Kansas and Pennsylvania, besieged by demands to present the "controversy," to "teach the debate." Under the public-relations cloak of fair and balanced presentation, this was an attempt by the Discovery Institute and other Christian fundamentalists to discourage, both in the classroom and in textbooks, the teaching of evolution. Five months after the cardinal's op-ed, the anti-Darwinian tide was temporarily but powerfully turned back by the judge's decision in a widely reported case involving the Dover, Pennsylvania, school board. Insisting that instructors read to their classes a statement asserting that Darwinian evolution was an inconclusive "theory, not a fact," the Dover school board had tried to mandate the teaching of an "alternate theory," Intelligent Design, as science. Federal District Court judge John E. Jones III—though a nonactivist conservative jurist, a Christian, and a Bush appointee—was scathing, even derisive, in rejecting what he characterized as a doubly duplicitous attempt: first, to "misrepresent well-established scientific propositions," and, second, to require the teaching of "an untestable alternative hypothesis grounded in religion." In trying to smuggle religious Creationism into the biology classroom, an "ill-informed faction" led by the board's chairman had driven the school board to act with what the judge called "breathtaking inanity."[4]

That decision, and, not least, the unexpectedly caustic language, was applauded by those residing within a secular, humanist, post-Enlightenment tradition. But the discontent of those who chose to make Dover a constitutional test case for Intelligent Design and the reaction of those disappointed or angered by the judge's ruling serve to remind us that for most Americans, and not only fundamentalists, science alone cannot provide the sense of transcendent meaning they

---

4. *Kitzmuller v. Dover*; the full ruling (December 20, 2005) is on the National Center for Science Education Web site: http://www.natcenscied.org/. On DVD, see the 2007/2008 Nova production, *Judgment Day: Intelligent Design on Trial*.

need in their lives.[5] In particular, Darwinian evolution seems antithetical to the purpose and design they perceive in the universe, and which they attribute to an intelligent Designer, usually in the form of the traditional monotheistic deity of the Bible: a God omnipotent, omniscient, and—though his purposes are often difficult to discern—benevolent.

"Does the universe have a purpose?" The answers to that question, recently posed by the John Templeton Foundation to a dozen distinguished scientists and scholars, ranged from *no* to *yes*, from *unlikely*, *not sure*, and *perhaps* to *I hope so* and *certainly*. Most scientists would agree with the respondent who answered "unlikely" that, "while nothing in biology, chemistry, physics, geology, astronomy, or cosmology has ever provided direct evidence of purpose in nature, science can never unambiguously prove that there is no purpose." But for some who answered "no," the rubric that "absence of evidence is not evidence of absence" was an axiom not to be abused: "that we do not yet understand anything about the inception of the universe should not mean that we need to ascribe to its inception a supernatural cause, a creator, and therefore to associate with that creator's inscrutable mind a purpose, whether it be divine, malign, or even whimsically capricious."

Of those who responded "yes," emphasis fell on the human as well as the divine. One observed that "the fact that we can ask such a question at all suggests an affirmative answer" since our "impassioned search for meaning" is itself part of nature. This respondent was John F. Haught, who testified as an expert witness in the Dover case (he opposed presenting biology students with information "inherently religious, not scientific in nature"), and whose work on the relationship of theology and science we will reencounter. Another of the affirmative respondents, astronomer Owen Gingerich, described himself as "psychologically incapable of believing that the universe is meaningless. I believe that the universe has a purpose, and our greatest intellectual challenge as human beings is to glimpse what this purpose might be." He thought that purpose might be "to provide a congenial

5. See Alfred I. Tauber, "Science and Reason, Reason and Faith," in Robert M. Baird and Stuart E. Rosenbaum, eds., *Intelligent Design: Science or Religion? Critical Perspectives,* 311.

home for self-conscious creatures who can ask profound questions and who can probe the nature of the universe itself," a universe that seems (and here he adopts an "anthropic" view other respondents thought "not readily reconcilable with what is known of the evolutionary origin of humankind") "magnificently tuned . . . for the emergence of intelligent life." Gingerich names that tuner or designer in his latest book, *God's Universe*, to which I also later refer.[6]

Given the prevalence of religious faith in contemporary America, a country in which 48 percent of those polled (in March 2007 by *Newsweek*) said God created humans in their present form within the past 10,000 years, the *range* of answers might shock many. Others might well be surprised by the affirmative, even theistic (or quasi-theistic) responses from some members of a scientific elite often thought to be uniformly secular. In fact, a minority of American scientists (40 percent, though only 7 percent of members of the elite National Academy of Scientists[7]) believe in a personal God and find their faith compatible with their profession.

On the more mundane level of politics, however, the ineradicable human longing for purpose and transcendence can pose, as in the Creationist challenge turned back in the Dover School Board case, a threat to the constitutional separation of church and state. In his 2007 study of the interaction of the political and the divine, Mark Lilla traces "the heritage of the Great Separation" between basic questions of "politics" and "questions of theology and cosmology." When looking to explain the conditions of political life and political judgment, "the unconstrained mind seems compelled to travel up and out: up toward those things that transcend human existence, and outward to encompass the whole of that existence." This "urge to connect is not an atavism." The "temptation to break the self-imposed limits of the Great Separation" and absorb political life into "some larger theological . . . drama has been strong in the modern West . . . because we are heirs to the biblical tradition. Political rhetoric in the United States, for example, is still shot through with messianic language, and it is only thanks to a strong

---

6. The most recent books of both Gingerich and Haught are briefly characterized at the end of Chapter 2. The responses to the Templeton Foundation question were widely published in October 2007. For the twelve essays in their entirety, see www.templeton.org/purpose.

7. Edward J. Larson and Larry Wilban, "Leading Scientists Still Reject God."

constitutional structure and various lucky breaks that political theology has never managed to dominate the American political mind."[8]

Secularists who currently fear, with good reason, that the intellectual values of the European Enlightenment are under assault, and who worry about threats to the separation of church and state, often see *only* irrationalism in the religious impulse, the human need for the sacred. Their dismay at current national and international trends, and their defense of enlightened rationalism, leads some, especially the "neo-atheists," to dismiss or ridicule as atavistic the religious impulse, not only at its most irrational, intolerant, or berserk, but even as what Lilla refers to as the urge to connect to wholeness and transcendence. For all their virtues, the authors of such recent books as *The End of Faith* (Harris), *The God Delusion* (Dawkins), *Breaking the Spell* (Dennett), *God: The Failed Hypothesis* (Stenger), and *God Is Not Great* (Hitchens), understandably fixated on their stimulus and bête noire, counter-Enlightenment fundamentalism, often seem unable to perceive *any* positive aspect of the religious impulse, let alone empathize with the discontent and need of those on, say, the other side of the Dover debate.

It was to that perceived discontent and need that Cardinal Schönborn addressed his op-ed, titled "Finding Design in Nature." His claim was that he was defending "Reason"—at least the metaphysical Reason that discerns God's cosmological design—against, not so much "evolution," as a materialistic ideology he and other theists refer to as "evolutionism." (Creationists try to smuggle religion into biology classes; atheists, it can be argued, try to smuggle their irreligion into evolutionary biology.) He was also defending the "design evident in nature" as "real," not to be explained away as the mere "*appearance* of design as the result of 'chance' and 'necessity.'" In subsequent lectures and papers, prompted by the spate of letters that followed his 2005 op-ed, Cardinal Schönborn continued to address the issues raised, issues that also confronted Emily Dickinson: the tension between faith and science (physics and evolutionary biology) and between divine design and random chance and, above all, the perennial problem presented for theists—most powerfully and inscrutably in the sublime masterpiece of the Hebrew Scriptures, the Book of Job, and in Shakespeare's deepest tragedy, *King Lear*—by the

---

8. Lilla, *The Stillborn God: Religion, Politics, and the Modern West*, 307.

sheer amount of undeserved suffering in a world presumably presided over by an all-powerful and all-loving God.

~

These were among the subjects I discussed with my friend Paul, who is "religious," though the precise nature of his essentially Christian belief is hard to pin down. I recited for him, as I had for Jim, Dickinson's "Apparently with no surprise," which raises precisely the questions Schönborn was trying to resolve. The poem was on my mind because I had recently sat in on the class of a colleague at a college "in the Jesuit Tradition." As it happened, this poem came up for discussion at the end of the period and there was simply no time for the students, or the professor, or me to do it justice. I was sufficiently frustrated that the same evening I e-mailed a copy of "Apparently with no surprise" to several friends, requesting *their* brief responses.

Like most readers of this poem, my friends leaped from Dickinson's miniature garden-drama to wider speculations—just as she intended. The poem invites us to contemplate, as Cardinal Schönborn had, the tension between design and accident, between faith in a providential, loving deity and overwhelming empirical evidence of a natural world of random, ruthless violence. Evolutionary science in particular has forced many to ask basic questions. Are reason and religion compatible? To *make* them compatible must we adopt the position that good fences make good neighbors? Paleontologist Stephen Jay Gould's attempt, a decade ago, to *separate* faith and science into "non-overlapping *magisteria*" is of course not without precedent, most dramatically visible in the philosophy of Immanuel Kant, who famously divided the realms of reason and faith, science and religion, into two separate spheres with functions so distinct that they need never conflict with each other.

Kant salvaged reason from the empiricist wrecking ball of David Hume, but at a high price, too high for many. Nonbelievers have faulted him for stopping short. By failing to assert reason's "precedence," he permitted it to "abdicate its powers"; thus faith is allowed to "go scot-free, and religion is saved."[9] Believers, on the other hand, have either been comforted or troubled by Kant's limiting of Pure Rea-

---

9. Michel Onfray, *Atheist Manifesto: The Case against Christianity, Judaism, and Islam*, 5. Onfray calls Kant's first *Critique* "a monument of timid audacity."

son's purview to the phenomenal world. For some, the rational demonstration by a great Enlightenment thinker of the limits of human knowledge confirmed their faith in a reality transcending the world revealed to us by the senses. Other believers have been *disturbed* by the limits imposed upon reason. Though it was ostensibly under Kantian auspices that Samuel Taylor Coleridge attempted *his* master project, the *reconciliation* of religion and philosophy, he could do so only by creative misreading, transforming Kantian Pure Reason into an "intuitive," higher Reason. As for Kant himself, as he acknowledged in the preface to the second (1787) edition of *The Critique of Pure Reason*, he could not "assume *God, freedom, and immortality.*" These ideas—the three postulates of what he calls Practical Reason—transcend a Pure Reason that, Kant conceded to Hume in this first *Critique*, can "reach only to objects of possible experience." Thus, he "had to deny *knowledge* in order to make room for *faith.*"[10] In the process of reconstructing theology on a moral foundation said to reflect ultimate reality, Kant pleased believers while compromising, for the more skeptical, his own Enlightenment project by an infusion, not of sophisticated epistemology, but of the pietist religion he inherited from his mother.

For Kant, Pure Reason is separate from the Practical Reason that is the basis of religion; Schönborn tries to fuse them—finally, like Coleridge, projecting his Christian faith onto the natural and human world. At first, he bases his position on human intelligence in the form of Thomistic reasoning, only to fall back—when it comes to the crucial Problem of Suffering, the great issue raised as well by Dickinson's poem—on the divine Logos and, especially, the redemptive sacrifice of Jesus. (Though attracted to Intelligent Design, Schönborn has too much integrity to endorse that facile "science"; but he, too, resorts to the Logos of the prologue to the gospel of John: the key text for Phillip Johnson, the architect of the ID movement, and William Dembski, its most prolific proponent, both of whom, avoiding the literalism of Genesis, identify Intelligent Design with the minimalist and mystical Logos theology of John 1.)

Despite the best efforts of the cardinal, the question remains: can science and religion—physics and theology, evolution and creation—

10. *Critique of Pure Reason*, Bxxx (117); B refers to the second edition, A to the first.

peacefully coexist? As we have already seen, and will again, for many they *can*; indeed, at a certain sophisticated level, the clash may present neither a real problem nor an adequate explanation for the loss of faith. The distinguished philosopher Charles Taylor, in a monumental study published in 2007, expressed dissatisfaction, on two levels, with what he acknowledged to be the widespread argument that modern Western secularism is to be explained in terms of science having refuted and crowded out religious belief. After registering two objections, he ends by making a crucial point about a range of possibilities:

> First, I don't see the cogency of the supposed arguments from, say, the findings of Darwin to the alleged refutations of religion. And, secondly, partly for this reason, I don't see this as an adequate explanation for why in fact people abandoned their faith, even when they themselves articulate what happened in such terms as "Darwin refuted the Bible", as allegedly said by a Harrow schoolboy in the 1890s. Of course bad arguments can figure as crucial in perfectly good psychological or historical explanations. But bad arguments like this . . . leave out . . . many viable possibilities between fundamentalism and atheism.[11]

Those other possibilities, those explanatory roads not traveled by literalists or by those who reduce religion to its worst or at least its most simplistic examples, are explored in this massive volume, a fusion of history and philosophy with Christian apologetics. Taylor is an orthodox believer, but his search would hardly be dismissed by Charles Darwin. That believer become gentle agnostic rather than adamant atheist refers, in the teasing final sentence of *The Origin of Species*, to "grandeur in this view of life, with its several powers, having been *originally breathed into* a few forms or into one." And, in a *Washington Post* column (November 18, 2005) written while the Dover case was still being argued, conservative commentator Charles Krauthammer rose eloquently to the occasion: "How ridiculous to make evolution the enemy of God. What could be more elegant, more simple, more brilliant, more economical, more creative, indeed more divine than a planet with millions of life forms, distinct yet interac-

---

11. *A Secular Age*, 4. That Harrow schoolboy, G. M. Trevelyan, would go on to become a major historian.

tive, all ultimately derived from accumulated variations in a single double-stranded molecule, pliable and fecund enough to give us mollusks and mice, Newton and Einstein?"

The "indeed more *divine*" is, of course, the more-than-metaphorical issue. For if evolutionary science and faith in a *personal, benign* God are *not* compatible, if neo-Darwinian natural science cannot be incorporated as part of God's eternal plan, how are we to perceive the universe? Is it the result of intelligent, beneficent Design, presided over by what Emily Dickinson calls in the poem "an Approving God"? Or is it the result of Darwinian evolution, random "accidental power" (another key phrase in her tiny but all-encompassing poem) directed by a selective force, *natural* rather than *divine*? Or is it that God exists and not only permits but "approves" of natural and human suffering, making God omnipotent but hardly benevolent?

In Emily Dickinson's era, as in our own, the tension between faith and science centered on the controversy ignited by Charles Darwin's theory of evolution. *On the Origin of Species by Natural Selection* (1859) and *The Descent of Man* (1871) had considerable impact on religious communities in New England. Unlike Unitarian Boston and Transcendentalist Concord, the Amherst of Emily Dickinson was still staunchly Calvinist. But despite the lingering shadow of the damnation-centered theology of Jonathan Edwards and her own family's religious orthodoxy, the nonconformist poet, always torn between religious faith and doubt, was aware of and open to dangerous Darwinian ideas. In her recent study of American women writers and science, Nina Baym remarks that many of the poems "sent across the hedge to Susan Gilbert Dickinson over the years questioned God's goodness, but few are scientific." But even if her "scientific affiliations" were "only provisional and strategic," Emily Dickinson wrote many antitheological poems "in which science demolishes orthodoxy," primarily the Calvinist Natural Theology taught at Amherst, including concepts of the afterlife.[12]

Nevertheless, the fine science faculty of Amherst College was conversant with Darwinism, and Dickinson would have encountered discussions of Darwin (including evolution parodies) in papers and

12. Baym, *American Women of Letters and the Nineteenth-Century Sciences: Styles of Affiliation*, 139, 143, 148–49.

periodicals she regularly read, especially the *Springfield Daily Republican,* whose associate editor, Josiah G. Holland, was a valued friend, and to whom Darwin himself wrote a complimentary letter in the summer of 1872. (About six months later, Darwin wrote another complimentary letter to another central figure in Dickinson's life, Thomas Wentworth Higginson.) Dickinson also read *Scribner's,* where she was likely to encounter a review of *Pater Mundi* (1872), a book on Darwinian evolution and Christianity by Amherst professor E. F. Burr. She was also a regular reader of the *Atlantic Monthly,* which featured several informed articles (July, August, October 1860) on the content and reception of *The Origin of Species* by Asa Gray, the distinguished botanist, theistic evolutionist, and friend of Darwin.[13]

The specific context in which Dickinson mischievously observed, in the draft of a letter to Judge Otis Phillips Lord, that "we thought Darwin had thrown 'the Redeemer' away" (*L* 728) is less significant than the year she made the remark: 1882, the same year in which she somberly registered the age's growing "abdication of Belief," a post-Darwinian, almost Nietzschean sense that the old verities seemed no longer to hold. Those who died in the past "Knew where they went." They went to "God's Right Hand." But "That Hand is amputated now / And God cannot be found—" (1551).

I will reengage this well-known poem, as well as an until recently neglected lyric that epitomizes my emphasis on Darwinian evolutionary theory, suffering, and Dickinson's flower-and-frost poems. In that poem, "There is a flower that Bees prefer" (380), Dickinson notes the aspiration of both the hummingbird and the pollinating bee for this "purple Democrat," the common clover. It is a "sturdy little" flower "Contending with the Grass," her "Near Kinsman," for "Privilege of Sod and Sun— / Sweet Litigants for Life." Her "Providence" is "the Sun," and her "Progress" is "by the Bee—proclaimed," until

---

13. Darwin's letter to the editors of the *Republican* is discussed in Chapter 2. In February 1873, Darwin informed Higginson, whom he and his wife had met the previous year, that they were impressed by his account of Civil War Negro solders, "Life with a Black Regiment" (*The Life and Letters of Charles Darwin,* 2:354–55). On Dickinson and Darwin, see the papers by Australian scholar Joan Kirkby listed in "The Dickinson Periodicals Project." As an addendum (see Bibliography) to a 2004 essay on Dickinson and the nineteenth-century "Darwin wars," she provides an online sampling of periodical discussions, parodies, and reviews of Darwin's work, focusing on the impact of Darwinian theory on religious belief.

she finally goes down, bravely if unaware, to "Defeat . . . / When cancelled by the Frost." In a 2007 essay titled "Darwinian Dickinson," James Guthrie suggests that Dickinson's frequent deployment of the bee/flower trope was influenced by the work of Darwin (whose later studies were almost exclusively botanical) on coadaptations between pollinators and flowers. He describes the clover of this poem as engaging in "heroic and Darwinian struggle, first to survive, then to ensure her reproductive viability."[14]

⌒

The principal idea of Darwin and his followers, evolution by genetic transformation and natural selection, is often seen by proponents and enemies alike as opposed to a divinely designed creation. It remains at the storm center of *contemporary* controversy in the United States. This animosity would be remarkable, given the massive, ever accumulating scientific evidence (the greatly expanded fossil record buttressed by genetics and molecular biology) supporting evolution, were it not for the fact that this is an essentially theistic nation, now debating, more acrimoniously than ever, the role of religion in public life. Theology and science have become politicized in a way that (as I soon discovered) peripherally affects even how contemporary American readers might interpret such a poem as "Apparently with no surprise."

With the emergence of the Moral Majority a quarter century ago, and culminating during the administration of an evangelical president, George W. Bush, the conflict between religion and science has become almost indistinguishable from our Blue/Red political polarization. Notoriously, during a Republican presidential campaign debate in May 2007, three of the ten contenders said they did not "believe" in evolution (Bush himself is on record opining that "the jury is still out"); and in his attempt to clarify his stance, one of them, Kansas senator Sam Brownback, limited his acceptance of evolution to "small changes over time within a species," insisting not only that "faith" must somehow "purify reason" but also that where science undermined religious "truth" about human origins, faith must prevail. Another, former Baptist minister Mike Huckabee, who would go on with strong evangelical support to remain the last challenger to the eventual nominee, John McCain, was praised by right-wing provocateur Ann Coulter for

14. James R. Guthrie, "Darwinian Dickinson: The Scandalous Rise and Noble Fall of the Common Clover," 73.

holding positions "upsetting to the mainstream media" but precisely what "normal Americans like": his "religiosity and his questioning of Darwinian evolution."[15]

Scientific naturalists, making a dogma of evolution, are too quick to dismiss nonscientific ways of knowing; at the other extreme, in the Religious Right's privileging of "faith" over "reason," we have a version of Kant, minus the mental labor. Here too, we glimpse, writ small, the Bush administration's more than occasional subordination of science to faith-based ideology. Many Americans, not only liberal and leftist, have long worried about the encroachments of religion—specifically, *fundamentalist* Christianity—into both domestic and foreign policy agendas of the Bush administration. But many more, most though not all on the political right, deplore the smug shrugging off of the beliefs of "people of faith" by an Unholy Trinity buzz-worded by the Fox Network's culture warriors as "Hollywood," the "mainstream liberal media," and a "bicoastal elite" dominated by "secular progressives."

Responding specifically to the much publicized emergence of the neo-atheists, a number of authors have lately reinforced tabloid defenses of religion. They include conservative polemicist Dinesh D'Souza (whose riposte is informed, readable, and often effective), as well as the harder to label Chris Hedges. Repelled by the "fundamentalist mindset itself," whether religious or atheistic, Hedges rejects both extremes in our increasingly polarized God-science debate. The most impressive of these books is also the most recent, the specifically targeted *God and the New Atheism: A Critical Response to Dawkins, Harris, and Hitchens,* by John F. Haught, senior fellow in science and religion at the Woodstock Theological Center at Georgetown University.[16]

---

15. Ann Coulter, Fox News, "The Big Story" (November 18, 2007). Brownback, *New York Times,* May 31, 2007; for responses, see letters to the editor, June 1, 2007. May 2007 also saw the opening, in Petersburg, Kentucky, of a "Creation Museum," intended to "counter evolutionary natural history museums that turn countless minds against Christ and Scripture" and featuring a display of Noah's ark and the spectacle—*sancta simplicitas!*—of dinosaurs and humans presented as coexisting neighbors. In its first two months (the director of the museum reported in July), there were more than a hundred thousand visitors.

16. Though acknowledging that there are valid challenges to the religious perspective, Haught criticizes the "new atheists" for theological shallowness, for a failure to engage religion much beyond fundamentalist varieties easy to caricature, and (in terms of my central theme) for their evasion of the problem of suffering by attributing the *cause* of suffering to faith. The two other books mentioned

It is hardly surprising that readers reflecting such a marked religio-cultural divide would have different responses to a poem encompassing the whole of the relationship of God to the universe. Had we world enough and time, I could further elaborate on the multilayered theological-scientific-political context in which, in the summer and autumn of 2007, I set about examining, and casually recording, a small sample of responses to Dickinson's "Apparently with no surprise," a poem in which an innocent flower is violently "beheaded" by frost, a grisly act apparently commissioned and endorsed by "an Approving God."

In pursuing the range both of conflicting responses to the poem and of Dickinson's exceptional and restless mind in her lifelong exploration of questions about the role of God in nature and what conception of God will withstand the accusation of unwarranted suffering, I felt obliged to engage both logical (*theo*logical) and imaginative (poetic) constructions. Thus, the various images of God presented by Emily Dickinson became the more immediate context in which I examined varying responses to the deity presiding over this particular lyric. In "Apparently with no surprise," by choosing to miniaturize the event and by adopting a stance of apparent utter detachment, she paradoxically compels each of *us*—her readers, especially the "country-men" into whose unseen hands she committed Nature's "message" (441)—to question the role played in this floral, human, and cosmic drama by that "Approving God." As in the case of another tiny poem, Tennyson's "Flower in the Crannied Wall," I even toyed briefly with the thought that, "if I could understand" the ramifications of *this* provocative Dickinson flower-poem, I might come closer to knowing, as Tennyson more confidently put it, "what God and man is."

---

are engaging but hardly at Haught's level of sophistication. D'Souza's arguments in *What's So Great about Christianity* are sometimes compelling, sometimes fallacious. The neo-atheists, accused of caricaturing religion, are themselves caricatured by Hedges, who reduces them to utopian optimists seduced by the rational myth of scientific progress. Still, the title of his new book, *I Don't Believe in Atheists* (2008), fails to convey the Niebuhrian aspect of Hedges's two-front assault, targeting religious as well as antireligious absolutism. In short, this new book, despite its title, complements rather than contradicts his earlier attack, in *American Fascists*, on the Religious Right, an alarmist study that pales in comparison with Michelle Goldberg's impressive deconstruction of evangelical "dominion theology" in *Kingdom Coming: The Rise of Christian Nationalism*.

I complete this Introduction as I began it, aware that some readers, particularly Dickinson scholars and other specialists in American literature, may have at least two criticisms of the book that follows. I've already addressed the first: what may seem my excessive emphasis on Wordsworth, a paradigmatic Romantic poet whose work, I believe, helps to illuminate Dickinson's. The second potential objection is more substantive. Some may find in the two parts of the book halves that do not make a whole. My premise is that they are not mutually exclusive but mutually *illuminating*, since the primary question addressed, in a contemporary scientific and theological context, in Chapters 2–4, is the same question confronted imaginatively by Emily Dickinson: the role of God in a world of violence and suffering, sickness and death. In addition, I meditate on spiritual and cultural life both at present and in Dickinson's work and period in an admittedly engaged and personal voice. Writing at this particular historical moment, amid a national and international culture war that is (in both senses of the word) *fundamentally* theological, I found it hard to separate my own existential and religious stance from a more detached "scholarly" viewpoint, even at the risk of mixing the time-bound with the timeless.

In fact, utter detachment—which is only the "apparent" stance even of the speaker in "Apparently with no surprise"—seems a luxury when the United States and some of its allies are engaged in conflict in Iraq and Afghanistan, and when forces unleashed by one platoon or another of those who consider themselves God's warriors may actually result in a version of Armageddon. We have, when it comes to the Middle East, our own share of religiously inspired militants, including apocalyptic Christian Zionists and theoconservatives certain that it is our messianic mission to extend to all cultures "the Almighty's gift of universal freedom," no matter the ethno-sectarian complexities or the cost, and even when getting bogged down in Iraq is strategically counterproductive in terms of our "global war" on Islamic terrorism.

The principal competing visions, American and Islamist, may both be described as apocalyptic.[17] But there is a difference in kind and

17. Writing in the first year of the Iraq war, psychologist Robert Jay Lifton argued, "We are experiencing what could be called an apocalyptic face-off between Islamist forces, overtly visionary in their willingness to kill and die for religion, and American forces claiming to be restrained and reasonable but no less visionary in their projection of a cleansing war-making and military power. Both

degree. Were Islamic jihadists (their spread helped rather than hin-
dered by the war in Iraq) to get their hands on a nuclear weapon, the
targeting of infidels might well be carried out in God's name by zealots
willing to engage even in mass murder in the name of religion. Theocratic Iran, the chief beneficiary of the Iraq fiasco, might develop a
nuclear capability, triggering a U.S. or Israeli preemptive strike. And
there is a more immediate nightmare scenario. The nuclear arsenal of
Pakistan, a state on the verge of chaos and with its northwestern
mountain enclaves providing safe haven for Osama bin Laden, may
fall into the hands of Islamic extremists sympathetic to Al-Qaeda and
willing to use such weapons in God's name.[18]

These will seem improbable scenarios only if those of us who think
of ourselves as rational actors in a reasonable world try to explain
away or simply deny a very long history demonstrating a willingness
on the part of fanatics, convinced that God is on their side, to kill their
fellow creatures because of absolutist religion. There is an understandable but dangerous tendency on the part of liberal Christians and
progressive, secular optimists committed to peaceful international
cooperation to *repress* evidence of man's primordial proclivity to violence. That is the theme of two of the most powerful poems of the

---

sides are energized by versions of intense idealism; both see themselves as
embarked on a mission of combatting evil in order to redeem and renew the
world; and both are ready to release untold levels of violence to achieve that purpose" ("American Apocalypse," *Nation*, December 2003, quoted in Hedges, *I Don't
Believe in Atheists*, 134).

18. Conflict might be ignited by war between old rivals. Muslim Pakistan came
into existence sixty years ago because of religious differences with predominantly
Hindu India, a dispute played out in the long-contested province of Kashmir. It is
estimated that some sixty million people would be killed in any all-out Indo-
Pakistani nuclear exchange. This would also be a religious war, since many of the
guerrilla groups operating in Kashmir are Islamic, linked not only to the Pakistani
military and intelligence services but also to Al-Qaeda. In short, we have, along
with the dangers presented by theocratic Iran, a potential marriage of nuclear
weapons with religious extremists and a confrontation between states, originally
partitioned over divergent religious beliefs, "now poised," as Sam Harris has
recently observed, "to exterminate each other with nuclear weapons simply
because they disagree about [theological] 'facts' that are every bit as fanciful as the
names of Santa's reindeer" (*The End of Faith*, 26–27). A hundred pages further on,
however, Harris himself contemplates carrying out what he acknowledges to be
an "unthinkable crime": a "nuclear first strike" on an "Islamist regime" that had
acquired "long-range nuclear weaponry" (*The End of Faith*, 129).

twentieth-century's preeminent visionary poet, W. B. Yeats: a writer as telepathically alert to the dangers of hubristic Enlightenment faith in reason and the utopian myth of collective moral progress as he was to the paradoxically related loosing of the blood-dimmed tides of irrational fanaticism.

In the twenty-*first* century, there is an even more terrifying twist on the visionary "nightmares" that rode upon Yeats's sleep in "The Second Coming" and "Nineteen Hundred and Nineteen"—as they rode on Wordsworth's sleep in passages of *The Prelude* describing the Terror during the French Revolution, passages Yeats echoes in both his poems. For today, the forces of irrationalism threatening civilization are quintessentially theological and, actually or potentially, armed with the most nightmarish, even apocalyptic, weapons. Our own strategy, however "accidental" the negative consequences, may be intended to achieve an ultimately positive end. But the injection of God into foreign policy can prove less providential than dangerous when the theological certitude of an evangelical commander-in-chief is combined with unparalleled military power. Ironically enough, and worst of all, in the case of such a stateless actor as Al-Qaeda, we confront a metastasizing religious fanaticism impervious to any traditional form of deterrence and driven by the mad conviction that any and all forms of terror against the infidel West are part of a Holy War carried out under the auspices of—to borrow Emily Dickinson's provocative description—"an Approving God."

Though I begin and end with Emily Dickinson's "Approving God" and focus primarily on her struggle between belief and unbelief, this book, as is already obvious, is almost as much a personal as a critical exploration. It is up to the reader to determine if I have succeeded in justifying that subjective approach, as well as my casting of an unusually wide contextual net. However personal this work's genesis and however widening the gyre in which I found myself turning, I hope that most if not all those who read the book will discover that the final result coheres. Above all, I hope they will find it *interesting*. Certainly, for all its range of reference, it was written with the general reader in mind: a reader intelligent and "interested" in literature, science, politics, and theology, without necessarily being a specialist in any of these fields, let alone in all of them. What is needful, in fact, is not expertise but a rejection of certitude: an acknowledgment of perplexity regarding the huge issues opened by Emily Dickinson's "little" poem. These include the challenges presented to theodicy by evolution and, implicitly, by the Problem of Suffering. If God exists, and he is all-knowing, all powerful, and all-loving, how can the natural and human world he created, and of which he "approves," be the site of so many violent forces—at once random, recurrent, and indifferent to all that is happy, beautiful, and innocent?[19]

19. Appearing too late to figure in the present text, but decidedly worth mentioning, is George Steiner's recent rumination, at once wide sweeping and movingly personal, on "theology and its bodyguard, theodicy." He insists on the futility of "words, words, words"—however acrobatic, eloquent, or repellent the arguments—to "render acceptable the bestialities and injustice of reality," to make "understandable" unmerited "suffering under God." The essay, "Begging the Question," appears as the coda to Steiner's *My Unwritten Books* (New York: New Directions, 2008). He does not mention the great German, but in his insistence on the futility of theodicy, skeptical Steiner is allied, philosophically though not of course religiously, with Kant. A believer and early defender of philosophic optimism and providential reasoning, Kant concluded in his late postcritical work *Failure of All Philosophic Attempts at Theodicy* (1791) that our limited reason is utterly incapable of gaining insight into the highest Wisdom, the mysterious ways of God.

Part I

Chapter 1

The Poem and Images of God

The dual subjects of this book—images of God in particular reference to the Argument from Design and the Problem of Suffering, and the specific theodicy of Emily Dickinson—both derive from a recent individual and communal reading of a late Dickinson poem:

> Apparently with no surprise—
> To any happy Flower
> The Frost beheads it at its play—
> In accidental power—
> The blonde Assassin passes on—
> The Sun proceeds unmoved
> To measure off another Day
> For an Approving God. (1624)

This well-known but rarely discussed Dickinson poem has provided, aside from a particular text to explicate, a *pretext*—a convenient occasion for a wide-ranging meditation. Though it compels us to confront the accident/design duality, as well as the conflict between an omnipotent, benevolent God and a violent natural world (and, by implication, a *human* world of pain and suffering), the poem itself seems something other than meditative. Simultaneously violent and detached, brutal yet coldly understated, its terse narrative recounts, though in the present tense at each stage, the course of a day. It is a day at once particular and universal: just "another" day. If I am repeating the word, I am in good company; *day* is by far the most frequently employed noun in Dickinson's poetry, appearing 232 times, its only remote rival being *sun*, which occurs 180 times, including in this poem. The setting is a garden, the central act the destructive (though some readers think merely damaging) impact of frost upon a flower, "any" flower. As in most traditional "flower poems," this blossom, "happy" but short-lived, epitomizes joy, innocence, and a beauty all the more to be cherished because of its transience and vulnerability. Whatever the poem's "unmoved" tone of distanced objectivity, no sensitive reader can fail to respond emotionally to the flower's sudden, brutal decapitation and to the human and theological implications of that "death"-by-frost.

While there is no lyric "I" in the poem, and a seemingly impersonal stance is maintained throughout, perspective is in fact present from the opening and governing word, "Apparently." In addition, not only are the key players (Flower, Frost, Sun, and God) personified; the crucial adjectives employed (*happy, accidental, unmoved, approving*) reveal value judgments that obviously transcend mere observation. In this case, the "I" may have seemed superfluous to Emily Dickinson since this is so clearly *her* territory: the setting, a garden; the occasion, the assault on a defenseless flower by a killing frost; the overarching issue, theology. As so often in Dickinson, God is present: the traditional God, but depicted with such apparent ambivalence that different readers may judge the dramatic speaker's tone as awed, or resigned, or dismayed, or angry, or even blasphemous.

On other almost identical occasions, Dickinson can be whimsical. In a poem written a quarter century earlier, "I had some things that I called mine" (116), "Dickinson's little-girl persona takes God to task for sending an unseasonable frost to kill her garden." I am quoting Jonathan Morse, who concludes the "Bibliographical Essay" appended to *A Historical Guide to Emily Dickinson* by citing the final lines of this poem, which had begun:

> I had some things that I called mine—
> And God, that he called his,
> Till, recently a rival Claim
> Disturbed these amities.
>
> The property, my garden,
> Which having sown with care,

He claims the pretty acre,
And sends a Bailiff there.

The speaker, seeking "Justice," but wishing to avoid a public squabble, threatens:

I'll institute an "Action"—
I'll vindicate the law—
Jove! Choose your counsel—
I'll retain "Shaw"!

Who the devil, one wonders, is the adversary the speaker chooses to send up against Jove himself? As Morse reports, no help is to be found in the annotations of either Johnson or Franklin, both of whom append a note by Mabel Loomis Todd identifying "Shaw" as a day laborer who "used to dig" for the poet. This hardly seems a qualification for taking on God in a court of law on a charge of having destroyed her carefully sown garden by sending his own court official in the form of a premature frost. Scholars have resolved the mystery of biographical reference, and so explained the joke.[1] I will be making few such ventures; what interests me is this early (1859) challenging of God and the adumbration of theological issues addressed rather more seriously in the frost-and-flower drama of "Apparently with no surprise."

In the case of the latter, all depends on the presentation of that moment when the silent but deadly frost, the "blonde Assassin," assaults the "happy" flower and "beheads it at its play," all under the auspices and with the explicit approval of an inscrutable God. Obviously, more is going on here than the registration of a passing incident in a garden. In microcosm, "Apparently with no surprise" engages the relationship between God and Nature; the pathos of mutability; and,

---

1. The reference is to the distinguished jurist Lemuel Shaw, chief justice of the Massachusetts Supreme Court from 1830 to 1860. (He was also the father-in-law of Melville, who dedicated his first novel, *Typee*, to him.) Summarizing work by previous scholars, Morse explains, "In the home of Edward Dickinson, the word 'Shaw' commanded reverence. Now that we know this, we can get the joke. Father's law office is upheld from season to season by Father's Shaw, says this poem, but in my garden I have a Shaw of my own—and *my* Shaw can plead before a court ultimately Supreme" (Jonathan Morse, "Bibliographical Essay," 266–67). Later, Emily Dickinson would mount *her own* defenses, and charges, in that Supreme Court.

by clear implication, the problem of the suffering of the innocent in a beautiful but harsh universe with or without discernible purpose.

By making the symbolic "victim" of violence floral rather than human, Dickinson anticipates and prescinds from two of the standard "answers" to the Problem of Suffering: pain as justified punishment for wickedness, or pain as attributable to the assertion of free will. A third classic solution—the redemptive argument that apparent or unintended evil can lead to a greater good—is at least potentially applicable in terms of the seasonal cycle of life, death, and rebirth. That vegetative version of the greater-good argument takes the form, in John 12:24, of Christ's parable of his own death and redemptive resurrection: "Unless a grain of wheat falls into the earth and dies, it remains but a single grain. Yet if it dies, it yields a rich harvest." Christ's death and resurrection is an element, in turn, of the "optimistic" argument that, as Alexander Pope put it in epistle 1 (lines 291–92) of his *Essay on Man*, "All discord" is "harmony not understood, / All partial evil, universal good." Or, as would seem to be the case, is the violence in "Apparently with no surprise" terminal, and thus emblematic of discord, pain, and death without an ultimately benign purpose? Dickinson's poem, minuscule as it is, raises momentous issues. It is only "apparently" surprising that it should have thematic precursors of enormous magnitude. Five come to mind, all of them texts with which Emily Dickinson was intimately familiar.

⌒

On the most profound level, there is the poetic core of the Book of Job, which, perhaps first and certainly most sublimely, dramatized the perennial problem of God's role in a world of undeserved suffering. As style and content make clear, the framing sections—the prose prologue and, especially, the pedestrian epilogue—are not the work of the master-poet who wrote the dialogues of chapters 3–42. In these exchanges, Job responds to the conventional arguments of his false comforters: that the evil inflicted on him must be the result of his own wickedness, since God would never "pervert justice" (7:2–3). Deprived of his possessions and his family, and physically afflicted, Job does not curse God; but, like the speaker in Dickinson's "I had some things that I called mine," he *does* seek justice and so challenges the Hebrew version of "Jove." Adamantly and accurately maintaining his innocence, he demands an "answer "from the "Almighty" (31:35–37).

But when God, interrupting one of these dialogues, in fact makes his dramatic appearance, it is not to answer his defiant victim but to imperiously reprimand him as a mere mortal who has no business confronting divinity. The magnificent Lord God who addresses the unjustly afflicted Job "out of the whirlwind" remains as enigmatic as the suffering he permits (even initiates) and unapologetically refuses to explain. Instead, he confronts Job with his own litany of unanswerable questions: "where were you when I laid the foundations of the earth" or when "the morning stars sang together, and all the sons of God shouted with joy?" Has Job "walked in the recesses of the deep? . . . Can you bind the chains of the Pleiades, or loose the cords of Orion?" If not, "Shall a faultfinder contend with the Almighty? He who argues with God, let him answer it" (Job 38–40).

The chapter that follows, 41, is devoted to the majestic and terrifying creature—the Hebrew original of Blake's Tyger and Melville's Whale—in whom this God takes particular pride and with whose fearful power he associates his own. Can Job "draw out Leviathan with a hook? . . . will he speak soft words unto thee? Will he make a covenant with thee?" Overwhelmed by the exuberant delight this sardonic, taunting God takes in his own creative power, a repentant Job, earlier and understandably absorbed by his own personal agony and horrific losses, responds with necessarily partial but now *direct* recognition of the awesome divinity who made and governs the universe. "I had heard of thee by the hearing of my ear, but now my eye sees thee" (Job 42:4).

The pious epilogue, a painful falling-off from the preceding sublimity, presents us with a cowed Job and an even more morally dubious divinity: a double-entry bookkeeper who compensates the guiltless penitent for all his losses, including, most disturbingly, "substitute" children replacing the ten God himself permitted to be senselessly destroyed by a storm. This vulgarization of the greater-good answer to suffering seems grotesque if not obscene. But what matters in terms of any theodicy worthy of the name is that Job does not endorse the "justice" of a God who seems no more interested than Leviathan in "covenants." Job submits instead to the irresistible evidence of the Almighty's *power:* sovereign and, finally, unchallengeable.

In its evocation of an omnipotent but ambivalent divinity and unfathomable mysteries, in its implication that suffering is not personal but universal, and in its varying perspectives, the Book of Job anticipates Shakespeare's greatest tragedy, which poses antithetical perspectives both on "Nature" and on "the gods."

Though *King Lear* is set in a remote pre-Christian past, pagan polytheism seems forgotten at that moment in the final act when Lear, projecting the imprisonment he will share with his wronged and now redemptive daughter, imagines them taking upon themselves "the mystery of things, / As if we were God's spies." Shakespeare's mask may have slipped for a moment (perhaps dangerously since a recent parliamentary ruling made onstage references to God blasphemous). Lear quickly resumes the play's polytheism, with the gods seemingly benign: "Upon such sacrifices, my Cordelia, / The gods themselves throw incense" (5.2.8–21). This divinely sanctioned and apparently redemptive anticipation of a caged but shared life for father and daughter is shattered by the hanging of the innocent Cordelia and the entrance of a brokenhearted Lear carrying her body: for the stunned onlookers, a pietà vision of the Apocalypse itself ("the promised end"), or the "image of that horror" (5.3.237–38).

The main tragedy, that not of an innocent Job but that of a flawed "man more sinned against than sinning" (3.2.60–61), is mirrored in the subplot. Gloucester invokes "kind" and "ever-gentle gods" (4.6.213), and Edgar claims, in a play supplying little evidence of either gentleness or justice, that the disproportionate retribution inflicted upon his father for his "pleasant vices" somehow proves "the gods are just" (5.3.171). But the gods in *King Lear* seem irresponsible and cruelly playful; brutally blinded so that he "feelingly" sees the truth, Gloucester himself cries out in his agony: "As flies to wanton boys are we to the gods; / They kill us for their sport" (4.1.36–37). That insight is tragically embodied in the cruel, almost gratuitous hanging of Cordelia—despite, pointedly enough, Albany's cry, "The gods defend her!" (5.3.230). And her death is, of course, closely followed by that of Lear, all too aware that his beloved daughter will "never" come again, yet deluded, at the moment he succumbs, that she may yet breathe: "Look on her, look, her lips, / Look there, look there!" (5.3.310–11).

Gloucester's comparison of the gods to capriciously cruel "wanton boys" is unforgettable. Emily Dickinson doubtless remembered it (as well, perhaps, as Lear's final poignant delusion) in chastising the bullying God who, unfairly allowing "Old Moses" only a glimpse of the Promised Land, subjected him to "tantalizing Play / As Boy—should deal with lesser Boy— / To prove ability" (597). Another victim of "play," the flower in "Apparently with no surprise," is casually beheaded by frost "at its play," a lethal act approved by God working through one of the forces of nature with which he is associated in the Book of Job: "By the breath of God frost is given" (37:10). In *King Lear*, "Nature" is herself a goddess, a divinity whose power is no less ambiguous than that of "the gods." She is invoked ("Hear, goddess, hear; dear goddess, hear") as an agent of retributive justice by the king as victim of a thankless child (1.4.266–80) and by the villain, Edmund, as his personal "goddess" (1.2.22), sanctioning his own morality-free code, that ruthless law of the jungle that Social Darwinists would later call the survival of the fittest.

The same mysterious forces, divine and natural, animating the Book of Job and Shakespeare's titanic tragedy are "at play," on the small scale typical of Emily Dickinson, in "Apparently with no surprise." And another connection may bind play and poem with Hebrew scripture. The companion text to Job, Ecclesiastes, actually alluded to in *King Lear* (4.6.176–81), may figure as well in "Apparently with no surprise."[2] According to Koheleth, "there is no new thing under the sun," and it would be better never to have been born than to see "the evil work that is done under the sun" (Eccles. 1:9, 4:3). Tone and setting alike suggest that Emily Dickinson, who alludes in many poems and letters to the bleak, almost nihilistic (and yet genuine, often carpe diem) wisdom of Ecclesiastes, may have that solar refrain in mind in a poem in which the eternally recurrent evil done under the sun takes the form of a sudden but unsurprising decapitation of a short-lived "happy Flower," while, overhead, "The Sun proceeds unmoved."

In terms of genre, Dickinson's minimalist lyric gestures toward grand forms other than Shakespearean tragedy and the problematic "theodicies" of Job and Ecclesiastes. Generically, Dickinson's "little" flower poem can be read as a variation on the pastoral elegy and—its exterior semblance again belying its thematic immensity—as a mini-epic. As the master of both genres in English and the most widely read

---

2. Though often associated with the Book of Job, *King Lear* may have even deeper affiliations with Ecclesiastes. That connection, advanced by Shakespeare critic Arthur Hirsch in terms of the play's "over-all conception," has been endorsed by Harold Bloom: "The enormous emptiness of Koheleth reverberates all through Shakespeare's darkest drama, which is also his wisest" (*Where Shall Wisdom Be Found?* 103).

poet in New England, John Milton may provide illumination. In "Lycidas," Milton confronts, as Dickinson implicitly does here, the issue of premature and violent death. Two of his symbolic equivalents of such death—frost-nipt flowers and the decapitation of Orpheus—may come together in the Frost's beheading of Dickinson's "happy" Flower. The "loss" of Lycidas, says the shepherd poet, "As killing as . . . frost to flowers that their *gay* wardrobe wear," is a loss as lamentable but unpreventable as the death and beheading of the Muse's son ("Lycidas," lines 45–49, 57–62). Since Milton's pastoral elegy moves from indictment to justification of God, it may be said to anticipate the Argument of his epic. He wrote *Paradise Lost*, Milton tells us, not quite to demonstrate, but "to assert eternal Providence / And justify the ways of God to men" (1:25–26). Is that why Emily Dickinson wrote "Apparently with no surprise"? Or *not*?

To raise such questions, to introduce the theodicy of Job and Ecclesiastes, Shakespeare and Milton, may seem disproportionate in the case of a tiny poem of thirty-six words. But that *distillation* of meaning is the key to the power of Emily Dickinson, who took "For Occupation—This— / The spreading wide my narrow Hands / To gather Paradise—" (657). "It was the peculiar genius of this poet to open out the soul of apparently little or familiar things."[3] Walter Pater was speaking of Wordsworth; it might as well have been of Emily Dickinson, whose little and familiar things—most often, her cherished flowers—provide symbolic equivalents of human life and death; whose beloved garden so often becomes the site where she wrestles with God. Her work brings to awareness what Shira Wolosky calls "the importance of theodicy as a core literary (as well as philosophical and religious) structure in, for example, Aeschylus, Augustine, and Milton, Herbert and Donne, or, closer to Dickinson, Melville and Hopkins." Questions involving theodicy, questions about suffering and its justification, "though surely Dickinson's private ones," are not private only, for

the problem of suffering is essentially the problem of history. This is expressly and centrally the case in Christian terms, whose metaphysics continue to frame Dickinson's own experience and understanding. In this model earthly events find their place and their

3. Walter Pater, "Wordsworth," 48.

meaning in a providential history . . . both comprehensible and redemptive. Each experience is thought to find its corollary, and hence its significant place in a meaningful order, eternally present to divine vision.[4]

The tension between private and public takes many forms in the poetry of Emily Dickinson. The passage just quoted occurs in an essay discussing that tension in Dickinson's wartime poetry. But, as "Apparently with no surprise" makes clear, Civil War battlefields are hardly the only site of struggle, the only "model of earthly events" thought to be "eternally present to divine vision." For Dickinson, a lifelong, expert gardener as well as a poet, the central issue of theodicy—what to make of suffering and death and possible rebirth in an ordered world presided over by a supposedly providential and loving God— was seasonally enacted year after year in her own beloved garden, over whose plants and flowers she doted as if she were the world's first gardener, Milton's "Eve, alias Mrs. Adam" (L 24). It was a garden as sequestered as the poet herself. But however retired and retiring Emily Dickinson may have been, especially after 1860, she epitomized in private what Emerson had publicly advocated: a self-reliant individual averse to conformity and, above all, willing to challenge God as traditionally conceived. Indeed, though she thought and wrote within an essentially Christian paradigm, Dickinson, like Melville, out-Emersons Emerson in the rebellious, sometimes blasphemous audacity of her critique. Whether or not *that* Dickinson is present in "Apparently with no surprise" depends not only on what is intrinsically present in the poem but also, in part at least, on the responses of readers and the various images of God *they* bring to the table.

Brief and "apparently" uncomplicated, the poem raises momentous issues, both textual and contextual. The contextual or extrinsic considerations are essentially "religious." As just suggested, there is the matter of reader response. Reactions to this particular poem are, as we might imagine and as I've recently confirmed by requesting brief responses from friends, influenced, at times determined, by a reader's religious beliefs or lack thereof. It matters, to begin with, whether one believes that the kind of "God" depicted in the poem does or does not

4. Wolosky, "Public and Private in Dickinson's War Poetry," 113–14.

exist. Beyond that, there are other questions: whether one conceives the universe to be with or without purpose or "Design," and what connection if any there is between a violent, evolving Nature and an omnipotent, omniscient, and all-loving Creator God, presuming that such a Being exists.

When, as mentioned in my Introduction, I solicited the responses of friends to this poem, they turned out to be of three sorts. The responses were brief (a sentence or two) and impressionistic. Unfolding (and expanding upon) their latent implications, I am taking considerable liberty in characterizing them as follows.

For some, the poem seemed an objective, "Darwinian" tracing of the automatic operations of an indifferent, ever-changing nature: an evolving process of destruction and creation, with the sun going through its accustomed round, measuring off another day for a Force (a supposed "God") presiding over a perishable world. These "objectivist" readers themselves fell into two camps: those whose response was as unsentimentally "neutral" as the process itself seemed to be, and those who responded to it with a more modest version of the quasi-religious awe expressed by Albert Einstein in contemplating the inexorable laws of the universe.

For others, lifting that "naturalistic" description to the level of theodicy and personalizing the process, the poem seemed a mini-Miltonic vindication of God's ways to man. The destruction of the flower by the frost was only "apparently" cruel—for some, in fact, it seemed more likely to be a damaging rather than a killing frost. As such, it promotes new growth in the spring, and so "plays" its part in a grand plan devised and approved by a guiding Intelligence who is also a loving God: a providential Creator who (in accordance with the redemptive or philosophically optimistic answer to suffering) brings good out of "apparent" evil, life out of "apparent" death.

Finally, there were those who stressed the random cruelty of the "beheading," the leisurely departure of the "Assassin," and the movement overhead of the "unmoved" (unfeeling) sun. In their estimation, Dickinson had presented a bleak indictment rather than a vindication of God: an "Approving God" coldly indifferent to "suffering" in the natural—and, by unavoidable implication, the human—world, perhaps even taking sadistic pleasure in it. To generalize: my friends' interpretations were based in part on close attention to the text, but even more (and here they mirrored the responses I had observed in the classroom) on the religious faith or skepticism they brought to that text.

Hence, the second and overarching contextual consideration. As already suggested, no matter how objective and attentive our close reading, this poem can scarcely be understood without "bringing in" as necessary background the image of "God" most familiar not only to its readers but to the author herself. This would be the traditional deity, the Creator God as presented in the Bible and elaborated by theologians and philosophers. In the case of those for whom the Hebrew Scriptures are at once altered and completed by the Christian Testament, the Father is buttressed by the Son: God incarnate in Jesus as Messiah. Ostensibly, this poem draws our attention exclusively to "God" as Creator of the natural universe, the Intelligence who presides over, participates in, and approves of every event that takes place in that supposedly orderly and purposeful cosmos, even its apparently "accidental" aspects. But the incarnate God is far from irrelevant to the poem since the "Design" many Christians perceive beneath the violence in nature and, especially, human suffering is embodied in and *resolved by* the redemptive crucifixion and resurrection of Jesus. At times, at least, the volatile thought and poetry of Emily Dickinson fit this redemptive pattern.

There is a third and related Abrahamic monotheism. The God of Islam, like the Judeo-Christian God, is a supreme, transcendent being who both creates and participates in the natural and human world he has brought into existence. Though Emily Dickinson, little given to prayer, once told Samuel Bowles that she was praying to "Alla" to bring him relief from his intense sciatic pain (*L* 382), the Islamic God seems far removed from Dickinson's New England. Nevertheless, mentioning Allah may entail more than a nod to religious diversity. Indeed, the spectacle of a deity "approving" beheading by an *assassin* (a Muslim word fusing violence and religion) might conjure up for contemporary, post 9/11, readers the Allah of the radical Islamic jihadists: that God whose greatness they cite as divine sanction for the slaying of the infidel, preferably by decapitation.[5] Though none of my

---

5. *Assassin* is the European name for a member of a secret order founded in the late eleventh century by Hasan Sabbah, a leader of the Ismaili sect of Islam. Assassins, often fueled by hashish, were distinguished by blind obedience to their spiritual leader and the use of murder as a sacred duty to eliminate their foes. The highest rank, the actual instruments of assassination, sought martyrdom.

respondents mentioned jihadism, comments about the barbarous brutality of the beheading suggested an unconscious link. More generally,
Islam figures in the current religious climate, a climate, as already indicated in the Introduction, likely to affect contemporary readers
encountering a poem presided over by "God."

When, in Dickinson's native land, we sit down to read a poem like
"Apparently with no surprise," we do so in a nation in which some 90
percent of the population professes belief in a personal God, more of
them believing in literal Creationism—as well as in Satan and the Vir-
gin birth—than in biological evolution. Their faith may range from the
strictly doctrinal to the soft and fuzzy, but the "God" in *whom* (not
which) this vast majority professes belief is not some vague cosmic
energy, or pantheistic deity, or even that disengaged God of the
Enlightenment Deists, the Watchmaker who wound it all up and then
retired from the scene. The "personal" God believed in by most Americans, especially the 26 percent who are evangelical Protestants, is the
traditional anthropomorphic God: the biblical Creator of the universe
who takes a continuous interest in every aspect of his creation and
who has the power to intervene in natural process—though, with the
advance of modern science, he is less likely to resort to miracles than
to governing through what he has set in motion. This God, people of
faith believe, listens to their prayers, prayers he always answers, even
if the answer is often No. Though he allows evil to flourish and even
the innocent to suffer, his ultimate purpose, which is necessarily
obscure to mere mortals, is benevolent, a divine providence working
in mysterious accord with the world he designed.[6]

⌒

This, with a Calvinist spin, is the image of God inherited as well by
Emily Dickinson: a God she alternately believed in, questioned, quar-
reled with, rebelled against, caricatured, even condemned, but never
ceased to engage. What Hawthorne said of Melville, characterizing
the state of mind the author of *Moby-Dick* had confided to him, also
applies to Dickinson. Though Melville thought himself excluded from
the Elect, he did not seem to Hawthorne "to rest in that anticipation;
and, I think, will never rest until he gets hold of a definite belief . . . he
persists in wandering to-and-fro over these deserts. . . . He can neither

6. For current information on religious sects in the United States, see John C.
Green's *The Faith Factor: How Religion Influences American Elections.*

believe, nor be comfortable in his unbelief; and he is too honest and courageous not to try to do one or the other."[7] Different in so many other ways, America's archetypal male Voyager and female Recluse engaged in a similar struggle between belief and unbelief.

A number of informed accounts describe Emily Dickinson's own vacillating struggle between belief and skepticism, her desire for an undefined but intuitive faith and her acknowledgment that God remains hidden, ultimately unknowable, often indifferent or worse. Something of her divided perspective is captured in the second and final stanza of "Bitter-Sweet" by the seventeenth-century poet-priest George Herbert, the 1857 edition of whose *Poetical Works* was in the Dickinson library: "I will complain, yet praise; / I will bewail, approve: / And all my sour-sweet days / I will lament, and love." In contrast to Herbert, Emily Dickinson did more complaining than approving. Dickinson's "recognition of the inadequacy of the Calvinist heritage to contemporary spiritual experience" inspired "some of her most intense, ferocious, and distressed verse."[8] Perhaps she took more seriously the divine proclamation to which Herbert may be responding: "I kill and I make alive; I wound and I heal" (Deut. 32:39). Yet even in rejecting the appalling God of her Calvinist tradition, Dickinson never ceased, in some sense, to *believe*. The two books I have found most helpful both contain forms of that word in their titles: Roger Lundin's *Emily Dickinson and the Art of Belief* and James McIntosh's *Nimble Believing: Dickinson and the Unknown*.

Lundin places Dickinson's "struggle with God" in multiple contexts: her Calvinist background; her absorption of the Romantic and Transcendentalist "turn in theology"; and her recognition of the "limits" of that anthropocentric turn, especially her intuiting of the limits of Romantic "optimism." Lundin is particularly interested in the historical context, defined by "the considerable challenges that arose to Christian belief in her lifetime." When Emily Dickinson was born, "the argument from design was securely in place on a six-thousand-year-old earth; at about the time that she began to write poetry regularly, Darwin published *The Origin of Species* and the earth had grown

---

7. The observation occurs in an 1856 journal entry; see Nathaniel Hawthorne, *The English Notebooks*, 433.

8. Magdalena Zapedowska, "Wrestling with Silence: Emily Dickinson's Calvinist God," 379.

suddenly older." Citing her "brilliant poem about the ebbing of belief," in which the divine "Hand is amputated now / And God cannot be found" (1551), Lundin observes that, like Melville, Dostoevsky, and Nietzsche—"contemporaries with whom she merits comparison"—Dickinson wrote about the loss of faith and "bravely tried to calculate the cost." He places her closer to Dostoevsky than to Melville and Nietzsche in that, like the Russian novelist, "she won her way through doubt to a tenuous but genuine faith." Lundin claims, "Unlike Nietzsche, she was not gleeful about the possible loss of God but profoundly sad about it, because," as she says in the amputation poem, "The abdication of belief / Makes the Behavior small." But he also acknowledges that, "in her moments of deepest uncertainty," she "registered her doubts with a vehemence as blunt as any oath of Melville's Ahab and a defiance as sharp as any hurled at the heavens by Nietzsche's Zarathustra."[9]

Obviously, these are questions of balance. One can dispute just how "gleeful" Nietzsche himself (as opposed to his Zarathustra) really *was* about a loss that he once compared to having the fibers of his heart torn out; and Dickinson, as Lundin concedes, was sometimes exuberant in her own denunciations of the Calvinist God.

In perhaps the best balanced of the studies of Dickinson's struggles with God, James McIntosh argues that, as in the case of Melville, Dickinson's lifelong wrestling with irresolution took a variety of forms, determined by what he calls, borrowing Dickinson's own term, "nimble believing." In the draft of a late letter to Otis Phillips Lord, she wrote: "On subjects of which we know nothing, or should I say *Beings* . . . we both believe and disbelieve a hundred times an Hour, which keeps Believing nimble—" (*L* 728). By nimble believing McIntosh means "believing for intense moments in a spiritual life without permanently subscribing to any received system of belief," an approach he describes as "a key experience, an obsessive subject, and a stimulus to expression for Dickinson."[10]

Though I differ somewhat from McIntosh (as well as from Lundin) in emphasis, his general argument is persuasive. Given her "dynamic" imagination, Dickinson "prefers not to adhere for long to any preconceived religious or philosophic doctrine." At different times and

9. *Emily Dickinson and the Art of Belief*, 4, 5, 148–49.
10. *Nimble Believing: Dickinson and the Unknown*, 1.

depending on shifting moods and contexts, she advances, as McIntosh points out, "opposed positions on such central questions as the goodness of God, the reality of heaven, or the presence of the divine in nature." Though the doctrines of her local religion, the Connecticut Valley Calvinist tradition in which she was raised, "are inscribed in her mind and heart," she "distrusts them and seeks an alternative faith that will be truer to her moral conceptions." Since Dickinson, a dialectical thinker, takes different positions on religious questions, commentators have found it difficult "to summarize her religious perspective."[11]

Those commentators are themselves (with unavoidable simplification) summarized by McIntosh. Some, like Jane Donahue Eberwein (*Dickinson: Strategies of Limitation*) and Dorothy Huff Oberhaus (*Emily Dickinson's Fascicles*), think of her as "essentially a traditional believer" and so tend to treat her skepticism as occasional and passing. Those who, like Cynthia Griffin Wolff (*Emily Dickinson*), Shira Wolosky (*Emily Dickinson: The Voice of War*), and Paula Bennett (*Emily Dickinson: Woman Poet*), think of her as "essentially a rebel" tend to treat her "quasi-orthodox poems and pronouncements as aberrations." Still others, including Vivian R. Pollak (*Dickinson: The Anxiety of Genre*) and Sharon Cameron (*Lyric Time: Dickinson and the Limitations of Genre*), address her religious concerns as "transformations of her psychological struggles and her religious language as the particular language she had available to address her personal needs as a nineteenth-century woman." In McIntosh's own view, Dickinson's "spiritual longings are genuine" and her "expressions of them central to her achievement as a poet. Yet she 'keeps Believing nimble' and does not allow herself to be assigned summarily to any ideological camp." What is needed is "a strategy that allows for her variety in order to present her range as a speculative artist and a thinker."[12]

As a number of critics have observed, while Dickinson's attitudes do not radically change in the course of her career, her work develops aesthetically and spiritually. McIntosh offers a useful synopsis. Her earliest poems (1858–1860) are "more sprightly and less troubled in spirit" than the prodigious output assigned to her most productive years (1861–1865), when Dickinson composed many lyrics with "dramatized speakers who anxiously explore religious questions." Speakers in the

11. Ibid., 35–36.
12. Ibid., 35–36.

poems from 1866 on are "apt to be confessionally meditative rather than dramatically afflicted." Our main poem, "Apparently with no surprise," was written in 1884, toward the end of her "last years" (ca. 1875–86), a period when, as McIntosh accurately notes, her poetry "reflects her awareness of the deaths of many closest to her and her contemplation of her own death." She turns often in this last period to what McIntosh characterizes as "general speculations concerning God, nature as God's creation, the relation between flesh and spirit, and the afterlife, often expressed in condensed and elliptical verse." In some of these late poems, Dickinson, at once acknowledging her Calvinist heritage and rebelling against it, "contemplates the abyss of God's unknown with terrified agnosticism."[13]

Nimble Believing, to quote the jacket blurb of Harold Bloom (who brought the book to my attention), may well be the "most subtly intelligent discussion of Dickinson's spirituality." At the risk of upsetting McIntosh's (as well as Lundin's) judicious balance, my own emphasis falls more on those instances when—as in "Apparently with no surprise"—the poet seems less "thankful" or "stimulated" confronting her inscrutable God than dismayed or denunciatory. "Apparently with no surprise," first published in 1890, may have been one of the "religious, or rather irreligious pieces" deplored by the considerably more pious Christina Rossetti, to whom Dickinson's publisher, Thomas Niles, sent a presentation copy of the posthumous 1890 *Poems.* A distinguished poet herself, Rossetti recognized the volume as "a very remarkable work of genius," but, as a conservative Christian, she also recognized blasphemy when she encountered it.[14]

———

The point remains that Dickinson's God, however inscrutable, is *personal.* She, of course, responded intensely—whether in love, awe, or terror—to the beauty, power, and often disturbing indifference or cruelty of Nature. But *her* God, like the God of the vast majority of contemporary Americans, is not pantheistic but personal: an intelligent Being who, however hidden from us, is concerned with life, especially with human life. In order to make it clear what I will *not* be talking about in subsequent references to "God," it may be useful to spend

13. Ibid., 37, 40.
14. Christina Rossetti quoted in Klaus Lubbers, *Emily Dickinson: The Critical Revolution,* 30.

some time contemplating the "religious faith" of Albert Einstein, with whose vision one of my friends associated the drama enacted in "Apparently with no surprise."

Despite that association, suggested by the remoteness and inscrutability shared by Dickinson's Calvinist God and Einstein's incomprehensible spirit manifest in the laws of nature, such a preamble would be irrelevant in a book concentrated *exclusively* (as mine is not) on "Apparently with no surprise." The theological, scientific, and literary net cast by the present study is wide enough to draw Einstein into the discussion. Aside from its considerable intrinsic interest, Einstein's "faith" in the at-least-quasi-divine, though impersonal, order of the universe can illuminate *both* Dickinson's religious thought and the larger issue of the relationship between God and Nature, God and humankind. More specifically, pondering "Einstein's God" enables us to move on to the contemporary debate between religion and science, God and Evolution, Design and Accident, divine benevolence or malevolence. These macrocosmic issues are all at "play," remarkably enough, within the microcosm of this brief lyric. Working within the compressed limits of her chosen genre, Dickinson manages to encompass, as Einstein did, both the infinitesimal and the infinite. And as for compression, not even our most concise and lapidary poet could rival the beautiful simplicity of Einstein's formulation of the theory that energy equals mass times the square of the speed of light. The leap from Emily Dickinson to Albert Einstein, who resorted to poetry himself in order to express his loving admiration of Spinoza, seems less unlikely when we consider that, in its own beautifully elegant way, $E=mc^2$ is a lyric poem.

Chapter 2

Religion and Science

Einstein's Spinozistic God

The archetypal twentieth-century genius, Einstein achieved what we would now consider rock-star celebrity, and he remains a recognizable icon around the world, even a figure in popular culture in the United States. During his life, as the world's most photogenic and publicly eminent scientist, he was endlessly questioned about his conception of God. His answers, though fascinating and even moving, did not exactly constitute a guide to the perplexed. That his answer to the Great Question continues to intrigue us has most recently been demonstrated by the essay "Einstein's God," which appeared in the April 16, 2007, issue of *Time* magazine. The essay was excerpted from the chapter of the same title in Walter Isaacson's splendid recent biography, *Einstein: His Life and Universe.*[1]

Like most of Dickinson's "religious" texts, our main poem treats the relationship—benign, malign, or indifferent—between Nature and the God who presumably created and governs the universe. Since Einstein devoted a lifetime's contemplation to a form of that relationship, I found it hard not to think of him in connection with such Dickinson

---

1. My own account is indebted chiefly but not exclusively to Isaacson's *Einstein: His Life and Universe,* and then not only to the chapter specifically entitled "Einstein's God" (384–93).

poems as "I know that He exists" and "Apparently with no surprise." And, since Einstein's conception of the "God" behind Nature is closely aligned with that of the great seventeenth-century idealist philosopher Baruch [Benedict] Spinoza, it seemed to me that a few words about Spinoza—as well as about the most celebrated passage of "Spinozistic" poetry in the canon of English literature—would also be in order, especially since the poet is Wordsworth, whose explorations of God and Nature sometimes provide, as I try to show in Part II, mutually illuminating comparisons and contrasts with the explorations of Emily Dickinson.

Excommunicated from his Amsterdam synagogue, cursed and vilified as a "heretic Jew," and condemned during the century following his death as the most monstrous of atheists, Spinoza was also, in the famous phrase of the German (Catholic) poet Novalis, "that God-intoxicated man." But Spinoza appealed as well to Nietzsche, that prominent atheist who pronounced his "precursor" a philosopher who "deified the All and Life in order to find peace and happiness in the face of it."[2] The "contradiction" is understandable. As enigmatically defined in part 4 of the *Ethics*, Spinoza's *Deus, sive Natura* (God, or Nature) either personifies Nature or depersonalizes God. Either way, God is not a person. The Nature with which Spinoza identifies God is "intelligible," that is, in principle capable of being understood through rational inquiry alone. This "deified" Nature is vital and creative, *natura naturans*, as opposed to *natura naturata*, passive nature, the mass of corporeal matter. As Spinoza says in part 1 of the *Ethics*, he took a "totally different view of God and Nature" than did "later Christians," in that his God was "the immanent, and not the extraneous, cause. All things, I say, are in God; and move in God." His view was not "*totally* different"; he wrote in Latin, the language of medieval philosophy, and his final phrase echoes Acts of the Apostles: "in him we live, and move, and have our being" (17:28).[3]

---

2. *Friedrich Nietzsche: Werke in drei Bänden*, 3:512. Nietzsche found in Spinoza "a *precursor*, and what a precursor." Spinoza had anticipated him by "making knowledge the *most powerful* affect" and by denying "the freedom of the will, teleology, and the moral world-order." Nietzsche's "lonesomeness" was "now at least a two-someness," he told his friend Overbeck in a July 1881 postcard (Walter Kaufmann, *Nietzsche: Philosopher, Psychologist, Antichrist*, 140, 246–47n).

3. Benedict Spinoza, *The Ethics of Spinoza*, part 1, proposition 18.

Spinoza insisted on strict causality. For all its seeming contingency from a human point of view, whatever happens, from a *philosophic* perspective, happens necessarily. There is no room in his universe for "purpose," intervention in events by an anthropomorphic God, or the illusion of divine, let alone human, free will. "Things could not have been produced by God in any manner or in any order different from that which in fact exists."[4] Yet readers of the God-intoxicated man vicariously experience something of his awed contemplation of a spirit immanent in the laws of the universe. That aspect of his vision was initially obscured, not only by his austerely geometric method and metaphysical vocabulary (substance, attributes, modes, and so on) but also by a scrupulous biblical scholarship that resulted in a devastating critique of popular religion. It took later German thinkers and writers (first Lessing, then Herder, Jacobi, Goethe) and, in England, Coleridge to resuscitate the reputation of Spinoza. Though, in the process, they reduced the Enlightenment philosopher and political prophet to a pantheistic mystic, they recognized in Spinoza a noble and profound spirit free of the burdens of dogma. What his contemporary Pascal "decried as the misery of man without the Biblical God, was for Spinoza the liberation of the human spirit from the bonds of fear and superstition."[5] It was Coleridge's friend Wordsworth who best expressed the Romantic conception of Spinozistic pantheism. In a famous passage (lines 88–102) of "Tintern Abbey," he magnificently if amorphously evokes an all-pervasive "presence," "motion," and "spirit":

> And I have felt
> A presence that disturbs me with the joy
> Of elevated thoughts; a sense sublime
> Of something far more deeply interfused,
> Whose dwelling is the light of setting suns,
> And the round ocean and the living air,
> And the blue sky, and in the mind of man:
> A motion and a spirit, that impels
> All thinking things, all objects of all thought,
> And rolls through all things.

4. Spinoza, *Ethics*, part 1, proposition 33.
5. Richard Popkin, *The History of Skepticism from Erasmus to Spinoza*, 237.

Though the phrase "whose dwelling" may evoke a numinous sense of what many would call "God" (a word seldom on Wordsworth's lips in 1798), it still located that "presence" in nature and in the mind of man. A quarter century later, Coleridge, who had introduced Wordsworth to Spinoza's *Ethics*, was troubled by—precisely—the Spinozistic impersonality of this passage. In *Aids to Reflection* (1825), he struggles to exonerate his old friend (and, not incidentally, his own earlier self) from the accurate charge that Wordsworth had substituted for the biblical Jehovah an indefinite "sense sublime." In citing the lines from "Tintern Abbey," Coleridge uses, he claims, "the language but not the sense or purpose of the great Poet of our Age." But he confesses to being deeply troubled by the contemporary "unwillingness to contemplate the Supreme Being in his personal Attributes," a "contagion" from which "even the sincerest seekers after light are not safe."[6]

At the same time that he was publicly clearing Wordsworth of the charge of pantheistic nature worship, in private correspondence Coleridge, by then somewhat estranged from his friend, was identifying the great poet of the age with that very "contagion" (a *topos* of high-church Anglican polemics). "I will not conceal from you," he told one of the most intimate of his later confidants, that this "vague, misty, rather than mystic, confusion of God with the world, and the accompanying nature-worship . . . is the trait of Wordsworth's poetic works that I most dislike as unhealthful, and denounce as contagious."[7] Whatever the reservations expressed by Coleridge and an increasingly orthodox Wordsworth (not to mention others who have found the passage poetically splendid but theologically vague and syntactically opaque), we still *have* those magnificent lines. They convey, if not the austerity of Spinoza, the impersonal majesty and sublimity of his vision.

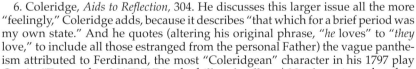

6. Coleridge, *Aids to Reflection*, 304. He discusses this larger issue all the more "feelingly," Coleridge adds, because it describes "that which for a brief period was my own state." And he quotes (altering his original phrase, "*he* loves" to "*they* love," to include all those estranged from the personal Father) the vague pantheism attributed to Ferdinand, the most "Coleridgean" character in his 1797 play *Osorio*: "To worship NATURE in the hill and valley, / Not knowing what they love." Wordsworth read *Osorio* in manuscript. The phrase from "Tintern Abbey" that the later, more orthodox Wordsworth was most defensive about was his description of his earlier self as, like Coleridge at the time, "a *worshipper* of nature" (line 151). I revisit "Tintern Abbey" in Chapter 11.

7. The remark is reported by the recipient of the letter. See Thomas Allsop, *Letters, Conversations and Recollections of S. T. Coleridge*, 1:107.

That vision appealed to Einstein, enthralled by Spinoza from the time he first read him in his early twenties. He remained impressed for the remainder of his life by Spinoza's concept of a God identified with the totality of Nature, his presence reflected in Nature's awe-inspiring beauty, rationality, order, and unity. Like Spinoza's, Einstein's impersonal God reveals himself in the partially discernible, ultimately mysterious, yet elegant and harmonious laws of the universe. Spinoza had written, in the third chapter of the *Tractatus Theologico-Politicus*, "By the help of God I mean the fixed and unchangeable order of nature, or the *chain* of natural events." For Einstein as well, Nature's laws were, above all, immutable; not even God could change them. In contrast to those for whom miracles were a proof of God's existence, for Einstein it was the *absence* of miracles that demonstrated a divine presence, revealed "in the harmony of all that exists." When "judging a theory," he told a friend, "I ask myself whether, if I were God, I would have arranged the world in such a way." The universe was determined, with no loopholes for "chance." If even a *few* things were random, he remarked in a 1942 letter, God would have "gone the whole hog," in which case "we wouldn't have to look for laws at all."[8]

And whether or not "*we* look" is irrelevant to those "laws." Though his own work (building on a suggestion by Max Planck in 1900) on the particle-like behavior of light had opened the way to quantum theory, Einstein stunned then elder statesman Wolfgang Pauli by objecting, in a conversation as late as 1954, to the principle fundamental to quantum mechanics, "that a system can be defined only by specifying the experimental method of observing it." No, insisted Einstein, who was never the "relativist" he is reductively thought to be. There was an objective, ontological "reality" independent of how we observed it. So much, in Einstein's erroneous estimation, for quantum mechanics and for Werner Heisenberg's "uncertainty principle."

Einstein's adherence (with some softening toward the end of his life) to strict causality ruled out any accommodation to randomness, an essential feature of quantum theory. The single greatest challenge to Einstein's deterministic paradigm came from the great Danish physicist Niels Bohr, who had developed a quantum theory of atoms as

---

8. Spinoza, *A Theologico-Political Treatise*, 44. The Einstein letters, as well as the 1954 exchange with Pauli and the 1926 letter to Max Born quoted in the next paragraph, are cited in Isaacson, *Einstein*, 335, 551, 538.

early as 1913. The challenge for Einstein was Bohr's Heisenberg-influenced "framework of complementarity," which involves two seemingly contradictory conceptual models. Two descriptions of nature are said to be "complementary" when both are true but cannot both be seen in the same experiment (as in the wave picture and the particle picture of an electron or a light-quantum)—a concept I revisit in my Conclusion, in the course of discussing Nietzschean "multi-perspectivism" as an approach to texts susceptible to apparently contradictory but sometimes equally valid interpretations.

By 1954, Einstein had been sparring over quantum theory for three decades with his friend the physicist Max Born. He had insisted, from the time of its full emergence in 1926, that quantum mechanics, at best a provisional step on the path to understanding atomic physics, could not be "correct" since it offered an incomplete, merely approximate description of phenomena at the level of the atom. "Quantum mechanics is certainly imposing," he conceded to Born in a 1926 letter. "But an inner voice tells me that it is not yet the real thing. The theory says a lot, but it does not really bring us any closer to the secrets of the Old One [*der Alte*]. I, at any rate, am convinced that He does not play dice."

The following year, when Einstein, during a conversation at a conference, once again trotted out his God averse to gambling, Niels Bohr reminded his friend of "the great caution, already called for by ancient thinkers, in ascribing attributes to Providence in everyday language." According to Heisenberg, present during the discussion, Bohr responded to Einstein's insistence that God would not and *could not* "play dice" with the good-humored quip: "But still, it cannot be for us to tell God how he is to run the world!"[9] In his mixture of determinism and pervasive God-talk, Einstein was following Spinoza. But despite the folksy anthropomorphism of his descriptions of dice-eschewing *der Alte*, Einstein, again like Spinoza, did *not* believe in a personal God who intervened in the universe, cared about human affairs, could be prayed to. Ethics was a purely human concern, with no supernatural input or sanction. Like Spinoza, too, Einstein did not believe in personal immortality.

Endearingly, Einstein responded in 1936 to a little girl in the sixth grade who wanted to know, "Do scientists pray?" He treated her

---

9. Heisenberg, *Encounters with Einstein,* 117.

question seriously. "Scientific research is based on the idea that everything that takes place is determined by laws of nature, and this holds for the actions of people," he explained. "For this reason a scientist will hardly be inclined to believe that events could be influenced by a prayer, i.e. by a wish addressed to a supernatural Being." Nevertheless, he continued,

> Everyone who is seriously interested in the pursuit of science becomes convinced that a spirit is manifest in the laws of the universe—a spirit vastly superior to that of man, and one in the face of which we with our modest powers must feel humble. In this way the pursuit of science leads to a religious feeling of a special sort, which is indeed quite different from the religiosity of someone more naïve.[10]

He had often been questioned at a more "sophisticated" level. At a Berlin dinner party in June 1927, Einstein, having dismissed astrology as sheer superstition, was asked why he didn't also reject as superstitious a religious belief in God. "Try and penetrate with our limited means the secrets of nature," he calmly replied, "and you will find that, beyond all the discernible laws and connections, there remains something subtle, intangible, and inexplicable. Veneration for this force beyond anything that we can comprehend is my religion." Two months later, sounding like both Spinoza (of whom he'd said in a poem, *Wie lieb ich diesen edlen Mann, / Mehr als ich Worten sagen kann*) and the Wordsworth who "felt / A presence" in "Tintern Abbey," he spoke of his "humble admiration of the infinitely superior spirit that reveals itself in the little that we can comprehend about the knowable world. That deeply emotional conviction of the presence of a superior reasoning power, which is revealed in the incomprehensible universe, forms my idea of God."[11]

Though Einstein's "faith" was notoriously difficult to pin down, there seemed to be—two years later—an almost concerted effort to do just

---

10. Letter to Phyllis Wright, January 24, 1936; cited in Isaacson, *Einstein*, 388.
11. The lines of Einstein's poem may be translated as "How I love this noble man, / More than I can say in words" (see http://www.AlbertEinstein.info/db/ViewImage.do?DocumentID+17814&Page=1). See also Einstein to M. Schayer, August 5, 1927, in Isaacson, *Einstein*, 388. For the Berlin dinner party, see Charles Kessler, ed., *The Diaries of Count Harry Kessler*, 322. For details in the following paragraph, see Isaacson, *Einstein*, 388–89.

that, or to condemn him. In a charge that appeared in *Time* on May 13, 1929, William Henry Cardinal O'Connell of Boston decried Einstein's speculations about time and space as "a cloak beneath which hides the ghastly apparition of atheism."[12] That blast prompted Rabbi Herbert S. Goldstein, longtime president of the Orthodox Jewish Congregations of America, to request that Einstein answer, "in 50 words," the question, "Do you believe in God?" Einstein's answer became famous: "I believe in Spinoza's God, who reveals himself in the lawful harmony of all that exists, but not in a God who concerns himself with the fate and the doings of mankind." The *New York Times* spread the word under the headline: "Einstein Believes in Spinoza's God." Though always awed and charmed by Einstein, many Americans, lay and clergy, were shocked by the idea of a God utterly indifferent to human affairs.

In a remarkable interview given shortly after his fiftieth birthday, Einstein described himself as "fascinated by Spinoza's pantheism." But he was only slightly more comfortable with that term than he was with being labeled either a believer or an atheist.[13] And he was called both by those who wished to enlist so distinguished a name in their cause. On several occasions over the years, some formal, but often, as we've seen, in response to letters, he tried to answer those who pressed him about his "faith." In 1930, he concluded his credo, "What I Believe," by defining what he *actually meant* in calling himself "religious":

> The most beautiful emotion we can experience is the mysterious. It is the fundamental emotion that stands at the cradle of all true art and science. He to whom this emotion is a stranger, who can no longer wonder and stand rapt in awe, is as good as dead. . . . To sense that behind everything that can be experienced there is something that our minds cannot grasp, whose beauty and sublimity reaches us only indirectly; this is religiousness. In this sense, and in this sense only, I am a devoutly religious man.[14]

12. We will return to a later public comment by a cardinal of the Catholic Church. But in 2005, the anger was to come from the other side, since Cardinal Schönborn's defense of theism in the *New York Times* seemed at the expense of evolution, rousing a reaction from scientists, some of them Catholic.

13. This revealing interview with George Sylvester Viereck was first published in the *Saturday Evening Post*, October 26, 1929. For details, see Isaacson, *Einstein*, 385–87, 617n4.

14. In Albert Einstein, *The World As I See It*; on audio: www.yu.edu/libraries/digital_library/einstein/credo.html.

Just as his observation at the Berlin party flabbergasted the sophisticated skeptic who challenged him, so "What I Believe" did not satisfy
orthodox believers. But Einstein never ceased exploring the perennial
issue: the relationship between "Science and Religion." In an op-ed of
that title (*New York Times*, November 9, 1930), Einstein claimed that his
"faith" inspired and supported rather than conflicted with his profes-
sional work. Indeed, "the cosmic religious feeling is the strongest and
noblest motive for scientific research." Such early scientists as Kepler,
Galileo, Robert Boyle, Bacon, and Newton, relating their scientific studies to their faith, explored creation as a way of finding out the wisdom
of God as revealed in it. Though Einstein was aware that something
remained missing from purely scientific accounts, he is not quite in
accord with the early scientists. And he stops short of the position of
modern scientist-theologians who argue that an understanding of cosmology and evolution can strengthen faith. In fact, some insist not only
that the human mind discerns the Mind of the Creator but also that "Science is possible because the universe is a divine creation."[15]

Despite the conflict he saw between science and the concept of a personal God, Einstein wanted to bridge the gap between two realms
many thought, and still think, must be kept separate. When Church
authorities silenced Galileo, whose work seemed to them to threaten
the necessary existence of God as creator of the physical universe, science responded to the attack by becoming increasingly secular, a
development climaxing in the Darwinian theory of evolution. Ever
since, frequently under Kantian auspices, theologians and scientists
have often worked out a modus vivendi, rendering unto the theologian the transcendent and moral realm, to the scientist the intellectually apprehensible natural world.

Where Darwin himself is to be located in the compatibility-
incompatibility debate is not always clear. Following the publication
of *The Descent of Man*, the *Springfield Republican* (the daily edited by
J. G. Holland and regularly read by Emily Dickinson) enthusiastically
announced the reception of a letter endorsing its June 24, 1872, edito-

15. John Polkinghorne, *Quantum Physics and Theology: An Unexpected Kinship*, 8.
In terms of evolution and faith, see, in addition to the more substantial books of
John F. Haught cited in the Introduction and in the next chapter, Michael Dowd's
*Thank God for Evolution! How the Marriage of Science and Religion Will Transform Your
Life and Our World* (2007).

rial arguing for compatibility rather than antagonism between science and religion. The writer of the letter was Darwin himself, who said of the *Republican*'s "Truths for the Times": "I admire them from my inmost heart, and I believe that I agree to every word." Modern science and religion, both based on "law" rather than "miracle," were, the editors claimed, "coming to a fair understanding"; that, "we trust and believe, is the real meaning of [Darwin's] words." Although many questions remain "open," the *Republican* editorial continued, "the most progressive science and the most progressive religion of the times are agreeing upon common principles and working for common ends—science ruling supreme in the world of intellect and religion ruling supreme in the world of morals." In discrediting "miracle," Darwin, the century's major scientist and one of the "greatest prophets of the new era," had "renovated the unity and harmony of nature's processes in a region which had been still sacred to superstition."[16]

The *Springfield Republican*'s Darwin sounds remarkably like the Einstein of natural (miracle-free) law and harmonious unity. But he is also presented as agreeing to a sharp division of labor between science and religion, a position closer to Kant than to Einstein. The most discussed, and debated, modern formulation of this division has been that of paleontologist Stephen Jay Gould. Making a case, in 1997, for "non-overlapping *magisteria*," he described the separation this way: "the net of science covers the empirical realm: what is the universe made of (fact) and why does it work this way (theory). The net of religion extends over questions of moral meaning and value."[17]

16. See "Darwin and Abbot[t]: An English Scientific Endorsement of American Free Religion," in Joan Kirkby, "The Dickinson Periodicals Project": http://ccs.mq.edu.au/dickinson/publications.html. Eight years later, in response to the direct question of a German student, a family member responded that Darwin "considers that the theory of Evolution is quite compatible with the belief in a God; but that you must remember that different persons have different definitions of what they mean by God." Unsatisfied, the student pressed the question, prompting a busy and unwell Darwin to respond, "Science has nothing to do with Christ. . . . For myself, I do not believe that there has ever been any revelation" (from Francis Darwin's chapter "Religion," in *Life and Letters,* 1:277). In passages written aboard the *Beagle* forty years earlier, Darwin describes how, though "unwilling to give up my belief," he felt himself compelled by the "evidence" to "disbelief," a process gradual but "at last complete" (1:278).

17. Gould introduced the concept in the journal *Natural History;* repeated in *Leonardo's Mountain of Clams and the Diet of Worms* (1998), it is available in Gould's posthumous collection, *The Richness of Life: The Essential Stephen Jay Gould,* 594.

This proposal for separate *magisteria* has come under attack from both sides, religious and secular. Among the so-called neo-atheists, it is rejected most strenuously by Oxford scientist and prominent nonbeliever Richard Dawkins, who wonders, in *The God Delusion*, why scientists are "so cravenly respectful toward the ambitions of theologians, over questions that theologians are certainly no more qualified to answer than scientists themselves." Instead, he insists, "the presence or absence of a creative super-intelligence is unequivocally a scientific question."[18] Physicist and astronomer Victor J. Stenger, in *God: The Failed Hypothesis,* also takes Gould to task for exempting supernatural religion from legitimate scientific scrutiny. Even philosopher Daniel C. Dennett, who finds Gould's peacemaking intention laudable, rejects his proposal, while making it clear that he "is not suggesting that science should *try to do* what religion does, but that it should *study,* scientifically, what religion does."[19]

This debate would not be alien to Emily Dickinson. In the 1870s in New England, no conflict was more heated than that between science and religion, and the compatibility or incompatibility of evolution with Design and religious faith. In the second series of his "Lectures on the Scientific Evidences of Evolution," given at Amherst College and published in 1872 as *Pater Mundi, or the Doctrine of Evolution,* the Rev. E. F. Burr argued that, while it was not absolutely inconsistent with theology (the human *interpretation* of religious beliefs) or with belief in a Supreme Being, the doctrine of Evolution was, "both in its practical influence and its logical sequences, . . . quite inconsistent with a reasonable faith in the Bible and in God," and so had to be combated by advocates of a Christian philosophy. Emily Dickinson would not have attended the lectures, but she may well have read the review of Burr's book in *Scribner's.*

~~

18. Dawkins, *The God Delusion,* 56. Dawkins's militancy recalls the 1993 controversy over the attempt to establish a lectureship in theology and the natural sciences, a lectureship handsomely endowed by the English author Susan Howatch. The plan was ferociously attacked as nonacademic in a lead article by the editor of the widely read scientific weekly *Nature* (April 1, 1993). His round dismissal of the suggestion that scientists had anything to learn from theology provoked many responses from scientists and theologians.

19. Stenger, *God: The Failed Hypothesis,* 10; Dennett, *Breaking the Spell,* 30.

Though Einstein was a nonbeliever in the biblical God, and not to be categorized as a scientist-theologian, he always tried in some sense to bring the separate *magisteria* together. At a 1941 symposium on science, philosophy, and religion held at the Union Theological Seminary in New York, he claimed that the spirit of genuine scientific investigation requires seekers "thoroughly imbued with the aspiration toward truth and understanding," an aspiration that "springs from the sphere of religion." The sense of awe he was referring to—the rapture attending "all true art and science"—may be clarified by his 1930s discussion with Saint-John Perse. When asked how a poem originated, the poet spoke of "intuition and imagination." Delighted, Einstein (whose revolutionary early work *was* nothing if not "intuitive") replied, "It's the same for a man of science. It's a sudden illumination, almost a rapture. Later, to be sure, intelligence analyzes and experiments confirm or invalidate the intuition." The speech at Union Theological Seminary "got front-page news coverage," reports Isaacson, and Einstein's "pithy conclusion became famous: 'The situation may be expressed by an image: science without religion is lame, religion without science is blind.'" Though Isaacson doesn't mention it, Einstein was adapting Kant's equally pithy synopsis in the "Transcendental Logic" section of the *Critique of Pure Reason:* "Thoughts without content are empty, intuitions without concepts are blind."[20]

One idea was totally *un*acceptable to science, Einstein added in a crucial caveat: that of a personal deity, a God who could and would meddle in events—altering his own laws. Indeed, second only to Darwin, no scientist has made belief in a personal God more difficult to accept than Einstein. Since the universe was precisely engineered, the divine "will" was no more "free" than human will; immutable laws governed all. One was the speed of light proposed by Einstein in 1905 as a universal constant. His foundation had been the 1887 Michelson-Morley experiment. At a 1920 party following a lecture at Princeton, someone informed him that new experiments on the Michelson-Morley technique seemed to confirm that the hypothetical "ether" existed and that the speed of light was actually variable. Einstein

20. Isaacson, *Einstein,* 390. Kant, *Critique of Pure Reason,* "Transcendental Logic" section, B75/A51, 193–94. Einstein was reading, and understanding(!), Kant as early as age thirteen, when he was introduced to the *Critique of Pure Reason* by a university student who dined weekly with the Einstein family.

calmly responded with his most memorable axiom: "The Lord God is subtle, but malicious he is not" (*Raffiniert ist der Herr Gott, aber boshaft ist er nicht*). Mathematics professor Oscar Veblen, who overheard the remark, remembered it and, when the new Princeton math building was built a decade later, requested permission to carve the words on the stone mantel of the fireplace in the common room. In cordially granting his approval, Einstein further explained to Veblen what he had meant: "Nature hides her secret because of her essential loftiness, but not by means of ruse."[21]

There is *some*thing of this in Emily Dickinson, whose God, though always a Person, was usually, in keeping with Puritan tradition, hidden and elusive. "The Puritan God," argues Perry Miller, "is entirely incomprehensible to man," a "realm of mystery." Fundamental to Puritanism is the idea that "God, the force, the power, the life of the universe, must remain to men hidden and unknowable," not "fully revealed even in His own [Biblical] revelation," behind which "always lies His secret will."[22] "Divinity dwells under seal," Dickinson ends one austere poem (662), an appropriate divinity for a poet who was not only an heir to the Calvinist tradition but also a recluse. Another, to which we will return, begins:

> I know that He exists.
> Somewhere—in Silence—
> He has hid his rare life
> From our gross eyes. (338)

Such poems seem as cryptic as Einstein's formulations, whether in his credo or in this most famous of his formulations. In his letter to Veblen he shifts gender (*Herr Gott* becomes a female Nature) while maintaining the anthropomorphism that has understandably confused so many. The point remains that Einstein's Spinozistic God, unlike Dickinson's, was impersonal, a reflection of the laws governing the universe and not to be thought of as concerned with human affairs. "I cannot conceive of a personal God who would directly influence the actions of individuals or would sit in judgment on creatures of his own creation," he wrote in 1927. "I do not believe in a personal God and I

---

21. Einstein to Veblen, April 30, 1930; in Isaacson, *Einstein*, 297–98.
22. Perry Miller, *The New England Mind: The Seventeenth Century*, 10, 21.

have never denied this but have expressed it clearly."[23] "The main source of the present-day conflicts between the spheres of religion and science," he insisted in concluding his Union Theological Seminary speech, "was this concept of a personal God."

⌒

As we have seen, and will again, there are those who would deny this "conflict." Though often resisted from both sides, the attempt to make science and religion compatible takes place in both the biological and the cosmological realms. There are many physicists who happen also to be believers, some of whom—Paul Davies, for example, in *The Mind of God* (1992) and later works—try to reconcile their religious faith with their scientific work. Theists often remind us that it was a Catholic priest, Georges-Henri Lemaître, who was the first (in 1927) to propose what would become known as the Big Bang theory. But it was not as a priest, who presumably accepted the idea of a divine creation, but as an eminent astronomer doing science based on Einstein's general theory of relativity that Lemaître advanced his proposal that the universe had a beginning. The idea that *God* caused the Big Bang, while it might be true, is not a *scientific* theory since it is not vulnerable to verification or falsification (there are no observations we can make to prove or disprove it). Lemaître himself insisted on keeping his theory separate from his religion, even going so far as to ask Pope Pius XII, who in 1951 interpreted the Big Bang as scientific proof of Genesis, to refrain from making that claim.

Others *reject* the Kantian truce between knowledge and faith, science and religion, an accommodation endorsed by such large-minded thinkers as the American pragmatists William James and John Dewey and reaffirmed by Gould. Believers who reject the notion of separate *magisteria* include theistic evolutionists (National Human Genome Resources director Francis Collins, for example, or philosopher Alvin Plantinga), as well as scientist-theologians such as Ian Barbour, Arthur Peacocke, and the physicist and Anglican priest J. C. Polkinghorne. But even Polkinghorne—the author of such books as *Science and Providence* (1989), *Belief in God in an Age of Science* (1998), and, most recently, *Quantum Physics and Theology* (2007)—begins the latter, subtitled *An Unexpected Kinship*, by acknowledging that, since theology and science

23. Einstein to M. Shayer, August 5, 1927, in Isaacson, *Einstein*, 387.

are usually considered antithetical, people "think it odd, or even disingenuous, for a person to be both a physicist and a priest."[24] Indeed, most scientists would agree with Einstein on a "conflict" between science and *belief in a personal God*—as we shall see in returning to the contemporary debate between science and religion.

In the next chapter, by way of balance, I will set against the position, already noted, of such prominent proponents of atheism as Richard Dawkins, Sam Harris, Victor J. Stenger, Daniel C. Dennett, and Christopher Hitchens an exemplary case for theism *and* science, reason *and* faith. Had I been writing a few months later, I might have chosen the new books, already mentioned, by Owen Gingerich and by John F. Haught. In *God's Universe* (2007), Gingerich, professor emeritus of astronomy and of the history of science at Harvard, carves out a "theistic space" from which it is possible to contemplate a universe of wonder and mystery in which God plays an interactive role, unnoticed yet not excluded by science. John Haught's *God and the New Atheism* (2008), a penetrating critique of the position shared by Harris, Dawkins, Hitchens, and Dennett, is both a polemic and a positive defense of Christian theology. Liberated from fundamentalist shackles, Christian faith is presented by Haught as fully compatible with scientific reason, specifically, with evolutionary theory. Unfortunately, Haught's book appeared when mine was already at the copyediting stage. In any event, and for reasons noted in my Introduction, I've chosen the case for coexistence between natural science and theology advanced, not always with the approval of John Haught, by Christoph Cardinal Schönborn.

Schönborn's new book, *Chance or Purpose: Creation, Evolution, and a Rational Faith,* evolved out of the widespread debate stirred by his earlier mentioned *New York Times* op-ed, a debate in which John Haught played a prominent part. Schönborn's book expands as well on two subsequent lectures. The result is a sustained attempt, carried on from 2005 to 2007, to rationally reconcile creation (*not* literalist "creation*ism*") and evolution (*not* ideological "evolution*ism*"), in the process

---

24. Polkinghorne, *Quantum Physics and Theology,* 1. Peacocke, who died in 2006, argued (more ingeniously than persuasively) that, by freely choosing to limit his omnipotence to accommodate random mutations as the raw material of Darwinian evolution, God displayed divine humility.

affirming the role of a benign and providential God in a world of injustice and suffering. In its defense of an overarching Design incorporating both evolution and a divine Logos, Schönborn's argument, however scientifically grounded, is ultimately providential and Christological. It therefore provides as well an opportunity to return to Emily Dickinson, who was drawn to Jesus as the very epitome of suffering humanity, but who was more often than not *dis*approving of the sort of "Approving God" she presents us with in "Apparently with no surprise" and in a considerable number of related poems.

Chapter 3

God and Evolution

The Contemporary Debate

For Einstein, the "main source" of the "conflicts" between religion and science was "the concept of a personal God." The same is true today in Einstein's adopted country. Few *leading* U.S. scientists believe in a "personal God," yet they live in what is by far the most theistic nation in the industrialized world. Surprisingly in such a milieu, a series of taboo-breaking, neo-atheist books—Sam Harris's *The End of Faith* (2005) and *Letter to a Christian Nation* (2006), Richard Dawkins's *The God Delusion* (2006), and Daniel C. Dennett's *Breaking the Spell* (2007)—have all hit best-seller lists. Two more appeared in 2007. The full title of Victor J. Stenger's *God: The Failed Hypothesis—How Science Shows That God Does Not Exist* synopsizes the shared, if not always expressed, position. In May, that formidable polemicist and maverick Christopher Hitchens weighed in with his provocative *God Is Not Great: How Religion Poisons Everything*. While these authors have been vilified by the faithful, most of their books are selling very well.[1]

---

1. And then there is *the* best seller. That international phenomenon, the seven Harry Potter novels (over 400 million copies sold thus far, in some sixty languages), fits into this secular, even neo-atheist pattern. Unlike Middle Earth and Narnia, the fantasy worlds projected by J. K. Rowling's precursors (Catholic J. R. R. Tolkien and Anglican C. S. Lewis), her magical world, both in the novels

The debate over religion in America is hardly new, but, witch trials aside and with the possible exception of the original Darwin wars in the 1870s, it has seldom been as fierce or as public. Reflecting the general interest in the recent atheist challenge to fundamentalist religion, *Newsweek* in April 2007 invited Sam Harris and Rick Warren, California pastor and author of the wildly popular *The Purpose-Driven Life*, to discuss what the informed moderator, Jon Meacham, called "the ultimate question: is God real?" The debate was won by Harris, who argued for Darwinian evolution instead of an intelligent Designer and, in addressing one of Warren's "great evidences" for the existence of God—"answered prayer"—challenged believers to an experiment: "Get a billion Christians to pray for a single amputee. Get them to pray that God re-grow that missing limb." As for the Bible and the Koran: it was "exquisitely clear" that neither "represents our best understanding of the universe." Subsequent letters to the editor attributed Warren's poor showing to the fact that "he had to try to present the Bible as something other than the very fallible creation of man that it is"; or regretted that he hadn't met Harris's onslaught in subtler ways—by, for example, conceding that "no all-controlling deity exists, but that there is a spiritual connection among us"; or by proposing a simple rather than a literalist spirituality: "a non-denominational sense of a benevolent higher power that calls us to serve mankind and the planet through love."[2]

These are valid points. But, of course, it is *precisely* the personal, highly sectarian, usually literalist interpretations of God as depicted in the Bible and Koran that Harris and his fellow atheists are most intent to refute, even when the exercise amounts to shooting fundamentalist

---

and in the film versions, is religion-free. As Christopher Hitchens notes in his August 2007 review of the final novel, "the schoolchildren appear to know nothing of Christianity." He pointedly cites Hermione's skeptical observation about the so-called Resurrection Stone: "How can I possibly prove it doesn't exist. . . . I mean, you could claim that anything's real if the only basis for believing it is that nobody's proved it doesn't exist." On the other hand, the children have a "strong moral code" (a "mystery," Hitchens rubs it in, only to the pope and "other clerical authorities who have denounced the series"). Harry's power derives not from God or nature but from the human emotion of love. Yet, in that final novel (as Hitchens does *not* mention), Harry's willing acceptance of death is followed by a "resurrection" in which he leads his friends to victory over evil.

2. "The Debate," *Newsweek,* April 9, 2007, pp. 55–63; "Letters," *Newsweek,* April 23, 2007, p. 16.

fish in a barrel. Not since the "death of God" controversy in the late 1960s has theology been so publicly discussed. Making his case and selling his book, Hitchens spent much of 2007 debating, on television (with Al Sharpton and, more substantively, with Jon Meacham) and at packed college events. In October alone, the month in which I happen to be writing, Hitchens debated the role of religious belief in the modern world with Alister McGrath, Oxford professor of historical theology and author of the four-volume *A Scientific Theology*, then with right-wing pundit Dinesh D'Souza, a skilled debater who, taking Kant for gospel, insisted, as he does in *What's So Great about Christianity, both* that believers have "faith" because they "do not claim to *know* God" *and* that theism "*knows* that there is a reality greater than, and beyond, that which our senses and our minds can ever apprehend."[3] Hitchens took his own book tour into hostile territory, the heart of the American Bible belt, where he repeatedly identified as the target of his animus the God of the monotheistic religions, for him a brutal "dictator in the skies." I raise the point since, to the extent that the God she addresses throughout her life is essentially the Calvinist deity of her childhood, Emily Dickinson is, if not completely, then largely in agreement. The difference is that, while she fearlessly and ferociously questions her Calvinist legacy, Dickinson seldom if ever questions God's existence.

There are focal and tonal distinctions among the neo-atheists, with Harris and Hitchens the most wide-ranging and polemical, Dawkins and Stenger the most relentlessly focused on hard science, and Dennett—neither biologist nor physicist, but a philosopher—the most even tempered. He might be appreciated by Einstein, who would find Harris, and, especially, the angry Dawkins and combative Hitchens too belligerent for his taste. At the risk of seeming churlish toward those from whom I have learned much, I cite Einstein. "What separates me from most so-called atheists," he said in 1953, "is a feeling of utter humility toward the unattainable secrets of the harmony of the cosmos." And in a letter a dozen years earlier, he compared "fanatical atheists" to "slaves . . . still feeling the weight of the chains which they have thrown off after hard struggle. They are creatures who—in their grudge against traditional religion as the 'opium of the masses'—cannot hear the music of the spheres."[4]

3. D'Souza, *What's So Great about Christianity*, 178.
4. Quoted in Isaacson, *Einstein*, 389, 390.

The neo-atheists cited above, though they certainly bear a grudge against traditional religion, *do* hear that music, even if they find it less harmonious than did Einstein, who was still trying, on his deathbed, to work out his elusive unified field theory. That quest, dominated by mathematical speculation and generally dismissed as a quixotic failure, may yet prove to have been anticipatory. Wrong in dissenting from quantum mechanics, Einstein may turn out to have been right in seeking, during his final three decades at Princeton, a new mathematics that might extend general relativity to a unification of all the forces and particles in nature. While it is too early to know, what has been going on recently in superstring theory certainly "looks a lot like what Einstein was doing in his Princeton years." One is moved though not surprised to learn that "the final thing [Einstein] wrote, before he went to sleep for the last time, was one more line of symbols and numbers that he hoped might get him, and the rest of us, just a little step closer to the spirit manifest in the laws of the universe."[5]

Of course, Einstein's spiritual quest has nothing in common with the religiosity prevalent in contemporary America. Amid our megachurches and televangelists, he would be compelled to align himself with the atheists and agnostics who find themselves an embattled, if increasingly assertive, minority. Always open to mystery, Einstein would not be militant. But, then, until the recent outbreak of the neo-atheists, most nonbelievers haven't been particularly combative. All but the most triumphal occasionally acknowledge the allure of the consolation associated with a majority belief they no longer share, and even doubters have their own doubts, though, as they must, they

5. Lee Smolin, "The Other Einstein," 83. For some, string theory has already reconciled those two equally valid but mutually incompatible theories: quantum mechanics, demonstrably true at the micro level, and the general theory of relativity, demonstrably true at the macro level. If that duality can be breached, who knows what other mysteries regarding the deepest truths of the universe may yet be unveiled, including, perhaps, the unifying Holy Grail Einstein was seeking. On one level, as Freeman Dyson has recently observed, string theory may be considered "the revenge of the heirs of Einstein against the heirs of Bohr" and his well-established concept of "complementarity." See Dyson, "Working for the Revolution," 47, and, for an accessible discussion of superstrings and "the quest for the ultimate theory," Brian Greene, *The Elegant Universe: Superstrings, Hidden Dimensions, and the Quest for the Ultimate Theory*. Einstein's "final" writing is reported in Isaacson, *Einstein*, 543.

value rationalism above spiritualism. Despite attempts to breach it (from Aquinas to Einstein; from Kepler and Newton to Schönborn, Polkinghorne, Gingerich, and Haught), the great gap remains that between "science" and "religion." That does not mean that nonbelievers never experience "an emptiness" that, as they might put it, "our big-brained architecture interprets as a yearning for the supernatural." For a science-oriented nonbeliever, seeking evolutionary explanations for why we believe in God, such an irrepressible yearning is "like an atavistic theism erupting when his guard is down."

The essay I am quoting—Robin Marantz Henig's "Darwin's God"— appeared in the *New York Times Magazine* in March 2007. Since they provide a convenient launching platform, I will be referring to two other pieces also published in the *Times*. The most recent, a February 2007 column by Nicholas Kristof to which I'll return in Chapter 4, inadvertently but graphically raised the perennial philosophical and theological problem: how an omnipotent, omniscient, and all-loving God can allow so much undeniable and unnecessary suffering in the world. But I'll begin with the earlier piece, by the Archbishop of Vienna, Christoph Cardinal Schönborn. When it appeared in the *Times* on July 7, 2005, that op-ed, as I noted in the Introduction, provoked a controversy that engaged me enough that I followed the cardinal's various responses to the challenging letters he received. Together, they offer a religious counterargument to those who, rejecting Gould's "non-overlapping *magisteria*," have recently marshaled evidence—or, rather, the *absence* of "evidence"—to demonstrate the nonexistence of the traditional God.

In addition, what Cardinal Schönborn has to say illuminates the context in which I am examining Emily Dickinson. While she was (obviously) not a Catholic, the challenges to which Schönborn is responding (hardly limited to Catholic thought, as indicated by the controversy he has stirred) seem to me relevant to Dickinson's concerns and especially germane to "Apparently with no surprise." In part, this is attributable to the coincidence noted in my Introduction. The same week that I found myself at a liberal arts college in the Jesuit tradition discussing with students "Apparently with no surprise," I had also been reading two recent lectures by Cardinal Schönborn, who seems to have emerged as the Catholic Church's official spokesman on questions involving creation, evolution, and design. These issues, obviously transcending and yet at the thematic and tonal heart of

Emily Dickinson's little poem, are engaging in their own right. They also provide a context in which to fully explore a miniature yet biological and cosmic drama in which the featured players are a "happy" Flower that a lethal Frost "beheads" while an "unmoved" sun measures off one more day "For an Approving God": an "apparently" grim, but perhaps merely realistic, illustration of what Alexander Pope referred to, in his famous couplet on Isaac Newton, as "Nature and Nature's laws," presided over by the Lawmaker, God.

In his *Times* op-ed, "Finding Design in Nature," Cardinal Schönborn, himself a future candidate for the papacy, dismissed "as vague and unimportant" a 1996 statement in which Pope John Paul II observed that "evolution," or, rather, the "*several* theories of evolution," constituted a valid "hypothesis," indeed "more than a hypothesis." Rather less casual than Schönborn implies, John Paul's statement (its thesis was that "Truth Cannot Contradict Truth") was issued to the Pontifical Academy of Sciences on October 22, 1996, and given front-page coverage around the world. The *New York Times* headline on October 25 was typical: "Pope Bolsters Church's Support for Scientific View of Evolution."[6] There was a more sensationalistic headline in the conservative *Il Giornale:* "Pope Says We May Descend from Monkeys." (He *didn't*, and we *don't*; we are related to, not descended from, monkeys.) The context of John Paul's statement, as he makes clear, was Pope Pius XII's 1950 encyclical *Humani Generis,* and what made John Paul's statement newsworthy was his revision of Pius's insistence that evolution had to be treated with caution, that, while having strong claims to legitimacy, and not necessarily "in opposition" to faith, it might still be untrue.

As Schonbörn notes, though John Paul was superseding *Humani Generis* by asserting that "new knowledge" has demonstrated beyond a reasonable doubt the origin of the "human body" from "pre-existing living matter," the pope did not define the "several theories of evolution" in 1996. Even so, his endorsement was troubling to others beside Cardinal Schönborn. John Paul's statement was accepted, but with

6. One indication of the favorable reception by Darwinians of John Paul's 1996 address is its appearance as the lead item in the section titled "Mainstream Religious Support for Evolution" in Philip Appleman's widely read *Darwin: A Norton Critical Edition,* 527–28.

pain, by a theist who, in a letter to the *New York Times* written shortly after the publication of John Paul's statement, confessed that the pope's "acceptance of evolution"

> touched the doubt in my heart. The problem of pain and suffering in a world created by a God who is all love and light is hard enough to bear, even if one is a creationist. But at least a creationist can say that the original creation, coming from the hand of God, was good, harmonious, innocent and gentle. What can one say about evolution, even a spiritual theory of evolution? Pain and suffering, mindless cruelty and terror are its means of creation. Evolution's engine is the grinding of predatory teeth upon the screaming, living flesh and bones of prey. . . . If evolution be true, my faith has tougher seas to sail.[7]

Emily Dickinson, who saw death and dissolution all around her and harbored few illusions about a gentle creation (frost "beheads" flowers with divine approval; nature "sears" saplings, "scalps" trees [314]), knew that when it came to religious faith, "the shore is safer . . . but I love to buffet the sea" (*L* 104). One nevertheless sympathizes with the believer for whom the pope's remarks left a faith with "tougher seas to sail." And his awareness of pain and suffering, as well as his sense of estrangement in an often terrifying post-Darwinian universe, was certainly shared by Emily Dickinson. In fact, interrupting both pope and cardinal, we may return for a moment to Dickinson and to the immediate reception and aftermath of the publication of *The Descent of Man.*

For many theists, Darwin's *Origin of Species* and, even more, *The Descent of Man* presented a painful, occasionally faith-destroying challenge. How was one to reconcile a biblical belief in divine creation of immutable species with Darwin's account of evolution through natural selection, especially given the inclusion of human beings among the creatures that had evolved? Many could not. For others, then and now, creation and evolution can peacefully coexist. An early compatibilist was Alfred Russel Wallace, the man who proposed, almost concurrently and independently of Darwin, the origin of species through natural selection. Articles and reviews in the papers and periodicals read by Emily Dickinson (and made conveniently available online by

7. *New York Times*, November 3, 1996.

Joan Kirkby) repeatedly distinguished between Darwin and Wallace. The *Springfield Republican* quoted Wallace from his *Natural Selection: What It Cannot Do* (1872): "The inference I would draw from this class of phenomena is, that a superior intelligence has guided the development of man in a definite direction and for a special purpose." In the previous year, the *Scribner's* reviewer of *The Descent of Man* emphasized Wallace's insistence that "there were evident proofs that a Higher Intelligence had modified and directed the operations of natural law." Nevertheless, the reviewer acknowledged in the very next sentence, "the most important contribution . . . to this subject is Darwin's long-promised *Descent of Man*," and Darwin had not found—and, as a scientist, had not sought—evidence of such a nonbiological, spiritual Higher Intelligence.[8]

Two of her letters reveal Emily Dickinson's awareness of Darwin. Writing to her friend Elizabeth Holland, Dickinson, thinking of pollinating bees, wittily noted, "Why the Thief ingredient accompanies all Sweetness Darwin does not tell us" (*L* 485). That was in 1871, the year a reluctant Darwin finally published *Descent*. In a sermon that year, famed Congregationalist minister Henry Ward Beecher praised Darwin, though he was "not prepared to accept all his speculations." In

---

8. The argument for compatibility continues. Philosopher Michael Ruse answered his own question affirmatively in his thoughtful *Can a Darwinian Be a Christian? The Relationship between Science and Religion* (2001); his characteristic virtues of scholarship and balance also inform his *Darwin and Design: Does Evolution Have a Purpose?* (2003). In short, Schönborn and Gingerich are not alone. In *The Language of God: A Scientist Presents Evidence for Belief* (2006), Francis S. Collins, director of the National Human Genome Resources Institute and an evangelical Christian, insists that there is scientific evidence for belief and that faith can coexist with science; with a sectarian emphasis alien to the spirit of Einstein, he claims that science is an "opportunity to worship." A similar case is made by biologist Joan Roughgarden in *Evolution and Christian Faith* (2006). Even Pope Benedict XVI, in July 2007, pronounced the supposed "clash" between evolution and faith "absurd." But the very next month, John Bowling, president of Olivet Nazarene University in Illinois, prohibited faculty member Richard Colling from teaching the general biology course and banned from all courses his 2004 book *Random Designer*, which argues that God "cares enough about creation to harness even the forces of Darwinian evolution." The problem was not Colling's yoking of religion and science. Instead, Bowling was responding to pressure typified by a letter from evangelical ministers expressing "deep concern regarding the teaching of evolutionary theory as a scientifically proven fact" and dismissing the unproven "theory" as "a philosophy that is godless, contrary to scripture and scientifically unverifiable." The Colling case was reported in *Newsweek*, September 17, 2007, p. 45.

regard to the crucial issue, the descent of man, he took an affably prag-
matic position, less focused on man's origin than on his destination.
He didn't "dread" the hypothesis of our animal ancestry. He wanted
only to be shown "how I got clear of monkeys" and to know that, now,
there is a "difference." In any case, "I had just as lief spring from a
monkey as from some men I know around here." That earned a laugh
from the congregation, even if the preacher *was* (inadvertently?) echoing T. H. Huxley's perhaps apocryphal riposte to the bishop of Oxford
a decade earlier. The Reverend Beecher concluded that he had "not the
least recollection of what happened a million years ago. All my life is
looking forward. I want to know where I am going; I don't care where
I came from."[9]

Not all responses to the impact of Darwin on religious faith were
this ostensibly lighthearted. New England in the 1870s was a central
site in the Darwin wars. *The Springfield Republican* reviewer of the
English translation of Louis Büchner's *Man in the Past, Present, and
Future* (1872) described the book as "Darwinism gone to seed" and
pronounced the results ("as evolved" by Büchner's self-proclaimed
"consistent and unprejudiced thought") "simply astounding to the
New England mind." What was most astounding was that Büchner,
going beyond an endorsement of evolution, denounced all monotheistic religions as "zealotic and intolerant." Buddhism, which "recognizes neither the idea of a personal God, nor that of a personal
duration," was commended; the rest, including Christianity, were to
be swept away by "that knowledge . . . destined hereafter to replace

9. Beecher would go on, in *Evolution and Religion* (1886), to attempt a reconcilia-
tion of evangelical Christianity and science. His 1871 sermon was quoted in the
Hampshire and Franklin Express, regularly read by Dickinson. Two years earlier, the
Springfield Republican had reported the legendary confrontation between Huxley
and Samuel Wilberforce, bishop of Oxford. Accounts differ, but according to the
Republican report, when the bishop turned to Huxley, wondering if he really
believed himself descended from a monkey, Darwin's "bulldog" allegedly replied,
"We are not here to inquire what we would prefer. . . . The true origin of man is not
a question of likes or dislikes, to be settled by consulting the feelings; but a question
of evidence, to be settled by strict scientific investigation. But as the learned bishop
is curious to know my state of feeling on the subject, I have no hesitation in saying
that, were it a matter of choice (which clearly it is not) whether I should be
descended from a respectable monkey, or from a bishop of the English Church, who
can put his brains to no better use than to ridicule science and misrepresent the cul-
tivators, I would certainly choose the monkey." A perfect squelch, *if* it occurred.

and render unnecessary every kind of religion." It is, in part, in this context that we are to read the "nimble Believing" letter to Judge Lord. In that draft letter, Dickinson goes on to note that some thought it "shocking" for the new governor of Massachusetts to seem to compare himself in his 1882 victory speech to Christ. The *precise* tone of her addition—"we thought Darwin had thrown 'the Redeemer' away" (*L* 728)—is difficult to gauge. But she raises a prospect cheered on by the German Darwinian Louis Büchner and never dreamed of in the theology, however liberal, of Henry Ward Beecher.

◦────

"We thought Darwin had thrown 'the Redeemer' away." John Paul (to return to Cardinal Schönborn's citation of the pope in his 2005 op-ed) may have thought the same. In his address to the Pontifical Academy, John Paul insisted that, whatever the body's origins, "the spiritual soul is immediately created by God"; and his more extended remarks of a decade earlier confirm the obvious: that he did *not* mean evolution in the "neo-Darwinian sense" defined by Schönborn (who agrees with other theists in distinguishing repeatedly and emphatically between scientific "evolution" and ideological "evolutionism") as "an unguided, unplanned process of random variation and natural selection." Instead, the evolution of living beings, said the pope in 1985, "presents an internal finality which arouses admiration," a "marvelous finality" that obliges us—if we are not to "abdicate human intelligence" by "admitting effects without a cause"—to "suppose a Mind which is its inventor, its creator."

As Cardinal Schönborn emphasizes in "Finding Design in Nature," the repeated word *finality* is an Aristotelian "philosophical term synonymous with final cause, purpose or design." He cites a 1986 general audience in which John Paul had concluded: "It is clear that the truth of faith about creation is radically opposed to the theories of materialistic philosophy," theories that "view the cosmos as the result of an evolution of matter reducible to pure chance and necessity." He also quotes a sentence from the 2004 International Theological Commission, stating that the Catholic Church had no problem with the "notion of 'evolution' as used by mainstream biologists." But, he adds, the commission's document reaffirms the Church's "perennial teaching . . . about the reality of design in nature" and cautions that John Paul's 1996 letter "cannot be read as a blanket approbation of all theories of evolution, including those of a neo-Darwinian provenance which explicitly deny to divine providence any truly causal role in the development of life in the universe." The dogmatic conclusion: "An unguided evolutionary process—one that falls outside the bounds of divine providence—simply cannot exist." In effect, John Paul and Cardinal Schönborn are addressing the theological issue raised imaginatively by Dickinson's presentation of an omnipotent Overseer she describes as "an Approving God."

The head of the 2004 commission was Cardinal Ratzinger, now Pope Benedict XVI. As Schönborn notes in his op-ed, the new pope proclaimed in the homily at his then recent installation: "We are not some casual and meaningless product of evolution. Each of us is the thought of God. Each of us is willed, each of us is loved, each of us is necessary." And Cardinal Schönborn, who happens to be its primary editor, cites the "authoritative" *Catechism of the Catholic Church,* which is, "naturally," in agreement with both pontiffs: "Human intelligence is surely already capable of finding a response to the question of origins. The existence of God the Creator can be known with certainty through his works, by the light of human reason. . . . We believe that God created the world according to his wisdom. It is not the product of any necessity whatever, nor of blind fate or chance." In short, and employing other words, "accidental power" is, in Cardinal Schonbörn's "Finding Design in Nature," part of, but subordinate to, the overall Design created by and endorsed by an "Approving God." In quoting the key phrases of Emily Dickinson's "Apparently with no surprise," I am *not,* I should point out, implying that she herself subordinates accident to Design.

ᘒ

The Schönborn op-ed ignited an international firestorm among scientists and even theologians, who saw in it, especially given the cardinal's close relationship with the new pope (whose student he had once been), less an "opinion" piece than a calculated institutional regression from the cautiously positive view of evolution expressed by John Paul a decade earlier.

As indicated earlier, one notable respondent was John F. Haught. In *God after Darwin* (2000) and *Deeper than Darwin* (2003) Haught had made a powerful case for compatibility, arguing that evolution and theology complement rather than compete with one another. Reading Schönborn, he was troubled—both by the original op-ed and by a front-page article two days later in the *Times* suggesting that the cardinal's stance might signal that the apparent truce between Catholicism and evolutionary theory was about to be renounced. In the August 2005 issue of *Commonweal,* Haught asked and answered that question: "Does Schönborn's essay mean that the church has changed its position on evolution? In a word, no." Nonetheless, he added, "it is a setback in the dialogue of religion and science." But was the "dialogue" just a staking out of separate *magisteria*? "Today most Catholic theologians and philosophers agree that it is not the job of science" to make reference to "God, purpose, and intelligent design," wrote Haught. "If some scientists go on to maintain that evolution is therefore conclusive evidence of a godless, purposeless universe, this is a leap into ideology, not a scientifically verifiable truth." Schönborn was right, he continued, to defend Catholicism against a materialism incompatible with faith; but when he "fails to distinguish neo-Darwinian biology from the materialist spin that many scientists and philosophers place on evolutionary discoveries," he "does no service to the nuances of Catholic thought."

Nevertheless, Haught insists (and Schönborn would later amplify the point) that evolutionary theory, providing it does not slip into a metaphysics beyond its competence, does raise a host of questions theology must address. "Evolutionary science has changed our understanding of the world dramatically," he wrote in *God after Darwin,* "and so any sense we may have of a God who creates and cares for this world must take into account what Darwin and his followers have told us about it." Peter Steinfels's synopsis of Haught's position seems relevant as well to the brutal, tragic aspect of such Dickinson poems as "Apparently with no surprise": "The role of chance events combined with the ruthless pruning by natural selection over vast, almost unimaginable expanses of time gives a picture of 'life's long journey as a wide trail of loss and pain' that cannot easily be reconciled with any traditional notion of a divine providential intelligence. [For Haught], arguments for intelligent design, even apart from their scientific weakness, do no theological justice to this tragic dimension of evolution."[10]

10. Haught, *God after Darwin: A Theology of Evolution,* ix. Steinfels, "Beliefs; A Catholic Professor on Evolution and Theology: To Understand One, It Helps to Understand the Other." Among others troubled by the Schönborn op-ed, Steinfels reports, was George Coyne, a Jesuit priest and director of the Vatican Observatory,

Clearly, a further response from the cardinal was required. On February 12, 2006, six months after his *Times* op-ed, he delivered in St. Stephen's Cathedral in Vienna a "catechesis" titled "'You govern all things . . .': Suffering in a World Guided by God." In this talk, later published in slightly altered form as chapter 7 of his *Chance or Purpose*, Schönborn referred to the "many letters" he had "received in recent months." He quoted from two. Taking up the theme that tormented Dostoevsky's Ivan Karamazov, and Dostoevsky himself, one correspondent emphasized, among many "absurdities," the "senseless and random suffering of innocent children." Another, Wolfgang Schreiner, a medical computer scientist who had been doing research for three years on the human genome, had come to the reluctant conclusion that "creation" was "an accumulation of unplanned steps," of which we see only what chanced to survive. He invited the cardinal himself to examine the genome: "You will see how chaotic everything is in it. . . . No technician would ever plan such a mess." As a Christian, he was "astonished" by what he had learned. In the final analysis, it seemed to him to come to this:

> God made use of evolution to create all of this. Granted this, however, the real problem is now on the table: How can God, the merciful one, allow all those frightful attempts and false trails with thousands of deaths [in the process]? And all these things are supposed to be the means used by his planned creativity? It contradicts the common picture [image] of God that we have received (as passed on [transmitted] by the Church). . . . It is certainly high time for us to look carefully [closely] at the world that God has made in order to find out how he has really intended it to be. I think no one yet knows.[11]

---

who contested the cardinal's position in the August 6, 2005, issue of the Catholic weekly *Tablet*. In addition, the distinguished British astrophysicist Sir Martin Rees expressed the hope that the Pontifical Academy of Science, to which he belonged, would dissociate itself from Schönborn's remarks.

11. Quoted by Schönborn in *Chance or Purpose*, 92–93. The book version (translated by Henry Taylor) differs somewhat from the online translation of the original lecture. Though at times I prefer that online translation (http://stephanscom .at/edw/katechesen/articles), for the reader's convenience, I cite (with some bracketed interpolations) from the book version. Subsequent citations, abbreviated *CP*, are included parenthetically in the text.

Summarizing the many letters he had received, the cardinal said he was "often" asked this question: "How can a rational plan of creation be found in a world full of absurd chance happenings?" (*CP*, 92). He responds by discussing the writer Reinhold Schneider. Though Schneider had converted to Catholicism, the pages of the Vienna diary he kept during the melancholy final months of a fatal illness (1957–58) were filled with what Schönborn characterizes as terror in the face of "the incomprehensible cruelties in nature"—in Schneider's own graphic phrase, the "process of eating and being eaten." Like Arthur Schopenhauer, David Attenborough, and Darwin himself (in passages I discuss in the chapter that follows), Schneider found himself fascinated and repelled by the spectacle of predatory creatures and parasites (octopi, starfish, leeches) "sucking the life" out of their prey, "nature" as so many "cycles of hell." He was also appalled by "the senselessly horrific world of men, filled with suffering and wars and groundless wickedness [unfathomable evil]." The stated purpose, both of Schönborn's talk and of this chapter of his book, is to reconcile the words of Genesis following the creation of man—God looked on his creation and "saw that it was very good" (Gen 1:31)—with "the fact of 'eating and being eaten' throughout the world of living being" (the online wording; compare *CP*, 97).

In exploring these issues, he insists from the outset that "the question concerning the origin of pain and its relation to the goodness of God should by no means be given too hasty an answer" and repeats in his peroration that we must "beware of 'glib' answers" to the questions of evil and suffering and their relation to divine providence (*CP*, 93, 102). He concedes that "evil is great, terrible, and not to be explained away." The decisive question is that of Augustine: "whence comes evil?" Augustine acknowledged that, while he "inquired into the origin of evil," he could find no solution, "no way out" (*CP*, 93–94, quoting *Confessions* 7.7, 11). But Augustine also supplies, for many believing Christians, the answer—not in the form of philosophical argument but as embodied in Jesus, who alone has conquered evil, sin, and death. Schönborn again quotes the *Catechism:* to the question of evil, "as pressing as it is unavoidable and as painful as it is mysterious," no quick answer will suffice. It can be answered only by "Christian faith as a whole," including, above all, faith in the ultimate "goodness of creation" and in the principal of God's covenants with man: the redemptive incarnation of his Son (*CP*, 94).

Despite the asserted "goodness of creation," Schönborn insists that we should be wary of applying the concept of "intelligent design." God is not a builder of perfect machines but a creator of imperfect "natures," limited expressions of a perfect and unlimited divinity. This distinction is an attempt to address a major, for some an insurmountable, problem. The Creator is perfect, but (in a passage from the lecture not repeated in the book) "in His creation, there is above all growth and becoming with all its groping, attempting, failing, breaking through, with all its synergy and struggle, its incomprehensible waste and unexpected and unintended results, fortunate and unfortunate." Fortunate and unfortunate. . . . The passage summons up *both* the staggering richness of life that has evolved on this resplendent earth *and* the extent of human and animal suffering on a planet where more than 99 percent of all species that have ever existed have become extinct.

Schönborn once again cites Wolfgang Schreiner, the medical computer scientist who had written to him about the human genome. We may talk, said Schreiner, about "*successful* design," but, when we consider mistakes in "design," the planning is emphatically not "careful" or "compassionate." And one would expect "intelligent" design to be "everything," not only successful but "careful and compassionate" as well (*CP*, 102). Without all three in harmony, we are left with the old question. It has been confronted by scientists who happen to be theists, and by thinkers like Augustine and Aquinas, as well as by innumerable philosophers and literary artists including (along with such a relatively minor figure as Schönborn's Reinhold Schneider) the author of the poetic dialogues in Job, Aeschylus, Shakespeare, and Milton. There is also, of course, G. W. Leibniz, who invented the term *theodicy*, and the devastating mocker of Leibniz's "best of all possible worlds," the Voltaire of *Candide*.

Of the nineteenth-century writers, one thinks first of Dostoevsky and the powerful challenge presented (in the "Rebellion" and "Grand Inquisitor" chapters of *The Brothers Karamazov*) by Ivan, for whom no ultimate divine resolution can justify the tears of a single tortured child. Like Ivan Karamazov, Emily Dickinson was no atheist but a challenger who, in her often oblique way, never ceased asking the same questions: Why does evil strike so meaninglessly? Why do the innocent suffer? How can a purportedly omnipotent and loving God approve of such an apparently random, brutally violent process?

Addressed from the perspective of a scientifically sophisticated and fully committed Christian faith, those questions provoke others: what is the *alternative* to evolutionary struggle, with all its waste, imperfections, suffering, and death? "If the universe were finished instantaneously," John Haught asks rhetorically, "where could it go from there?" He proposes a "mental experiment" for the imagination: "what would it be like to exist in [a] perfectly designed universe" of the sort idealized by (as he would have us believe) the new atheists. Such a universe would be "finished to perfection on the first day of creation. An instantaneously completed initial act of divine prestidigitation would guarantee that there would be no suffering, no evil, and no need for the creation to evolve into something different over immensely long periods of time. . . . There would be no growing pains, no death . . . ; no theodicy problem either, since there would be no evil to reconcile with the existence of God." There would also be no room for indeterminacy, accidents, freedom, or creativity. The universe would be "locked eternally into splendid perfection," and "human beings, if we can imagine them at all, would be puppets and statues." But for another major philosopher of religion, John Hick, "suffering remains unjust and inexplicable, haphazard and cruelly excessive. The mystery of dysteleogical suffering is a real mystery, impenetrable to the rationalizing mind. It challenges Christian faith with its utterly baffling, alien, and destructive meaninglessness."[12]

As Schönborn himself concedes, "there is no 'design' to be recognized [discerned] here; far more, [we see] the destruction of any meaning and plan." He concludes by quoting chapter 8 (verses 20–22) of Paul's Epistle to the Romans: "the whole creation has been groaning in labor," says Paul, "until now." For *now*, this Jewish-Christian apocalyptist was convinced, the "eager longing" of all creation for deliverance is at hand. Like Jesus himself (Mark 9:1, 13:30) and, later, the author of the Book of Revelation (22:20), Paul believed the End was imminent. For Paul, the crucifixion and death of Jesus brought salvation, symbolized and incarnated in the resurrection, which ushered in the Kingdom of God. Apocalyptists keep moving the goalposts; even in Cardinal Schönborn's formulation, the verb tenses are unstable. To

12. Haught, *God and the New Atheism*, 105–6; Hick, *Evil and the God of Love*, 335.

quote the final words of his Pauline lecture and chapter, we will be delivered from pain and death because of the sacrifice and resurrection of "Christ the Redeemer, in whom the sufferings of creation come to [will find] an end, and in whom the new creation has [will have] its beginning and its goal" (*CP*, 102).

⎯⎯⎯

Revealingly, Emily Dickinson also quotes the eighth chapter of Romans, not to affirm the deliverance through Christ's sacrifice of a world groaning in travail, but to challenge Paul's rhetorical question: "if God is for us, who can be against us?" (8:31). Lamenting the killing of her flowers, first by worms, then by an unexpected "Midwinter Frost," in the early autumn of 1881, she quotes Paul: "when God is with us, who shall be against us," adding, in a bitter addendum conceding God's omnipotence while denying his benevolence: "but when he is against us, other allies are useless" (*L* 746). Dickinson's omnipotent deity is personal, though more likely to be an antagonist than a friend, exercising his power unpredictably and often cruelly.[13] Even the Son who suffered and died on the cross is a victim of that power. *There* is the crucial difference between those who "keep believing nimble" and those orthodox/apocalyptic Christians for whom Jesus provides the supreme example of pain as redemptive, of partial evil leading to a greater good. For Cardinal Schönborn, it is in the sacrifice of Christ the Redeemer that "the sufferings of creation will find an end" and a "goal." Though attracted to the crucified Jesus, Dickinson is less drawn to final ends than to painful process, less persuaded of redemptive purpose than of the reality of natural and human suffering.

That emphasis reflects Dickinson's remarkable capacity, in poems such as "Apparently with no surprise," "Longing is like the Seed," or "Through the Dark Sod—as Education," to experience empathetically what it might be like, for example, to *be* a flower. It might be the "happy Flower" cut down by frost. And even in her more "redemp-

13. Given her emphasis on a personal and powerful God operating through nature, one can imagine Emily Dickinson endorsing the 1997 revision of the U.S. National Association of Biology Teachers' official "Statement" on evolution. The original statement had defined evolution as "an unsupervised, impersonal, unpredictable, and natural process." Belatedly recognizing the limitations of science and acknowledging human ignorance of whatever inexplicable, possibly divine, purposes may underlie evolutionary change, the association, in 1997, deleted the first two adjectives, *unsupervised* and *impersonal*. Dickinson would have concurred.

tive" imaginings, she recaptures the organic process in its *entirety;* what it *feels* like for the "Lily" that "passes" through the "Dark Sod," then emerges "Swinging her Beryl Ball— / The Mold-life—all forgotten—now— / In Ecstasy—and Dell—" (392); or for a "Seed" to "wrestle" in the dark earth "Before it see the Sun!" (1255). As she had informed her "Preceptor," T. W. Higginson, in 1862: "My Business is Circumference" (*L* 412). That famous and multilayered term has been best defined by Thomas H. Johnson: "As nearly as one can judge from the nature of her thinking and the pattern of her poems, the term 'circumference' meant a projection of her imagination into all relationships of man, nature, and spirit."[14]

Dickinson's capacity to empathetically project into, and humanize, other life-forms—reminiscent of Keats and Whitman, or the Theodore Roethke of the "greenhouse poems"—evokes for me a truly great contemporary poem, one that also happens to allude crucially to the eighth chapter of the Epistle to the Romans. In the Appendix, I discuss Derek Mahon's "A Disused Shed in Co. Wexford." In this compassionate and uncanny poem, we are made to experience, to *feel*, the otherwise impenetrable life of a colony of neglected mushrooms. Our response to their abandonment by man and God, and their longing for "deliverance," radiates out to include our own yearning for deliverance from *human* suffering, natural or manmade.

14. *Emily Dickinson: An Interpretive Biography*, 140.

Chapter 4

Design, Challenged and Defended

To take up Emily Dickinson's twist on the Pauline terms: *is* God "with us" or "against us"? It seems no "accident" that the issue comes up repeatedly in Dickinson in connection with her beloved flowers— as it does in the 1881 letter just cited and, most dramatically, in "Apparently with no surprise." No matter how we intellectualize the question of Design, believers must depend on faith in a providential God. Astute and moving as it is, the argument advanced by Cardinal Schönborn (in his "catechesis" and chapter) will persuade only those who have made the leap from science to faith. Schönborn himself tried to bridge that gap in a September 2006 lecture to the Pontifical Colloquium on Creation and Evolution. He began his talk, titled "Reasonable Science, Reasonable Faith," by citing the scientist par excellence, Isaac Newton. To book three ("The System of the World") of the second edition of *Principia Mathematica*, Newton appended a *scholium generale* (first published in 1713 and revised in 1726). There, sounding like Thomas Aquinas, Newton wrote that the "supremely exquisite structure . . . visible to us," comprising the sun, planets, and comets,

> could come into being solely through the decision and under the dominion of an intelligent and powerful being. . . . He steers everything, not as a world-soul, but as the Lord of all things. A God lacking in dominion, providence, and final causes is nothing other than mere fact and mere nature. No possibility of change in things may

be derived from blind metaphysical necessity. . . . The entire manifold of things ordered according to place and time could originate solely from the idea and the will of a truly existent being, one that exists as a matter of necessity.[1]

When Newton famously remarked in 1675 to Robert Hooker, "If I have seen further it is by standing on the shoulders of Giants," the shoulders were presumably not those of mythographers and theologians. But that is the case here, a background omitted by the cardinal but worth mentioning. The Design argument, adumbrated by the pre-Socratics, was not fully articulated until Plato, especially in the *Timaeus*. Aristotle credited Anaximander, whose primal stuff vaguely "steers all," with originating the concept, though his "divine" directing substance was not supernatural. In Heraclitus, the universal flux seems ordered by a Logos, though not as unambiguously intelligent and purposive as later Stoic and Christian interpreters claimed. But the most significant contributor prior to Plato was Anaxagoras, who posited "mind" as the knowing power governing change. Mind "controls all things," though as an ordering principle only, not as a moral agent. Building on Galileo's and his own scientific demonstration of a unified world system, Newton went beyond both the mythical portrayal of a cosmic Designer in Plato's *Timaeus* and Aquinas's theological affirmation in the *Summa,* extending, for the first time, the Design Argument to what he presented as a monotheistic conclusion based on science.[2] The Newtonian System required universal control—here anthropomorphized as "counsel and dominion"—over limitless space and time; thus, the Cosmic Intelligence is none other than God, "the Lord of all things."

1. Schönborn quoting Newton. I quote Schönborn's lecture in its initial English translation, in *First Things,* April 2007, pp. 21–26. Henceforth cited in the text as "RSRF." (The full text of the conference proceedings was subsequently published by Ignatius Press.)

2. In "To the Royal Society on Newton's Bicentennial" (March 1927), Einstein, again disputing his nemesis, quantum mechanics, insisted that "the last word had not been said. . . . May the spirit of Newton's method give us the power to restore union between physical reality and the profoundest characteristic of Newton's teaching—strict causality." Einstein had once whimsically summarized the history of physics: "In the beginning (if there was such a thing) God created Newton's laws of motion together with the necessary masses and forces" (quoted in Isaacson, *Einstein,* 333, 91).

In a passage from the "General Scholium" not quoted by Schönborn, Newton describes this Lord God as "omnipotent and omniscient," his "duration" eternal, his "presence" infinite; "he governs all things, and knows all things that are or can be done." Newton *needed* an eternal and infinite God since he knew that such concepts as "absolute time" and "absolute space" could not be directly observed. In a 1933 Oxford lecture, "The Methods of Theoretical Physics," Einstein would remember this Newtonian scholium in relying on "God" to get him out of the dilemma: "The Deity endures forever and is everywhere present, and by existing always and everywhere, He constitutes duration and space." Schönborn makes no reference to Einstein, but it is in the comfort zone of this Newtonian context that he refers to the "vehement" responses elicited by his *Times* piece a year earlier. In a crucial statement at the outset of "Reasonable Science, Reasonable Faith," he poses the issue this way: "The question whether the universe and the place human beings have within it owe their origin to blind chance or to a supremely wise and good plan arouses us all" ("RSRF," 21).

This opening formulation must be questioned before we can proceed. The introduction of "blind chance" muddies the waters and establishes a false dichotomy, since, in neo-Darwinian theory, randomness and blind chance refer *not* to natural selection, the second step in evolution, but to the *first* step, the mutations that indifferently generate genetic variations. These variations are then ordered by the winnowing force of natural selection, which is not at all a chance or random, let alone "blind," process.

Darwin himself was occasionally caught on the horns of this dilemma, this false choice between divine design and blind chance. On May 22, 1860, he wrote to his friend Asa Gray, the American botanist who in that year introduced *The Origin of Species* to New England readers like Emily Dickinson. His subject was divine beneficence, against which he set a striking example of natural cruelty. As we saw in the preceding chapter, Reinhold Schneider was disturbed by the incomprehensible cruelties of nature, the "process of eating and being eaten" exemplified in the cannibalism of predatory and parasitic animals and insects: a spectacle Cardinal Schönborn tried, in his account of "Suffering in a World Guided by God," to reconcile with the words of Genesis, in which God looked on his creation and "saw that it was very good." For Arthur Schopenhauer, that great pessimist appalled by the blind urge of an individuated and insatiable "will" that "feasts on itself," the paradigm example from nature was the Tasmanian bulldog-ant. Unlike other killer ants, highly toxic bulldogs engage in fierce individual combat to the death—a ferocity that takes the even more relentlessly aggressive form remarked by Schopenhauer. If one cuts this insect in half, he notes, "a fight begins between the head and the tail—each attacks the other with bites and stings, and this struggle goes on bravely for half an hour, until they die, or are carried away by other ants. This happens every time."[3]

The example, also from the insect world, that particularly disturbed the tenderhearted Darwin, and in fact shocked most Victorians when they were made aware of it, was that of *Ichneumonidae* wasps. They are also known as "assassinator wasps," though their behavior makes Dickinson's "blonde Assassin" benign by comparison. There are some 3,300 species, all of whom reproduce in the same macabre way. The female wasp stings a prey animal with her ovipositor and lays her eggs inside the paralyzed prey. The eggs then hatch into larvae, which slowly devour the living prey from the inside, destroying the less essential parts first and eating the essential parts (and thus killing the victim-host) only at the very end, at which point the prey's shell becomes a cocoon containing the baby wasps about to hatch. Asa Gray, a devout Protestant, believed that evolution was compatible with divine Design, a concept developed in his influential study *Darwiniana* (1876). That thought occasionally "pleased" Darwin himself. But in the 1860 letter to his American friend, Darwin rejected divine Design. Not for the first time, he set aside his scientific awareness that nature is not to be judged in terms of *human* morality, while still—despite confessing himself "bewildered" by a subject "too profound for the human intellect"—apparently holding the traditional *God* to account:

> With respect to the theological view of the question. This is always painful to me. . . . I had no intention of writing atheistically. But I own that I cannot see as plainly as others do, and as I should wish to do, evidence of design and beneficence on all sides of us. There seems to me too much misery in the world. I cannot persuade myself that a beneficent and omnipotent God would have designedly created the Ichneumonidae with the express intention of their [larva] feeding

3. Arthur Schopenhauer, *The World As Will and Representation*, vol. 1, sec. 27.

within the living bodies of Caterpillars, or that a cat should play with mice.[4]

Though she refers to death as something that "worries one like a wasp" (*L* 364), Emily Dickinson has nothing to say of Ichneumons. But the cat playing with a poor mouse was for her, precisely as it was for Darwin, an emblem of the teasing cruelty of life, an illustration of sadistic "Murder by degrees": "The Cat reprieves the Mouse / She eases from her teeth / Just long enough for Hope to tease— / Then mashes it to death—" (762). She had earlier employed the cat-and-mouse example, imagining a distanced Father God, as improbably tender as herself, fulfilling the pledge of his Son, who promised to "prepare" for us a "place" in his "Father's house," consisting of "many mansions" (John 14:1):

> Papa above!
> Regard a Mouse
> O'erpowered by the Cat!
> Reserve within thy kingdom
> A "Mansion" for the Rat!
>
> Snug in Seraphic Cupboards
> To nibble all the day,
> While unsuspecting Cycles
> Wheel solemnly away! (61)

But such a charming scenario, in which God would reserve a cozy nook in heaven for one of life's perpetual victims, would require pre-

---

4. Darwin, *Life and Letters*, 2:105. Gray did not give up easily. The following year, he raised the crucial issue again. Darwin responded: "Your question what would convince me of Design is a poser. If I saw an angel come down to teach us good, and I was convinced from others seeing him that I was not mad, I should believe in design. If I was convinced thoroughly that life and mind was in an unknown way a function of other imponderable force, I should be convinced. If man was made of brass or iron and no way connected with any other organism which had ever lived, I should perhaps be convinced. But this is childish writing." In a letter three months later (December 1861), Darwin, no more able than Gray to "keep out of the question," began, "With respect to Design, I feel more inclined to show a white flag than to fire my usual long-range shot"; yet were he to accept Design, "I should believe it in the same incredible manner as the orthodox believe the Trinity in Unity" (*Life and Letters*, 2:169–70, 174).

cisely that divine beneficence for which Darwin could find no evidence, and Dickinson precious little, her God often less a playfully
addressed "Papa" than a Blakean Nobodaddy. Darwin noted that he
could not "look at the universe as a result of blind chance"; but—in
this 1870 letter cited by Schönborn—neither could he find "evidence
of beneficent design, or indeed any design of any kind, in the detail."
In this, he differed from Augustine, Aquinas, Newton, and the author
of *Natural Theology* (1802), William Paley, whose rooms at Cambridge
Darwin later occupied. Writing to his great friend and fellow scientist
Joseph Hooker on July 13, 1856, he coined a phrase that would later
supply a book title for Richard Dawkins. Playfully yet seriously rejecting the concept of divine Design, Darwin exclaimed: "What a book a
Devil's Chaplain might write on the clumsy, wasteful, blundering low
and horribly cruel works of nature." Agreeing with his friend about
the blundering cruelty of nature, Hooker later informed Darwin (who
had used the same example in a letter to Gray) that he found the idea
of a designed "Creation . . . no more tangible than that of the Trinity &
. . . neither more nor less than superstition."[5]

As Cardinal Schönborn acknowledges—or, rather, insists—the recognition of any form of Design "will indeed be difficult on a strictly scientific, quantitative, measure-oriented methodology." Yet we often depict
nature as purposive. As Schönborn notes ("RSRF," 24), even strict Darwinists can at times speak of nature "in this anthropomorphic manner,
even when they afterward correct themselves and say, with someone
like Julian Huxley, 'At first sight the biological sector seems full of purpose. Organisms are built as if purposely designed. . . . But as the genius
of Darwin showed, the purpose is only an apparent one.'"

Schönborn doesn't go into detail on this point in "Reasonable Science, Reasonable Faith." But what Darwin and his followers
"showed," to the satisfaction of mainstream science, was that the
"apparent" design—the "ingeniously" fine-tuned functioning—of
these organisms was actually attributable to competition and natural
selection. The emergence of even the most improbable complexity
(including the eye, that Creationist favorite) is the result neither of
Design nor of pure "chance" but of countless minute developmental

---

5. *The Correspondence of Charles Darwin*, 2:178. The Richard Dawkins book
referred to is *A Devil's Chaplain: Reflections on Hope, Lies, Science, and Love* (2003). *Life
and Letters of Joseph Dalton Hooker*, 1:474.

stages, in each of which chance—"accidents" frozen in the evolution-ary history of trial and error—plays a part in a process ultimately determined by a selective force favoring (to borrow Herbert Spencer's momentous coinage) the "survival of the fittest."[6] The adaptations of organisms to their environments result from small mutations in the genetic material. The consequence of this combination of physical forces operating over billions of years in accord with the theory of her-itable variation is the emergence of complex life.

For many, the old question posed by skeptics—"Who created God?"—has its parallel when it comes to the ultimate cause puzzled over by scientists. The mystery that baffled Darwin has been solved: the source of heritable variation is genetic mutation. Since we have known since 1953 what the genetic material is, the question becomes: "What is the origin of DNA?" Though we now understand a great deal about accidental changes in the sequence of DNA, the consequence of molecular replication during cell division, the full complexity of DNA (and of RNA, its significance only recently discovered) may or may not prove ultimately explicable within the limits of nonteleological physical law. Unlike God, DNA and its workings can be observed; but observation is not the same as ultimate explanation. At this founda-tional level, neo-Darwinian theory may offer only limited help. That would leave us with mystery and, hence, with what may "appear" to be, or *actually* be, teleological "purpose."

We need not succumb to the Creationist pseudoscience of "Intelli-gent Design," but even nonbelievers will probably always be haunted by the anthropomorphic image, vestigial even in Einstein, of a Designer, a God who doesn't play dice with the universe. Augustine, Aquinas, and Newton notwithstanding, most philosophers agree that the existence of God can be neither proved nor definitively refuted. Himself a theist, Kant rebutted most of the traditional "proofs" (only to accept his own "moral" proof), and, despite its title, J. L. Mackie's

---

6. For the 1870 letter, see "RSRF," 24. Spencer, *Principles of Biology* (1864), 1:444. Thirty years later, in his brilliant *Evolution and Ethics*, T. H. Huxley opposed human "goodness and virtue" to the "gladiatorial" struggle for existence in the natural world (81). Defending Darwin and rejecting *Social* Darwinism's thesis that the struggle for existence was an "ethical" competition and that the self-assertive vic-tors in that struggle somehow "merited" their triumph, Huxley accused Spencer of "fanatical individualism" and "reasoned savagery."

The Miracle of Theism (1982) exposed with particular force and philosophic rigor the weaknesses in the traditional arguments for God's existence, including Kant's Moral Argument. On the other hand, for most of us, a reductive materialism seems no more satisfactory—even if purposive design in *its* more facile form *has* indeed been exposed by "the genius of Darwin" and his followers to be "only apparent."

We will be revisiting that final adjective in its adverbial form, *Apparently:* the opening and governing word of our main Dickinson poem. But at this point it is necessary to return to "Reasonable Science, Reasonable Faith," specifically to Cardinal Schönborn's crucial citation of Thomas Aquinas ("RSRF," 24). Arguing on the basis of the *Summa Theologica,* Schönborn claims that nature does not merely "act" *as if* it had goals. According to the fifth of Aquinas's proofs of God's existence, natural bodies cannot have their *own* intentions since they lack cognition.

> Yet they act for an end, and this is evident from their acting always, or nearly so, in the same way, so as to obtain the best result. Hence it is plain that they achieve their end, not fortuitously, but designedly. Now whatever lacks knowledge cannot move toward an end, unless it be directed by some being endowed with knowledge and intelligence; as the arrow is directed by the archer. Therefore some intelligent being exists by whom all natural things are directed to their end; and this being we call God. (*Summa* I.2.3)

Here Aquinas, whose other four proofs of God's existence share an Aristotelian foundation, is more dependent on Plato. Too perfect to partake in any original design let alone necessary corrections, Aristotle's Unmoved Mover is above and beyond the changing natural world, which is thoroughly immanent. "The best illustration," says Aristotle, "is the case of a man being his own physician, for Nature is like that—agent and patient at once" (*Physics* 199B). Plato's *Timaeus,* on the other hand, had by the thirteenth century become a text often deployed to reinforce the biblical conception of a God actively concerned with his own creation. The Demiurge of Plato's dialogue is a cognizing agent, a cosmic craftsman whose ordering of the universe is motivated by benevolent efficiency: "Desiring, then, that all things should be good and, so far as might be, nothing imperfect, the god took over all that is visible—not at rest, but in discordant and unordered motion—and brought it from disorder into order, since he judged that order was in every way the better" (*Timaeus* 29E–30A).

In the Thomistic extension, completing Aristotle with Plato, the Creator endows nature with immanent, self-unfolding, end-oriented principles, *and*—unlike the Designer of the Greek philosophers or the impersonal God of Spinoza and Einstein—personally participates in that creation. What Schönborn calls the "self-evident experience of nature"—being "directed toward an end, as ordered, and as beautiful"—leads to the question: "Where do these marks of intelligence come from?" No answer can be expected from what Schönborn calls evolutionary theory's "self-limited" methods of "measurable and mechanical cause" ("RSRF," 24), but for believers the answer is as self-evident as the experience of nature itself. The Designer directing this ordered, beautiful nature, he who does not merely work *through* natural laws and biological process but *actively* "*steers* everything" as the archer in Aquinas's memorable image steers an arrow, "we call God."

And what if—as in the cases of incomprehensible brutality and waste earlier noted—nature seems anything *but* ordered and beautiful? In his exploration of "Suffering in a World Guided by God," Cardinal Schönborn quoted Reinhold Schneider and Wolfgang Schreiner, believers besieged by doubt. Two other, more skeptical, modern witnesses may serve for many.

Nobel Prize–winning physicist Steven Weinberg summarized his widely read *The First Three Minutes* with the much-noted (and much-debated) declaration that "the more the universe seems comprehensible, the more it also seems pointless."[7] But his rejection of a Designer God and a designed universe rests less on purely scientific than on moral grounds, on his "distress in coping with the existence of evil in our world, whether it is the Holocaust or the evolutionary struggle for survival or the starvation of children in Africa or Afghanistan." By "God" Weinberg means a deity with "some sort of personality, some intelligence, who created the universe and has some special concern with life, in particular with human life." Speaking in April 1999 at the Conference on Cosmic Design of the American Association for the Advancement of Science, he said, "You may tell me that you are thinking of something much more abstract, some cosmic spirit of order and

---

7. *The First Three Minutes: A Modern View of the Origin of the Universe*, 154.

harmony, as Einstein did. You are certainly free to think that way, but then I don't know why you use words like 'designer' or 'God', except perhaps as a form of protective coloration." Speaking in personal terms, he described his own life as "remarkably happy," yet he had seen his mother die painfully of cancer, his father's personality destroyed by Alzheimer's, and scores of second and third cousins "murdered in the Holocaust":

> Signs of a benevolent designer are pretty well hidden. The prevalence of evil and misery has always bothered those who believe in a benevolent and omnipotent God. Sometimes God is excused by pointing to the need for free will. Milton gives God this argument in *Paradise Lost*. . . . It seems a bit unfair to my relatives to be murdered in order to provide an opportunity for free will for Germans, but even putting that aside, how does free will account for cancer? Is it an opportunity of free will for tumors? I don't need to argue here that the evil in the world proves that the universe is not designed, but only that there are no signs of benevolence that might have shown the hand of a designer.[8]

Coming from the other side of the science-religion divide, there is the testimony of New Testament scholar Bart D. Ehrman. In an addendum to his best-selling *Misquoting Jesus*, Ehrman—once an evangelical Christian, later a mainstream one—notes that he has become an agnostic. He found himself no longer able to reconcile "a good and loving God who was actively involved in this world" with that world's "rampant evil" and "senseless pain and suffering," including the starvation "of millions of innocent children." Though aware of the theological "answers" to the problem, it was "ultimately my dissatisfaction with these answers that led me to a place where I could no longer believe in God, or even know if he exists." That, he added, will be the subject of "my next book." In that book, titled *God's Problem*, Ehrman argues that the Bible fails to answer "our most important

8. First published in the *New York Review of Books*; available in *Science and Religion: Are They Compatible?* ed. Paul Kurtz, 31–40 (37–38). Weinberg's reference is to *Paradise Lost* 3:124–28, where God says of humankind, "I formed them free," and concludes, "they themselves ordained their fall." Weinberg's "moral" objection to a Designer God was synopsized in a 2001 conference paper by astronomer Owen Gingerich, "Science and Religion: Are They Compatible?" For Gingerich, as we have seen, they *are*. His position is summarized in his 2007 book, *God's Universe*.

question, why we suffer."[9] Though it appeared in February 2008, when my own manuscript was with the publisher, I was able to insert several last-minute observations reflecting at least some of the many insights in this cogent and humane study.

Ehrman reminds us of innumerable, horrific examples of mass human suffering. Along with the death toll resulting from tsunamis and earthquakes, there are the preventable tragedies: sickness and death caused by drinking water contaminated by parasites; the 2.7 million who die every year, most of them children and almost all from sub-Saharan Africa, as a result of malaria caused by mosquito bites. (Though he doesn't mention it, the resurgence of malaria is a negative consequence of evolution: parasitic adaptation to antibiotics formerly effective in combating the disease.) In any case, "Solve malaria, and then you have the problem of AIDS," which is of course epidemic in Africa. Ehrman is asking, not the "scientific question of why mosquitoes and parasites attack the human body," but, rather, "the theological and religious question of how we can explain the suffering in the world if the Bible is right and a good and loving God is in charge."[10]

Undeserved suffering in Africa in particular returns us to the previously mentioned Nicholas Kristof column, which itself had triggered for me a recollection of a comment made some years ago by British naturalist and broadcaster David Attenborough. Kristof, traveling in Ethiopia with Jimmy Carter in February 2007, reported on the former president's visits to projects he had set up to try to wipe out the Guinea worm, "a horrendous two-foot long parasite that lives inside the body and finally pops out, causing excruciating pain." Carter met a woman with a Guinea worm coming out of one nipple, another from her genitals, and one from each foot. There were also little children "screaming uncontrollably with pain" because of the worms emerging from their flesh. Though, according to Kristof, Carter "cried, along with the children," his religious faith apparently remained unshaken: a different response to undeserved suffering than that just noted in the cases of Weinberg and Ehrman.

In this column, appropriately titled "Torture by Worms," Kristof goes on to note that Carter has also worked in Africa to alleviate suf-

9. *Misquoting Jesus: The Story behind Who Changed the Bible and Why*, 248, 258; *God's Problem: How the Bible Fails to Answer Our Most Important Question—Why We Suffer*.
10. *God's Problem*, 198–99, 200, 273–74.

fering caused by a tiny worm, the parasite that causes river blindness (*onchocerciasis*): the very example cited by David Attenborough when challenged by viewers of his BBC Nature programs. "People sometimes say to me, 'Why don't you admit that the humming-bird, the butterfly, the Bird of Paradise, are proof of the wonderful things produced by Creation?'" He found himself responding with his own challenge: "Well, when you say that, you've *also* got to think of a little boy sitting on a riverbank, like here, in West Africa, that's got a little worm, a living organism, in his eye and boring through the eyeball and is slowly turning him blind. The Creator God that you believe in, presumably, also made that little worm. Now I personally find that difficult to accommodate."[11]

Cardinal Schönborn, though he humanely recognizes that every child that suffers is "an unrepeatable being with its own destiny," and though he repeatedly urges us to "beware of 'glib' answers" (*CP*, 102), would respond in part by pointing to humanitarians like Carter and Kristof. "How much love," he exclaims in "Suffering in a World Guided by God," has "come into the world by this way of pain!" The argument is less than persuasive. "If the world was without any natural evil and suffering," argued theologian Richard Swinburne in 2003, "we wouldn't have the opportunity . . . to show courage, patience and sympathy." That dice-loading "any" cannot blunt the obvious questions about gratuitous suffering, especially when it is endured by the innocent: "Does God really need so much pain and suffering to achieve his ends? Is there any conceivably good purpose behind so many children dying every day of starvation and disease? How are they helped by the rest of us becoming more sympathetic?"[12]

Saint Paul finds in the crucifixion and resurrection of Jesus the response to a whole world groaning for deliverance. Yet, for many, the rhetorical questions just posed are hard, perhaps impossible, to answer, whether we are empathizing with the undeserved suffering of children or focusing (for the traditional God is supposed to be present in everything, no matter how small), with Schopenhauer, Darwin, and Attenborough, on the horrifying micro-world of bulldog ants, *Ichneumonidae*

---

11. Cited in Jack Huberman, ed., *The Quotable Atheist*, 30.

12. Stenger, *God: The Failed Hypothesis*, 219. For Swinburne's neo-Augustinian argument, see Julian Baggini and Jeremy Stranghorne, eds., *What Philosophers Think*, 109.

wasps, and parasitic worms. The poets I will be discussing later—who present us with destructive scenarios juxtaposing Frost and Flower, Spider and Moth, Tiger and Lamb, Canker-Worm and Rose—might be able to answer such questions having to do with the Problem of Suffering. But the poems themselves suggest otherwise: that they, like Attenborough, might find his eyeball-boring worm—which makes Schopenhauer's bulldog-ants and Darwin's larval wasps feeding within the living bodies of caterpillars pleasant by comparison—difficult to accommodate within a beneficent, providential "Design" presided over by a loving "Creator God."

The truths inconvenient to any facile theodicy range from ants, worms, and wasps to supernovas, from the biological and microscopic to the macrocosmic. According to Pope's epitaphic couplet, "Nature and Nature's laws lay hid in night. / God said, 'Let Newton be!' and all was light." But, to quote the answering couplet by John Collins Squire, "It did not last; the Devil howling 'Ho! / Let Einstein be!' restored the status quo." The things of nature, as revealed by modern science, have certainly not returned to the pre-Newtonian darkness; but they have shrunk to the subatomic, and expanded, even exploded, beyond the orderly confines of the "supremely exquisite structure" visible to Newton, even granted (in Wordsworth's tribute) the range of that extraordinary "Mind for ever / Voyaging through strange seas of Thought, alone" (*Prelude* 3:62–63). Like Emerson in the first half of his powerful essay "Fate" (in *The Conduct of Life*), Cardinal Schönborn is fully—honestly and eloquently—aware of the challenges attendant to the concept of a designed let alone theistic universe:

> We consider the world-picture drawn by modern science and ask why we have this laborious, complicated path of cosmic evolution. Why its countless trials and blind alleys, its billions of years of time and expansion of the universe? Why the gigantic explosions of supernovae, the cooking of the elements in the nuclear fusion of the stars, the excruciating grind of biological evolution with its endless start-ups and extinctions, its catastrophes and barbarities, right up to the unfathomable brutalities of life and survival to the present day? Does it not make more sense to see the whole as the blind play of coincidences in an unplanned nature? Is this not more honest than the attempts at a theodicy of a Leibniz ["pre-existent harmony"]? Is it not more plausible simply to say, "Yes, the world is just that cruel"? ("RSRF," 25–26)

Excellent questions, for the brutalities *are* "unfathomable" from a "merely" scientific or philosophic perspective. If even Emerson was compelled to fall back on divine "Providence" (along with human "power") as an antidote to the litany of horrors laid out in the first, brutal half of his essay "Fate," we can hardly be surprised if, in his peroration, a Catholic cardinal should rely on not only a theological but also a specifically Christological "explication" of the "purpose" underlying the seemingly "cruel," blind play of coincidences in an unplanned nature. One thing is clear, he argues, and it "requires a frankly theological explication," an explication centered on the Logos of the theologically crucial prologue to the Gospel of John:

> Let us not be excessively hasty in wanting to demonstrate "intelligent design" anywhere as a matter of apologetics. Like Job, we do not know the answer to suffering and chaos. We have been given only one answer—but that from God himself. The *Logos*, through whom and in whom everything was created, has assumed flesh; the cross is the key to God's plans and decisions. . . . It is only through God's self-revelation in Christ, and our response of faith, that we can begin to glimpse the ultimate purpose of the cosmos and to trust in God's provident care of all cosmic details. It is not that "the path [the "complicated path of cosmic evolution"] is the goal." Rather, the Resurrection and the Second Coming are the purpose of the path. ("RSRF," 26)

The crucial emphasis here is repeated by Cardinal Schönborn in *Chance or Purpose*, both in his chapter on Christ as "The Goal of Creation" (*CP*, 29–43) and in his concluding pages. From Joachim Illies, a natural scientist who also focuses on the incarnation of Christ, he borrows the metaphor of two "Ladders," those of Darwin and Jacob, an image meant to symbolize "the ascending movement of evolution and the movement of the Creator Spirit coming down from God." A truly inclusive view emerges only when we attend to both movements, which "have their center in Christ, and their meaning and inner goal in him" (*CP*, 166–67). Each ladder is indispensable: that of evolutionary science and that which connects this ascending and descending movement with "the Logos, through whom and toward whom everything has been created. . . . For what kind of evolution would it be if resurrection and eternal life were not its ultimate goals?" (*CP*, 175). Schönborn's rhetorical question in effect echoes and scientifically "updates" the rhetorical question posed in the final sentence of the *City of God*. Augustine concludes his self-described "huge work" with "the resurrection of Christ": the teleological event that resolves all "suffering," in the process "foreshadowing" our own "eternal rest." We are to "Behold what will be, in the end, without end! For what is our end but to reach that kingdom which has no end?"[13]

This resolution of an otherwise insoluble problem—a theodicy shared by Paul, Augustine, Aquinas, and Cardinal Schönborn—fuses the general lesson of Greek tragedy—out of Suffering comes Wisdom—with the specific mystery of Christianity, a religion centered on the incarnate God who died on the cross and rose from the dead. "So he dies, / But soon revives": the archangel Michael's stunningly terse Pauline formulation in *Paradise Lost* (12:419–20) reminds us that, for believing Christians, the Crucifixion/Resurrection *fusion* epitomizes and embodies in action the sustained philosophical-theological arguments of Augustine and Aquinas. In the *Summa* (I.2.2), Aquinas aligns himself with his precursor: "As Augustine says, 'since God is the highest good, He would not allow any evil in His works unless His omnipotence and goodness were such as to bring good even out of evil.' This is part of the infinite goodness of God, that He should allow evil to exist and out of it produce good."

Paradise lost, paradise regained; out of evil, good; out of death, immortal life. For both Christian philosopher-saints, Augustine and Aquinas, as for Milton and Schönborn, the supreme example is of course Jesus's all-redeeming Resurrection: the "good" fruit both of the original Fall (a *felix culpa*) and of the agonizing love-sacrifice on the cross. Though the Crucifixion was indelibly impressed on the mind and memory of Emily Dickinson, she is, as we will see in the chapter that follows, much more centered on the suffering Jesus than on the transcendent Redeemer; and her "paradise," however imperfect, tends to be earthly.

---

13. Augustine, *Concerning the City of God against the Pagans*, book 22, chap. 30, p. 1091.

Chapter 5

Emily Dickinson on Christ and Crucifixion

Emily Dickinson's depiction of an approving God who sanctions the decapitation of flowers is not an isolated rendering of divine cruelty or indifference in her work. She once referred to Jehovah as a tyrannical "Mastiff" who rescinded his command for Abraham to kill Isaac only because he was "Flattered by Obeisance" (1317). These negative characterizations of a patriarchal God who inflicts sacrifice and suffering did not extend to her feeling for Jesus, himself a sacrificial victim. There are a few exceptions to her separation of Jesus from Jehovah. In one poem, she seems to fuse them, referring to "'The Father and the Son' himself" (1258). In another, she rather promiscuously embraces the entire Trinity, imagining herself

> Given in Marriage unto Thee
> Oh Thou Celestial Host—
> Bride of the Father and the Son
> Bride of the Holy Ghost.
> Other Betrothal shall dissolve—
> Wedlock of Will, decay—
> Only the Keeper of this Ring
> Conquer Mortality— (817)

There was to be no mortal nuptial for Emily Dickinson, and this celestial marriage also remained unconsummated. Though she came closest to being the bride of Jesus, her groom was less the conqueror of mortality (she was more absorbed by his sacrifice on the cross than by the salvation it entailed) than the Jesus who suffered and died on Calvary.

For the most part, Emily Dickinson distinguished sharply between Father and Son. Of course, she is hardly alone in making a distinction between the harsh God of the Hebrew Law and (playing down the statements of Jesus regarding eternal damnation[1]) the gentler God of the Christian gospels. Dickinson did not go as far as the second-century philosopher-theologian Marcion, who was pronounced heretic for positing *two entirely different deities:* the God of the Jews, who created the world and imposed stringent law on his Chosen People, and the God of Jesus, who sent his Son into the world to save people from the wrathful vengeance of the Jewish Creator God. But at times her position *almost* resembles that of Schopenhauer and Nietzsche, unbelievers who rejected Christianity as a religion of transcendence while still admiring Jesus. For Schopenhauer, Jesus was an emblem, one finally impossible to emulate, of the endurance of existential suffering. Valuing Jesus, while detesting the religion founded in his name, Nietzsche once said that, based on the criterion of authentically living up to the standards of the gospels, "There has been only one Christian, and he died on the cross."[2]

In her more orthodox moods, Dickinson's Jesus is an omnipotent pardoner who, inviting his "small" petitioner into "my House," assures her (as in Luke 9:48) that "The Least / Is esteemed in Heaven the Chiefest" (964). Jesus is the "Tender Pioneer" who must be fol-

---

1. In Dickinson's poetry, hell "Defies Topography" (929), with one exception: an undated emblem poem in which Jesus's crown of thorns becomes an instrument of vengeance on the Roman procurator who turned him over to those who crucified him. Pilate's lavabo notwithstanding, the "crown" whose "stigma deified" Jesus will find Pontius Pilate, in "whatsoever hell" he lives: "That coronation pierces him / He recollects it well" (1735).

2. Nietzsche, *The Antichrist* §39. For Schopenhauer, affirmation of life required the sort of superhuman strength displayed by the tortured Jesus, said to have taken upon himself the world's guilt and pain. Faced with a world of suffering and without a god to fall back on, Schopenhauer and Nietzsche came to different conclusions. Relinquishing the struggle to affirm life, Schopenhauer chose a quasi-Buddhistic withdrawal and pain-transcending peace of mind. Nietzsche, in contrast, struggled heroically to affirm life, rejecting Christian morality and, in effect, replacing Jesus with the *Übermensch* who endures and overcomes suffering: the symbol of those who assert that what does not destroy them makes them stronger.

lowed (698). The "brittle" bridge "on which our Faith doth tread" was "built" by God, who "sent his Son to test the Plank, / And he pronounced it firm" (1433). But her Jesus is far more often the human Sufferer admired by Schopenhauer and Nietzsche than the divine Son of Jehovah. "When Jesus tells us about his Father," she notes in a late letter, "we distrust him. When he shows us his Home we turn away, but when he confides to us that he is 'acquainted with Grief' [Isaiah 53:3], we listen, for that also is an Acquaintance of our own" (*L* 837). Her Jesus is less the divine Redeemer than a fellow sufferer, another victim.

Here Dickinson anticipates some modern if more orthodox incarnational insights. In *The Creative Suffering of God* (1992), Paul S. Fiddes devoted a chapter to "the central place of the cross." In his 1974 book *The Crucified God*, theologian Jürgen Moltmann emphasized "the concept of divine participation in creaturely suffering through the cross of Christ," a crucified God-man who, in the words of John Polkinghorne, is "not just a compassionate spectator of the suffering of creatures but a fellow-sharer in the travail of creation. The concept of a suffering God affords theology some help as it wrestles with its most difficult problem, the evil and suffering present in the world."[3] Though the thought is initially consoling, it is hard to see how the suffering of a man who is, for the orthodox, also an omnipotent God is at all comparable to the suffering of powerless mortals. Dickinson's response is more radical. In an 1877 letter to Thomas Wentworth Higginson she insists, sounding like William Blake and W. B. Yeats, "To be human is more than to be divine, for when Christ was divine, he was uncontented till he had been human" (*L* 592). Christ's suffering and death registered more powerfully than the Resurrection, and even that resurrection was to Dickinson testimony to the humanity of Jesus. A late (ca. 1882) single-quatrain poem insists that it was "Christ's own personal Expanse / That bore him from the Tomb" (1543).

Nevertheless, the *full* trajectory of the Christian paradigm remained compelling. As Shira Wolosky notes, that "biblical and providential vision, encoding events in . . . an overarching divine pattern, continued to be strongly felt in the habits of orthodox, antebellum Amherst." Directly descended from the Puritanism of Jonathan Edwards, Amherst's Calvinist community was largely immune to the liberalizing

3. Polkinghorne, *Quantum Physics and Theology,* 21–22.

Unitarianism and Transcendentalism of Boston and Concord. Yet Emily Dickinson, who refused to submit to any fixed theological position, had been affected by her reading of Emerson and Thoreau and was encouraged to think for herself by a number of progressive preachers, including Charles Wadsworth, as well as by her friendship with Elizabeth and Josiah G. Holland, the coeditor of the *Springfield Republican*. As Emily fondly remembered on the occasion of his death, Holland thought that "God must be a friend—*that* was a different God," a "warmer," more "sunshiny" Deity than the remote God she was used to. Though Holland's theology struck her as comforting and enlightened, he was committed to the authority of biblical revelation. Nevertheless, his 1854 Amherst lecture on "Manhood" was sufficiently liberal-minded that it was criticized by a reporter in the *Hampshire and Franklin Express* as "a creedless, churchless, ministerless christianity, so called."[4]

Yet even for so heterodox a nonconformist as Emily Dickinson, the problem of suffering remains inextricably connected with the patterns of her religious heritage, with Thomas à Kempis's fifteenth-century meditation, the *Imitation of Christ,* a favorite text. Dorothy Huff Oberhaus calls into question "secular interpretations" of many poems that diminish their Christian symbolism to the merely personal. At the very least, one can agree, such poems are enriched by an understanding of the tradition in which they are embedded.[5] Summarizing a view persuasively fleshed out by Oberhaus and, especially, Jane Donahue Eberwein, Shira Wolosky agrees that Dickinson was "profoundly torn" regarding her religious inheritance, a dialectic of faith and denial, conformity and resistance. Though she herself places Dickinson in the camp of resistance, Wolosky readily concedes that there "is an extent to which the Christian metaphysical tradition inevitably informs" Dickinson's work, "and indeed never ceases to do so."

> Dickinson never entirely divests herself of the Christian, and specifically Calvinist, context in which she grew up in Amherst, although her relation to it is often one of rebellion and contention. The very

4. The reporter is cited in Jay Leyda, *The Years and Hours of Emily Dickinson*, 1:296. For Wolosky's comments on Amherst orthodoxy, see her "Public and Private in Dickinson's War Poetry," 114.

5. Oberhaus, "'Tender Pioneer': Emily Dickinson's Poems on the Life of Christ," 113.

fact that poems of more or less definite religious displacement or conflict take their place alongside poems of more or less religious devotion and conformity (and the arrangement is not simply chronological: there is no clear evolution in Dickinson's work from one stance definitively into another) argues for a continuous metaphysical pressure on her. This would not make Dickinson a "religious poet," nor is conversion from deprivation to transcendence in art, if not religion, her fundamental and overarching poetic structure. She is, instead, a poet of religious engagement, whose very criticism of religion reflects her deep involvement in it.[6]

Her deepest involvement was with the suffering and death of Jesus, specifically the crucifixion, whether attended to devotionally *or* personalized and poetically transmuted. As the "Queen" or "Empress of Calvary" (348, 1072), Dickinson sometimes insists that the one "recorded" crucifixion is not unique: "There's newer—nearer Crucifixion / Than That" (553). Oberhaus rejects the Brooks-Lewis-Warren argument that, in "One Crucifixion is recorded—only," Dickinson "bend[s] the Biblical vocabulary to an account of her own psychic condition," a commonsensical reading amplified by Robert Weisbuch, who argued two years later that Dickinson here finds Christ's crucifixion "unique only in that it was made historically public," while "'newer-nearer Crucifixion' [is] most worthy of attention."[7] It is true, as Oberhaus says, that Dickinson keeps Christ's Crucifixion "before the reader's attention throughout the poem," and some interpretations do overstate a secular priority, even exclusivity. Yet in one poem, somewhat confusing in regard to the antecedents of the final pronouns, Dickinson can go so far as to proudly acknowledge, "See! I usurped *thy* crucifix to honor mine!" (1736).

At the same time, it comforted her to know that, through the suffering of Jesus, God was aware of the human condition; that her own pain and "renunciation" had the "Flavors of that old Crucifixion" (527). One substantial, ten-stanza poem, written at the height of her powers, resembles Blake's "London," in which the Bard of Experience, walking the streets of the fallen city, "mark[s] in every face I meet / Marks

6. Wolosky, "Emily Dickinson: Being in the Body," 132.

7. Cleanth Brooks, R. W. B. Lewis, and Robert Penn Warren, eds., *American Literature: The Makers and the Making*, 1245–46; Robert Weisbuch, *Emily Dickinson's Poetry*, 80–81; Oberhaus, "'Tender Pioneer,'" 113–15.

of weakness, marks of woe." Moving beyond the "apparently" ego-centric "I" that opens so many (some 150) of her poems, an empathetic Dickinson wonders if the woes of others, however various they may be, resemble her own crucifixion.

> I measure every Grief I meet
> With narrow, probing, Eyes—
> I wonder if It weighs like Mine—
> Or has an Easier size.
>
> I wonder if They bore it long—
> Or did it just begin—
> I could not tell the Date of Mine—
> It feels so old a pain—
>
> I wonder if it hurts to live—
> And if They have to try—
> And whether—could They choose between—
> It would not be—to die—

She wonders if the passage of years might "give them Balm," alle-viating whatever harm "hurt them early," or if they "go on aching still," perhaps even "Enlightened to a larger Pain— / In Contrast with the Love." There are many forms of grief, she has been "told," with many causes; "Death—is but one—and comes but once— / And only nails the eyes." There is also "Grief of Want—and Grief of Cold— / A sort they call 'Despair.'" While she may not be able to precisely "guess the kind" of grief experienced by others,

> yet to me
> A piercing Comfort it affords
> In passing Calvary—
>
> To note the fashions—of the Cross—
> And how they're mostly worn—
> Still fascinated to presume
> That Some—are like My Own— (561)

In one powerful and possibly blasphemous poem, she can, because she too has been forsaken, take Jesus's cry from the cross—*Eli, Eli, lama sabachthani?* ("My God, my God, why hast thou forsaken me?"—and make that double biblical echo (Matthew 27:46; Psalm 22) her own: "That scalding One—Sabachthani— / Recited fluent—here." Since, "without the Calvary," there can be no triumphal "Palm," she utters a startling plea and near command: "So Savior—Crucify." The final stanza, though dense with biblical imagery, conveys a bitter skepticism that victory will in fact follow defeat, that Gethsemane-like human suffering (the "Reefs") will be rewarded by finally reaching the desired, and divinely promised, recompense, "the Coast— beyond!":

> Defeat—whets Victory—they say
> The Reefs—in old Gethsemane—
> Endear the Coast—beyond!
> 'Tis Beggars—Banquets can define—
> 'Tis Parching—vitalizes Wine—
> "Faith" bleats—to understand! (313)

Despite what "they say" ("they" being, here as elsewhere in Dickinson, the conformist guardians of religious orthodoxy), despite our hunger and thirst for God's mercy (couched in characteristic Dickinsonian form, in which presence is defined by absence),[8] despite Christ's Agony/Crucifixion/Resurrection, human pain and deprivation remain a mystery. And so-called Faith—in a plaintive, angry, and ironic reduction of the image of Jesus as Good Shepherd and Paschal Lamb—pathetically *"bleats*—to understand!"

Crucifixion, dramatizing sacrifice in the name of love, figures in many poems; but the Resurrection is, depending on specific poetic context, either accepted or questioned, altered or rejected. One poem affirming the Resurrection, subjected to an impressive close reading by Oberhaus that appropriately climaxes her essay, also illustrates Dickinson's obsession with botanical imagery. Jesus "gave away his Life," which would be "To Us—Gigantic Sum." For him it was a "trifle," but "magnified—by Fame." His death and the empty sepulchre "burst the

---

8. Compare "Success is counted sweetest," where it is the defeated and dying who best understand the meaning of victory (67), and "I had been hungry, all the Years," where hunger is discovered to be "a way / Of Persons outside Windows— / The Entering—takes away—" (579).

Hearts" of the apostles, but Jesus's body "slipped its limit— / And on the Heavens—unrolled": a Resurrection-image fusing the stone rolled back from the tomb with Dickinson's own lovely though alien image of the bird who "*unrolled* his feathers / And rowed him softer home" than oars dividing an ocean or "Butterflies, off Banks of Noon / Leap, plashless as they swim" (328). The Resurrection poem ends:

> 'Tis ours—to wince—and weep—
> And wonder—and decay
> By Blossoms gradual process—
> He chose—Maturity—
>
> And quickening—as we sowed—
> Just obviated Bud—
> And when We turned to note the Growth—
> Broke—perfect—from the Pod— (567)

While we weep, wince, wonder, and—in accordance with the organic process we share with blossoms—"decay," Jesus, in slipping the limits of the grave and prefiguring our own potential transcendence of death, fulfills the promise of Psalm 126 that "They that sow in tears shall reap in joy." According to John 20:14, when Mary Magdalene "turned herself back" she "saw Jesus standing"; in this poem's fusion of botanical and Christian imagery, when we "turned to note the Growth," Jesus "Broke—perfect—from the Pod."

One love poem, apparently commemorating that day in August 1860 when the Reverend Charles Wadsworth visited Emily, features secularized but finally transcendent apocalyptic imagery. There "came a day at Summer's full," a day the speaker thought reserved "for the Saints, / Where Revelations—be." As usual, the sun shone and flowers blossomed, "As if no soul the solstice passed / That maketh all things new" (Rev. 25:5). The precious time was "scarce profaned" by speech, needless "as at Sacrament / The Wardrobe—of our Lord." Although "each was to each The Sealed Church," the two were at last permitted to "commune" so as not to appear awkward "at Supper of the Lamb." Though "clutched tight," the "Hours slid fast," the would-be lovers like those on the decks of passing ships, "Bound to opposing lands." But "when all the time had leaked," each is also "bound the Other's Crucifix," no "other Bond" required:

Sufficient troth that we shall rise—
Deposed—at length, the grave—
To that new marriage,
Justified—through Calvaries of Love— (322)

This "new" if posthumous nuptial seems closer to Swedenborg, with his vision of frustrated earthly lovers enjoying angelic connubial bliss, than to Jesus, who ruled out marriage in heaven. There are other, even more familiar erotic secularizations (or profanations) of the sacred. "Wild Nights—Wild Nights!" animates projected sexual ecstasy as "Rowing in Eden" (249), imagery played on again in "Come slowly—Eden!" (211). Though this is not precisely what Jesus had in mind, for Christians (and others), the central message of Jesus *is* love—epitomized in Paul's sublime celebration of that paramount virtue, without which we are as sounding brass, or a tinkling cymbal (1 Cor. 13:1–13). Interestingly, it was a skeptic and classicist, the poet A. E. Housman, who most succinctly synopsized the lesson of Calvary. His Shropshire lads might condemn "Whatever brute and blackguard made the world" ("The chestnut casts his flambeaux") and hold that "malt does more than Milton can / To justify God's ways to man" ("Terence, this is stupid stuff"). But Housman's poem "The Carpenter's Son" ends with three condemned men on the gallows, all doomed, "Though the midmost hangs for love."

Still, in her radical alterations of Eden and of the Christian Afterlife, Emily Dickinson can go so far as to imagine herself, at least as a dramatic speaker, *eternally* doomed for "love." The well-known "I cannot live with You" (640) combines her recurrent imagery equating "frost" with "death" (imagery relevant to a full interpretation of the "blonde Assassin") with a litany of "could nots" that most conventional Christians would find troubling. She could neither "live" with the beloved, nor "die" with him. How could she stand by "And see You—freeze— / Without my Right of Frost— / Death's privilege?" She could not "rise" with him since "Your Face / Would put out Jesus'." While the beloved lived, he "served Heaven," or "sought to." She "could not,"

Because You saturated Sight—
And I had no more Eyes
For sordid excellence
As Paradise.

Here she extends her earlier expressions of skepticism, as in "Going to Heaven!" (79), with its initial dubiousness ("How dim it sounds! / . . . Perhaps you're going too! / Who knows?"), its almost astonished repetition of the opening exclamation, and the climactic reversal and rejection of the promised heaven: "I'm glad I don't believe it." Heaven and its opposite appear more metaphoric than literal in the often anthologized "My life closed twice before it closed" (1732), with its shift from personal sorrow (*My . . . me*), to shared tragedy (*we*) in the final stanza: "Parting is all we know of heaven, / And all we need of hell." But the more audacious, climactic claim in "I cannot live with You" is that heaven and hell really *are* psychological rather than onto-logical, not posthumous places but present states of mind. Were the beloved "saved," and she "condemned to be / Where You were not, / *That self—were Hell to me.*" Readers familiar with the deployment of dramatic personae, and of the long tradition in which poets in biblical cultures secularize and eroticize the supernatural, would grant Dickinson her poetic license. Many if not most would be likely to take in stride even her allusion, anticipated by Emerson and Margaret Fuller, to Milton's Satan, that "lost archangel" who declares "*myself am Hell*" and, bidding farewell to "celestial light," hails "profoundest Hell" as its "new possessor," one who brings "A mind not to be changed by place and time. / The mind is its own place, and in itself / Can make a Heav'n of Hell, a Hell of Heav'n."[9]

One suspects, however, that even if such a poem were to pass muster with Cardinal Schönborn, it would not with his close personal and doctrinal friend, the current pope, who recently and strenuously reaffirmed the traditional church teaching on hell. His predecessor had referred to damnation vaguely as an "eternal emptiness." Bene-dict, registering the widespread modern phenomenon often described as "the decline of Hell," complained in March 2007 that the place of everlasting torment was no longer much talked about. He described Satan as a "real, personal, and not merely symbolic presence" and pro-

9. *Paradise Lost* 1.75, 243–55. Borrowing Satan's phrase, Emerson chose as the chapter title of a projected book "the mind as its own place"; *The Journals and Mis-cellaneous Notebooks of Ralph Waldo Emerson*, 3:316. Margaret Fuller acknowledged that it was from Emerson "that I first learned what is meant by the inward life . . . that *the mind is its own place* was a dead phrase until he cast light upon my mind." See Moncure Daniel Conway, *Emerson at Home and Abroad*, 89.

claimed, while sparing us any fire-and-brimstone details, that hell, far from being a state of mind, is an actual place, one that "exists and is eternal."[10]

Despite moments when the beloved's face extinguishes that of Jesus, Emily Dickinson seldom wavered in her empathy with the crucified Christ. For her, that was, precisely, the crux. Through his acquaintance with grief, the Jesus who suffered and died on the cross emerges as a central figure in her poetry and thought. "The sentimental religionists" of Dickinson's place and period did not, in Cynthia Griffin Wolff's secular yet empathetic synopsis, trouble themselves much with the "paradox of the God-man in the throes of death."

> Their belief in God had become too attenuated, too secularized and domesticated and comforting, for them to recognize the savage implications of this element in the myth that formed their faith. The rich irony of Emily Dickinson's position was that although she could not relinquish reason and accept the reassurance of some "birth" after death, neither could she shake her tenacious belief in the existence of the God who had become man only to die on the cross. The strength of this belief impelled her to confront the dark implications of that execution in the ancient past.[11]

Though Dickinson contemplated the agony of Christ crucified, and invested any hope for immortality in Jesus's Resurrection, she resisted, often defiantly, the God offered by the Bible and clergymen, by philosophers and theologians: a Creator supposedly omnipotent, omniscient, and benevolent—a God who, moving in mysterious ways his providential wonders to perform, invariably (with the notable

10. One wonders if looking down upon the agonies of the damned is, as in Tertullian's *On Spectacles* and in the *Summa,* still conceived of as enhancing the bliss of the saved: an unedifying spectacle chosen by Nietzsche, in *On the Genealogy of Morals,* to illustrate his crucial concept of *ressentiment.* Not long before, John Stuart Mill, attacking the divine Judge directly, had declared, "I will call no being good who is not what I mean when I apply that epithet to my fellow-creatures; and if such a being can sentence me to hell for not so calling him, then to hell I will go" (*Examination of Sir William Hamilton's Philosophy,* in *The Collected Works of John Stuart Mill,* 10:103).

11. Wolff, *Emily Dickinson,* 263. We can only wonder what additional "dark implications" might have been fleshed out in the extended Dickinson essay that astute critic Randall Jarrell was contemplating shortly before his death in 1965 (almost certainly by suicide); its tentative title was "The Empress of Calvary."

exception of hell) wrought good even out of the worst evil and suffering. There is no question, even for believers, that this God allows us, those we love, and—most problematically—the innocent and children to suffer. The real question is: does one trust that such a God actually *does* bring good out of evil and, therefore, that he acts out of love rather than indifference or cruelty? Both believer and nonbeliever may vacillate, but ultimately the former trusts in this God and his provident care; the latter doesn't, and so rejects—or denies the existence of—a "God" who fails to meet at least one of the three criteria mandated by the traditional definition.

Those in the middle, torn between belief and doubt, wrestle, as Dickinson did, with the Great Question: given the "apparently" random evil and undeserved suffering all too evident in a world often groaning in vain for deliverance, how *could* God be simultaneously omnipotent, omniscient, and omnibenevolent? At the outset of his chapter on providence in *Chance or Purpose*, Cardinal Schönborn wonders "what kind of God" would ignore the tears of the suffering. "Can God not help? Then he is powerless. Does he not want to help? Then he is cruel and merciless" (*CP*, 71). He is silently echoing a famous passage, itself derivative. As Hume has the more skeptical of his two spokesmen ("Philo") note in part 10 of his posthumously published *Dialogues Concerning Natural Religion* (1779), "Epicurus' old questions are yet unanswered": "Is God willing to prevent evil, but not able? Then he is not omnipotent. Is he able, but not willing? Then he is malevolent. Is he both able and willing? Whence then cometh evil?" Of course, if he is neither able nor willing, why call him God?[12]

For Christians, even for those simply raised in a Christian tradition, Jesus is central to any attempt to answer these questions. And for orthodox Christians, it is not simply a matter of what Jesus said or taught as a great prophet (the merely humanist perspective), but what he *did* as the Son of God: namely, atone for our sins through his sacri-

---

12. *Dialogues Concerning Natural Religion*, 75. Compare the three questions posed by Nietzsche in *Daybreak* 91, cited as one of my epigraphs (above, p. v). One (unpersuasive) way around the Riddle is the argument for evil as mere privation, and so nonexistent. An Epicurus-like exchange is presented by the fifth-century Christianized pagan Boethius: "'There is nothing that an omnipotent God could not do.' 'No.' 'Then, can God do evil?' 'No.' 'So that evil is nothing, since that is what He cannot do who can do anything'" (*The Consolation of Philosophy*, 290).

fice on the cross and, by rising, conquer death. To those who believe in
the centrality of Christ's Crucifixion and Resurrection, the Problem of
Evil or Suffering seems to be resolved. An otherwise inscrutable moral
mystery—the purpose of an omnipotent and loving God's apparent
refusal to eliminate evil and suffering—is resolved in the redemptive
suffering and death of Jesus on the cross. In the miracle of his resurrection from the dead, believers see a harbinger of their own survival
beyond this vale of tears.

For others, those for example who admire the Jesus who suffered
and died on the cross without accepting him as the Son of God, and
who see this world as an existential crucible (in Keats's great
metaphor, a "vale of Soul-making"), the problem is not so much
resolved as movingly epitomized. Keats's metaphor has been powerfully evoked by John Hick. Having rejected most of the traditional
attempts to reconcile evil with the concept of a God of love, and
emphasizing the problem of suffering as a particular challenge for
Christians, Hick concludes, "The only appeal left is to mystery." This
is "not, however, merely an appeal to the negative fact that we cannot
discern any rationale of human suffering. It may be that the very mys-
teriousness of this life is an important aspect of its character as a sphere
of soul-making."[13]

As prolegomenon to my focus on Emily Dickinson's poems about
God, especially "Apparently with no surprise," I have recapitulated
Augustinian-Thomistic-Newtonian arguments as updated by an eminent spokesman for that tradition, one who acknowledges the vulnerability at least of the more facile arguments, old and new, for
"Design." But the Epicurean Riddle, epitomizing the "very mysteri-
ousness of this life," still resonates, especially with those who, like
Dickinson, "keep Believing nimble." More generally, this would
include all those who—despite the efforts of someone of the caliber of
Cardinal Schönborn—remain moved by the example of Jesus but
resistant to the Christian "solution" to the primary mystery, the Problem of Suffering.

13. *Letters of John Keats*, 2:102; Hick, *Evil and the God of Love*, 333–34.

Part II

Chapter 6

Destroyers and Victims

"Apparently with no Surprise" and Related Scenarios

As noted earlier, these thoughts about God and Design, and my reading of the various responses of Cardinal Schönborn to the challenges faced by defenders of an omnipotent, omniscient, and all-loving Deity, coincided with a recent classroom experience. I sat in on a colleague's class that ended with a rushed discussion of several of Dickinson's late poems. Because we were running out of time, I felt compelled to dispute several interpretations offered in regard to the last of them, which happened to be "Apparently with no surprise." That evening, still frustrated by the truncated class discussion, I copied the poem and e-mailed it to several friends, inviting them to jot down, in a sentence or two, whatever seemed to them salient to say about this brief lyric. I was particularly interested in what they thought might have provoked the differing interpretations in class. Here, once again, is the poem:

> Apparently with no surprise
> To any happy Flower
> The Frost beheads it at its play—
> In accidental power—
> The blonde Assassin passes on—
> The Sun proceeds unmoved

To measure off another Day
For an Approving God.

I've already noted the gist of the responses I received. The first of them was also the shortest: "Frost happens." This seemed wittily succinct, capturing something of the poem's this-is-the-way-it-is toughness. This most concise of the responses sent me quickly became the lengthiest. The following day, an elaboration followed, in the form of a rapidly recorded flurry of thoughts and surmises. My respondent had asked his wife for her thoughts,

> not expecting surprise, but finding it. Beyond the "frost happens" remark, I'd say that nature runs its course, raising questions: is God good? etc. There also seems to be a sexual dimension, with a happy male flower facing uncertainty, possible danger. But frost *does* happen. That frost is totally ignored, unseen; casual, at play, yet cold, stinging, causing hurt, but leaving the flower, maybe, to rise again, next spring. Sylvia, however, sees the Frost as young and masculine—careless, thoughtless, wreaking havoc on nature.
> Go figure.

Several of these remarks, to which I'll return, raise the very issues rehearsed in my preamble. I'll also return to the "sexual dimension" in the poem, but it was interesting to note that my friend, presumably taking the "blonde Assassin" as a castrating femme fatale, emphasized a threat to the *male,* even if it meant identifying with a flower, more typically thought of as "female." On the other hand and more persuasively, his wife saw the Frost as a *masculine,* destructive force, wreaking havoc on an implicitly female "nature." Though the text is far more supportive of her reading, gender had apparently helped shape interpretation.

Before unpacking points raised about the course of nature, the duality of frost, and the crucial question "is God good, etc.," I should note that, despite my long contextual preamble, I might have responded to my own assignment by initially focusing on the textual and biographical fact that Emily Dickinson jotted the poem, two years before her death, on the back of an envelope addressed to her aunt Elizabeth Currier; or on purely *intrinsic* features: content and genre, as well as the poem's structure, meter, rhyme, and so forth. After all, we have before us an eight-line poem written in the common meter ballad stanza of which Emily Dickinson is one of our most skilled practitioners. A formalist would note that the poem consists of two linked quatrains of alternating iambic tetrameters and trimeters, rhymed *abcbdece;* that "Day" in the second quatrain picks up "play" in the first, leaving only the first line of each quatrain unrhymed; that there is one slant or partial rhyme (*unmoved/God*) and one feminine rhyme (an unstressed final syllable): *Flower/power.* Most crucially, I would have attended to the elements of the poem that enable us to tactfully adjudicate *tone:* the speaker's attitude toward her subject and toward her implied auditors.

But let me adhere to the spirit of my own assignment by taking off from my friends' comments and responding to their response by going off on tangents suggested by them, before reengaging the poem more intrinsically. In the ruminations that follow, I will be attempting to clarify my own thinking—with, in this case, the added enjoyment of not cogitating in isolation but being stimulated by the thoughts of others, whether students or friends, theologians or skeptics.

In this poem, to be sure, "nature runs its course, raising questions." That course incorporates the destruction of beauty and what appears to be divine acquiescence in the whole life-death process. So: "is God good?" My friends, like most of the respondents, had moved, understandably but abruptly, from poetry to theodicy—the attempt to vindicate divine justice given the existence of perceived evil. Once we move beyond the poem's literal scene to its symbolic implications, this *is* the central theological question raised. Besides, poetry as theodicy has the epic precedents already noted: the poetic dialogues in the Book of Job and *Paradise Lost,* where Milton set out to "assert Eternal Providence / And justify the ways of God to men." As we have also seen, those ways *need* to be justified to human understanding, faced with and often perplexed by the problem of suffering, by the spectacle of God presiding over a creation mingling good and evil, light and darkness.

The model for Dickinson's "Approving God" is biblical. On occasion (as in the 1882 poem she characterized, in an accompanying note to her nonconformist nephew Ned, as her "Diagnosis of the Bible"), Emily Dickinson could dismiss Scripture as "an antique Volume— / Written by faded Men / At the suggestion of Holy Spectres" and inferior to "Orpheus' Sermon," which "captivated— / It did not condemn—" (1545). Nevertheless, the Creator God who haunted Dickinson creates order out of chaos and separates light from darkness, at the outset of the book of Genesis: "And God saw that it was good." Is this the "Approving God" of this poem? It could well be; indeed, the Latin root of "approve" is *approbare*: "to make good, admit as good." The tradition we have been discussing makes the same claim: whatever the challenges presented by post-Darwinian physicists and biologists, whatever the brutalities of nature and the problems that arise from human suffering, the universe created by this God must be, ultimately, "good." Certainly, the God presiding over the world of Dickinson's poem regards its operations favorably. Viewing things from the aspect of eternity (*sub specie aeternitatis*), unlike mortals of limited understanding, this God presumably *comprehends* (in all senses of the word) the whole of his creation: a designed and providential cosmos in which—as Augustine, Aquinas, and Cardinal Schönborn insist—good is brought forth even out of evil, real or "apparent."

But if Dickinson's Deity in this poem regards all favorably, how do *we* regard *him*? This was the question raised in most of the responses I received. Does God's approval of what *seems* in this poem to be a randomly cruel process—the "accidental" beheading of a "happy Flower"—make him seem less benign than indifferent (like the "unmoved" sun)? Or, worse yet, "cruel" himself: "an Approving God" as smiling sadist. In a bitter poem in which the speaker at first prays, somewhat tongue in cheek, for the fulfillment of "but modest needs— / Such as Content—and Heaven," she is greeted by just such a derisive expression: "A Smile suffused Jehovah's face— / The Cherubim— withdrew." And so

> I left the Place, with all my might—
> I threw my Prayer away—
> The Quiet Ages picked it up—
> And Judgment—twinkled—too—
>
> That one so honest—be extant—
> It take the Tale for true—
> That "Whatsoever Ye shall ask—
> Itself be given You"—
>
> But I, grown shrewder—scan the Skies
> With a suspicious Air—
> As Children—swindled for the first
> All Swindlers—be—infer— (476)

This "shrewdness" comes to define Emily Dickinson's stance toward God, and, as we shall later see at some length in discussing the anguish caused for believers by a God who absents himself, she almost obsessively cites the knocking-and-asking passage from Matthew (7:7) as a promise unfulfilled. In the present poem, God is not only blasphemously accused of being unresponsive but also revealed, despite his reputation for honesty, as a smiling "Swindler" who has defrauded us with a "Tale" gullibly taken as "true" by the faithful. The futile "prayer" for fulfillment of "modest needs" received with smiling indifference will remind us of the torturing "Inquisitor" in Dickinson's most blasphemous parody of a prayer, a bitterly sardonic declension of increasingly minimal petitions that can still shock:

> The Heart asks Pleasure—first—
> And then—Excuse from Pain—
> And then—those little Anodynes—
> That deaden suffering—
>
> And then—to go to sleep—
> And then—if it should be
> The will of its Inquisitor
> The privilege to die— (536)

Does the "Approving God" of our poem resemble Dickinson's smiling Jehovah as Swindler, or, worse, this Torquemada? Though any answer to such a question must derive from close attention to the rhetoric and tone of the text before us, it seems worth noting that precisely this divine ambiguity (a smiling God as benign or sadistic) occurs in Blake's "The Tyger"—a fearful symmetry Robert Frost may well play off, and exceed, in his terrifying sonnet titled, with cunning and characteristic mischievousness, "Design."

Just as Dickinson's God created both happy Flower and killing Frost, Blake's Jobean creator God would seem to have "made" both happy Lamb and predatory Tyger. The questions posed to that creature of terrible beauty by the poem's speaker (a Bard of Experience either sublimely awed or frightened out of his wits) apply to Dickinson's poem as well:

> Did he smile his work to see?
> Did he who made the Lamb make thee?

Tyger! Tyger! burning bright
In the forests of the night,
What immortal hand or eye,
Dare frame thy fearful symmetry?

The "assorted characters of death and blight" brought together in Robert Frost's post-Blakean and post-Darwinian sonnet include predatory spider, flower, and the spider's victim, a now dead moth. All are "white." But what had that particular flower, a normally "blue and innocent heal-all," to do "with being white," and "what" was it that

brought the kindred spider to that height,
Then steered the white moth thither in the night?
What but design of darkness to appall?—
If design govern in a thing so small.

This malevolent illustration of "Design" is certainly frightening. Worse yet, especially to a religious sensibility, is the thought that there may be *no design at all*, just an amoral purposelessness: a nihilistic universe bereft of meaning, as in Dickinson's "More than the Grave is closed to me," in which she cries out, "I cling to nowhere till I fall— / The Crash of nothing, yet of all— / How similar appears" (1503). Deconstructing its own carefully chosen title, Frost's sonnet presents its readers not with the theists' "supremely wise and good plan," a "Design" governed by an agent demonstrating benevolent Intelligence, but with another deadly acting out, in miniature, of pitiless indifference, of random "accidental" power. The alternative to this Darwinian universe is divine brutality. In that case, the image of the predatory spider would extend from Nature to Nature's God, if such a God exists at all. However we read the poem, the vision cannot but "appall."[1]

---

1. The remark, by his biographer Jay Parini, that Robert Frost's poems "live on that perilous fault line between skepticism and belief" applies as well to Emily Dickinson. Having focused on Frost's spider, I should add that, in her own poetic handling of that emblematic arachnid, Dickinson emphasizes not its destructive but its *constructive*, aesthetic role, its intricate artistry: a "female" weaving, though her spiders are invariably male. Such poems—605, 1138, 1423, and especially 1275 ("Neglected Son of Genius / I take thee by the Hand")—offer a welcome respite to those we are examining.

If Frost's repeated, equally unanswerable questions evoke "The Tyger," the striking verb "appall" may be imported from Blake's "London," where the "cry" of victimized chimney sweeps "Every blackning Church appalls." (As a "child" pondering the "portentous" mystery of a Calvinist "Father and the Son," Dickinson's speaker in Poem 1258, engaging in "inference *appalling*," hopes "at least they are no worse / Than they have been described.") I will discuss in a moment a third grim masterpiece from *Songs of Experience:* Blake's "The Sick Rose," a poem with an obvious family resemblance to "Apparently with no surprise."

Dickinson's Flower and Frost, though inanimate, are transformed by the poet's use of pathetic fallacy and personification into an innocent, "happy" victim and an assassin, whose display of power had, for my initial respondents, a "sexual dimension." If so, the beheaded flower is not to be thought of as a threatened or castrated male. Though here the Flower is referred to as "it," Dickinson's preferred pronouns are almost invariably "her" and "she," a reflection less of literary tradition (or of botany, since many flowers possess both male and female sexual organs) than of the tenderness she felt toward the flowers she cultivated in her garden and sent as tokens of her love to friends, often accompanied by poems to form "bouquets." Emily Dickinson's lifelong, intensely intimate, and *spiritual* love of flowers—"The older I grow, the more do I love spring and spring flowers" (*L* 66), "If we love Flowers, are we not 'born again' every Day?" (*L* 899)—reinforces the emotional dynamic beneath this poem's laconic surface. "Since the garden was her cherished metaphor for the world, the careers and fortunes of her flowers signified [in miniature] the bitter struggles of humanity." In her "complex vision of flowers," a happy blossom is beheaded, "murdered by forces like frost, intrinsic to divine design."[2]

My friend's wife rightly identified the Frost as "careless, thoughtless, wreaking havoc on nature," envisioning a *female* Flower, victim of a destructive *masculine* violence. That aggressiveness, as well as the fact that, as she noted, Frost is at first "ignored, not seen," allies this Dickinson poem (and others, later discussed) with "The Sick Rose,"

2. Judith Farr, *The Gardens of Emily Dickinson,* 116. Farr's plural "gardens" (in this beautifully produced book) include the "actual spaces" where Dickinson cultivated her plants and flowers; the "imaginative realm of her poems and letters"; and "the ideal Garden of Paradise" (1).

also written in two *abcb* quatrains, but an even more powerful and concentrated lyric than Dickinson's:

> O Rose, thou art sick!
> The invisible worm
> That flies in the night,
> In the howling storm
>
> Has found out thy bed
> Of crimson joy,
> And his dark secret love
> Does thy life destroy.

Set in darkness and a howling storm, "The Sick Rose" suggests something awry at the very heart of the sexual principle itself; indeed, the Rose seems to be "sick" even before the worm's arrival. Like "Apparently with no surprise," Blake's violent poem functions on a literal, horticultural level as well as on a deeper, darker, symbolic one; and in both poems, victim and destructive agent are personified. A canker winged, the invisible worm "flies in the night," its mission to "destroy" the flower. The symbolic role shared by Blake's worm and Dickinson's Frost is emphasized in "Lycidas," cankerworm and frost supplying Milton, Dickinson's "great florist" (*L* 900), with natural equivalents to the human loss of Edward King as Lycidas—"As killing as the canker to the rose," or "frost to flowers that their gay wardrobe wear." What impels the life-destroying agent in "The Sick Rose" is not *wholly* negative; it is neither a ruthless, unadulterated death-drive nor mere lust, but "his dark secret *love*." Still, it *is* dark and secret.

In a late poem in which the rose is again a victim, Dickinson goes so far as to make the usually benign bee almost as destructive a sexual force as Blake's worm. A bold lover, the bee arrives in golden splendor, has his way with the acquiescent flower, then, "Their moment consummated," swiftly flees the scene, leaving the ravished rose humbled and resigned:

> A Bee his burnished Carriage
> Drove boldly to a Rose—
> Combinedly alighting—
> Himself—his Carriage was—

The Rose received his visit
With frank tranquillity
Withholding not a Crescent
To his Cupidity—
Their Moment consummated—
Remained for him—to flee—
Remained for her—of rapture
But the humility. (1339)

To that sexual treachery, and to the destructive violence of "Apparently with no surprise," several Dickinson poems provide life-affirming counterexamples. In the Keatsian "Come slowly—Eden!" the visiting bee/lover *does* "come slowly": "Lips unused to Thee— / Bashful—sip thy Jessamines." Open to that gradual approach, this flower, unlike those violently assaulted in both "The Sick Rose" and "Apparently with no surprise," is ready "To let the warm Love in"— to quote the final line of Keats's "Ode to Psyche." Dickinson's bee,

Reaching late his flower,
Round her Chamber hums—
Counts his Nectars—
Enters—and is lost in Balms. (211)

In a letter Keats advised a friend, "let us open our leaves like a flower and be ... receptive ... taking hints from every noble insect that favors us with a visit."[3] In Dickinson's poem, we have eroticism without the overriding sense of transience, of "Beauty that must die," Joy's hand "ever at his lips / Bidding adieu; and aching Pleasure nigh, / Turning to poison while the bee-mouth sips" ("Ode on Melancholy"). Instead, in "Come Slowly—Eden!" the "rapture" is tantalizingly delayed but unalloyed; the Original Fall from innocence in the Garden of Eden becomes a sexual Paradise gained rather than lost.

In "I tend my flowers for thee" (339), a Miltonic Eden is again evoked, in the form of what seems to me an echo of Eve's most beautiful speech. In this poem, a lyric lush with flowers (fuchsias, geraniums, daisies, carnations, and more), even the most voluptuous, the

3. Keats to John Hamilton Reynolds, February 18, 1818 (*Letters of John Keats*, 1:232–33).

crimson roses, waste their riches when the beloved, the "Bright Absentee," is not there:

> Globe Roses—break their satin flake—
> Upon my Garden floor—
> Yet—thou—not there—
> I had as lief they bore
> No Crimson—more— (339)

Dickinson seems to be recalling (along with Hamlet's "I had as lief . . .") one of the most exquisite passages in *Paradise Lost*, Eve's litany of all the beauties of heaven and earth, including "herb, tree, fruit, and flower, / Glist'ring with dew"—*none* of which, she tells Adam, "without thee is sweet" (4.639–56).

But "The Sick Rose" and "Apparently with no surprise," in which joy and happiness are abruptly terminated, are poems set in the fallen world of painful Experience. Just as Blake's nocturnal worm, exercising "his dark secret love," destroys the life of the rose, the Frost's beheading of the Flower goes well beyond what my friends termed "*possible* danger." Their point was that the cold but "casual" Frost, "at play," may damage rather than destroy, "causing hurt, but leaving the flower, maybe, to rise again, next spring." This "Assassin" certainly seems a "killing" frost, and the poem's tone austere. But, to judge from the classroom discussion and from the brief e-mail responses I requested, many readers, wishing to find the presiding God benevolent as well as approving, also find the seasonal *cycle* the poem's implicit theme. Gardener as well as poet, Emily Dickinson was acutely aware of seasonal transition, often using the flowers and plants in her essentially "perennial" garden as parables of the life-death cycle, even as reaffirmations of, or, more often, challenges to, a providential theodicy.

Since the evidence (to which we will return) in "Apparently with no surprise" would seem to confirm the action of a "killing" rather than a damaging frost, we may, before moving on, recapitulate the lethal insights provided by juxtaposing Dickinson's scenario of victimized Flower and destructive Frost with Blake's victimized rose and destructive worm, as well as with Robert Frost's victimized moth and destructive spider. It seems safe to say that, whatever may have "steered" the victim and the spider to their rendezvous "in the night," whatever directed the invisible worm that "flies in the night" to "his" victim in "her bed of crimson joy," it certainly does *not* seem to be the Thomistic or Newtonian God, who "steers everything": that Cosmic Intelligence who directs, as an archer does his arrow, all natural things toward a benignly intended, ultimately "good" goal.

In the next two chapters, we will explore the tension between Design and Accident as it seems to play out in "Apparently with no surprise," focusing on Frost as the blonde Assassin performing, "apparently," at the behest of a God who approves of its exercise of "accidental" but nevertheless lethal power.

Chapter 7

Design and Accident

Is the exercise of "accidental power" in "Apparently with no surprise" purely arbitrary, or is there an underlying Design detectable beneath the surface violence? Of course, Nature itself—A. E. Housman's "heartless, witless nature," that can "neither care nor know"—is "unthinking." I'm quoting Dickinson's "I dreaded that first robin, so" (348). Bird and grass, blossoms and bees, are cherished but alien ("What word had they, for me?"). When, despite her dread of hurtful beauty, they arrive in the spring, each "salutes" her as it passes in parade, "And I, my childish Plumes / Lift, in bereaved acknowledgement / Of their unthinking Drums." Thought is the province, on any supernatural level, of God, and, on the human level, of the one creature in the universe capable of cognition. "We live between two divergent realities": on one side, the world "in our heads and in our lives," and on the other, "the world beyond our human life—an equally real world in which there is no sign of caring or value, planning or judgment, love or joy. We live in a meaning-rupture because we are human and the universe is not."[1]

---

1. Jennifer Michael Hecht, *Doubt: A History*, xii. Though "Emily Dickinson" concludes the list of "Great Doubters" in Hecht's second subtitle, she receives in the body of the book only two (perceptive) paragraphs (425–26). The Housman poem, perhaps his most haunting, is "Tell me not here, it needs not saying" (*Last Poems*, XL, in *The Collected Poems of A. E. Housman*). Czeslaw Milosz—responding to

Dickinson was painfully aware of that cleavage. "This Consciousness that is aware / Of Neighbors and the Sun" is also necessarily the "one aware of Death." In utter solitude ("itself alone"), "Traversing the interval" between birth and death, the human spirit is "condemned to be— / Attended by a single Hound / Its own identity" (822). Emily Dickinson was torn between a Romantic celebration of the autonomous self and a growing realization of the isolation and limits of what philosopher Charles Taylor calls "secular," or "immanent," or "exclusive humanism." In contrast with the Wordsworthian egotistical sublime or Emersonian self-reliance, "the Dickinsonian self," as Roger Lundin has noted, "is cut off," both from "the infinite consciousness of God" *and* "from the serene unconsciousness of nature."[2]

The exhilaration of autonomy is offset by the sense of being alone in a perhaps purposeless universe. Related concepts widely accepted at the time of Emily Dickinson's birth—a benevolent Deity, the Argument from Design, a sense of harmony between religion and science—were, as earlier noted, under intense challenge in the period following the publication of *The Origin of Species* in 1859, the year Dickinson began to write poetry regularly. That Darwinian challenge was intensified by the carnage of the Civil War, the period of her most intense creativity. As an example of the "sobering changes" and "profound shifts" marking the mid-nineteenth century, Lundin considers the fate

of an idea that had enchanted Emily Dickinson as a student but that had become badly discredited by the time she began to write poetry. At the Amherst Academy and Mount Holyoke Seminary, Dickinson had been trained thoroughly in the argument from design, which held, in its various forms, that we can read nature like a book and discover the loving intentions of its author in the text. Science reinforced the truths of revealed religion, and the study of nature brought comfort to the troubled soul. . . . Dickinson, however, quickly detected the discordant notes being sounded by Darwin. . . . As an adult, the poet found it impossible to believe in what had

---

Blake, Goethe, and Erich Heller's *The Disinherited Mind*—is also sensitive to the "Romantic crisis of European culture" unleashed by "the dichotomy between the world of scientific laws—cold, indifferent to human values—and man's inner world" (*The Land of Ulro*, 94).

2. Taylor, *A Secular Age*, 19–21, 26, 251–52, 367; Lundin, *Emily Dickinson and the Art of Belief*, 154.

comforted her as a child. In many poems written during the Civil War, she tested the argument from design and found it wanting.[3]

In one poem (354), a butterfly freshly emerged from its chrysalis—an image, as Lundin notes, for the youthful Dickinson, "of God's design and a sign of the resurrection"—meanders "Without Design," at least as detectable by the human observer. Yet it exhibits a seemingly *benign* purposelessness. Occupying a middle stage in this development is her poem on the "four trees," in which purposelessness can be read as either a bald fact of nature teasing us into speculation or as an absence of design no less appalling than it is in Robert Frost's sonnet. The "Four Trees—upon a solitary Acre," though they "Maintain" their existence, are "Without Design / Or Order, or Apparent Action." Their nearest "neighbor," aside from sun and wind, is "God," but the stark poem, syntactically and metrically gnomic, ends in mystery:

> What Deed is Their's unto the General Nature—
> What Plan
> They severally—retard or further—
> Unknown— (742)

Defying definitive interpretation, the poem presents us with a God at once a "neighbor" and, as McIntosh has noted, eminently "suited to the designless space of the first stanza and the message of inscrutability conveyed by the whole poem."[4]

Purposelessness, then, can be benign, enigmatic, or malign. Acting with apparently *malign* purposelessness, the Frost in "Apparently with no surprise" nevertheless maintains its own form of radical innocence, brutally beheading, but "in *accidental* power." That adjective is as teleologically loaded a term as "Design" in Frost's sonnet and in Dickinson's poems about the butterfly and the four trees.

In a passage I focus on in Chapter 11, lines widely read in Dickinson's New England, Wordsworth describes an infinitely benevolent and powerful Being whose "purposes embrace / *All accidents*, converting

---

3. *Emily Dickinson and the Art of Belief*, 151.
4. *Nimble Believing*, 159. But see Judith Farr, who emphasizes the "*fact* of the trees" (which "Maintain" themselves) as well as "the *mystery* of their purpose" (*The Passion of Emily Dickinson*, 294–95).

them to good" (italics added). Contemporary exponents of "Intelligent Design," repackaged old Creationism fused with the Argument from Design, try to account for a cosmos that, having evolved from the dense heat of the Big Bang, formed galaxies and planets, on at least one of which living beings have also evolved. It would appear that the universe has precisely those characteristics that allow life—through cyclical creation, destruction, and re-creation—to emerge and evolve. Can it *all*, on either the cosmological or biological level, be "accidental"? No, say the proponents of ID, who insist that the underlying Design displays, in some instances, so much evidence of what Michael Behe has termed "irreducible complexity" that it must entail an implicit if imperceptible Designer: a cognizing creative agent that Augustine and Aquinas, even Newton and later Wordsworth, have no problem calling "God" but that goes unnamed by those promoting Intelligent Design as science rather than what it is: a more sophisticated version, elaborately camouflaged, of religious Creationism.[5]

The reference to Creation suggests additional connotative weight in the word *accidental*. In Genesis as in *Paradise Lost,* human suffering and death derive from an "accident"— in the root sense of *ad-cadere* ("to fall"), a disastrous mis-"chance" (from the same Latin root, *cadere*)— on the part of Adam and Eve, who fall and are expelled from the Garden. In the different yet related garden in Dickinson's poem, it is less the fall of the hitherto "happy Flower" (an intriguing variation on the theological *felix culpa*) than the destructive power of the *Frost* that is "accidental." This introduces precisely that unintended, random chance unacceptable to most exponents of Design. In a sense, the designation of its blow as "accidental" makes the poem's Assassin not only "blonde" but *blind*—an instrument of that "blind chance" almost as dismaying to Darwin as to Cardinal Schönborn, though not to Richard Dawkins, who titled one of his books *The Blind Watchmaker:*

5. Behe introduced the term *irreducible complexity* in 1996 in *Darwin's Black Box: The Biochemical Challenge to Evolution.* A conservative-evangelical Christian organization, the Discovery Institute, promotes and often funds the work of both Behe and his colleague William Dembski. For devastating refutations of Intelligent Design, see the essays in *Intelligent Thought: Science versus the Intelligent Design Movement,* ed. John Brockman; *Science and Religion,* ed. Kurtz; and "The Great Mutator," a *New Republic* review by Jerry A. Coyne of Behe's last-ditch defense of ID, *The Edge of Evolution: The Search for the Limits of Darwinism* (2007).

Why the Evidence of Evolution Reveals a Universe without Design (1987). Such "accidents," however, *do* present a challenge to theists, who have to go beyond Darwinism to accommodate the "apparently" cruel and accidental within a larger ordered and ultimately benevolent Design.

I placed "apparently" in quotation marks because our poem's opening word emphasizes perspective, how things *appear* from a given vantage point. What we see, and how we interpret it, depends on perspective, as crucial in poetry as it is in life. To some, Nature reveals intelligent, purposive design; to others, random chance. Benign harmony, malign brutality, meaningless flux: much of it is in the eye, and often in the faith or skepticism, of the beholder. On both the celestial and the terrestrial planes, Dickinson's Nature appears less ordered than meandering. "The Moon upon her fluent Route" is "Defiant of a Road," and the poet seems dubious that "The Star's Etruscan Argument / Substantiate a God." Even *if* there *is* purpose in the celestial movements, we who "know" know that the Designer has either forgotten that Newtonian-Enlightenment order or is himself forgotten:

> If Aims impel these Astral Ones
> The ones allowed to know
> Know that which makes them as forgot
> As Dawn forgets them—now— (1528)

In the earlier mentioned poem in which a butterfly emerges from its cocoon, the wayward insect displays, from the speaker's human perspective, a *benign* purposelessness:

> Without Design—that I could trace,
> Except to stray abroad
> On Miscellaneous Enterprise
> That Clovers understood. (354)

Of course, what we cognizant mortals understand is that *all*—the butterfly, the summer day, the clovers, the farmer depicted making hay— are ultimately extinguished, engulfed in death's tidal sunset. Of this, the apparently privileged clovers know nothing. Despite our empathetic bond with Nature, there is an irremediable cognitive gap between the natural and the human. Even Emerson, who claims in *Nature* that "Every appearance in nature corresponds to some state of the mind," insists in the introduction to that seminal work that there is a profound distinction between Mind and Nature, between the Soul and all else: the ME and the NOT ME,[6] what the philosopher Fichte, influencing Emerson by way of Carlyle, contrasted as the *Ich* and *Nicht Ich*. However deep the analogy between human and external nature, the latter, the NOT ME, remains emotionally unmoved and incapable of thought. At the other extreme, the God looking down upon this "purposeless Circumference" is also unmoved, not only aloof but scornful: "This Audience of Idleness / Disdained them from the Sky—" (354)

The cleavage between the human and the natural is not only Aristotelian, Thomistic, and Cartesian. It is also the dark undersong of Romanticism, inherited by Emily Dickinson, whose sentimental poems about Nature are offset by those stressing its inscrutable mystery. Her late poem "What mystery pervades a well!" anticipates Robert Frost's "For Once, Then, Something." Looking, for once, "Deeper down in the well," beneath the merely self-reflecting surface, Frost's speaker detects at the bottom "something white, uncertain, / More of the depths," but "then I lost it." Dickinson's poem presents a world of nature even more ghostly, alien, and impenetrable:

> What mystery pervades a well!
> That water lives so far—
> A neighbor from another world
> Residing in a jar
>
> Whose limit none have ever seen,
> But just his lid of glass—
> Like looking every time you please
> In an abyss's face!
>
> The grass does not appear afraid.
> I often wonder he
> Can stand so close and look so bold
> At what is awe to me.
>
> Related somehow they may be,
> The sedge stands next the sea—

6. *Emerson: Essays and Lectures,* ed. Joel Porte, 20, 9.

Where he is floorless
And does no timidity betray

But nature is a stranger yet;
The ones that cite her most
Have never passed her haunted house,
Nor simplified her ghost.

To pity those that know her not
Is helped by the regret
That those who know her, know her less
The nearer her they get. (1400)

When it comes to the irrevocable otherness of nature, the transatlantic precursor, overtly for Emerson, covertly or perhaps unconsciously for Dickinson, is Wordsworth. "Knowing that Nature never did betray / The heart that loved her" ("Tintern Abbey," lines 122–23), Wordsworth also knew that Nature was often—as in Dickinson's "haunted house" in "What mystery pervades a well!"—alien, other, *and* inferior to human consciousness: "the Mind of Man," celebrated in Wordsworth's canonically crucial "Prospectus" to *The Recluse* as "My haunt, and the main region of my song" (lines 40–41). As Pascal memorably put it,

> Man is only a reed, the weakest thing in nature, but he is a *thinking* reed [*un roseau pensant*]. The whole universe does not need to take up arms to crush him; a vapor, a drop of water, is enough to kill him. But even if the universe were to crush him, man would still be nobler than what killed him, because he knows he is dying and the advantage the universe has over him. The universe knows nothing of this.[7]

In "Apparently with no surprise," Dickinson has it both ways. While this lack of conscious knowledge is inherent in both the fate of the Flower and the pivotal act of the Frost, *we* sympathize with that slain Flower, because we "know" that we too will be cut down by impersonal forces that have "the advantage" over us. The speaker in this poem, in which perspective is as important as in Pascal's *Pensée*, is an observer and commentator, a "thinking" reed aware of things of

7. Blaise Pascal, *Pensées*, 64.

which the Flower and Frost know nothing, but whose own perspective is limited. Thus, the Flower is *apparently* both "happy" and unsurprised, the decapitating Frost *apparently* deploying "accidental power," the Sun *apparently* unmoved, God *apparently* approving. As Charles R. Anderson notes, "'Apparently' not only modifies the opening words but controls the whole poem. This is not necessarily the way things *are*, merely the way they *appear* to the mortal view."[8]

Here Anderson makes explicit what is implicit in Dickinson's opening word: her intuitive acceptance ("apparently") of Kant's epistemological version of the Copernican Revolution, his insistence that *things* correspond to *thoughts*, rather than the reverse. But the shaping, orchestrating power of the human mind comes at a price. Limited by our own modes of perception, we live, Kant informed all subsequent philosophy, in a phenomenal world of "appearances," cut off from knowledge of the *ding an sich*, things as they "really are," the *noumena*. What Anderson refers to as the control of the "whole poem" by its opening word extends, I would add, to *sound*, for "Apparently" initiates the plosives that recur in all but the penultimate line (surprise, ha*pp*y, *p*lay, *p*ower, *p*asses, *p*roceeds) and that culminate in the crucial description in the final line of God as "A*pp*roving." This alliterative design would appear to be *not* "accidental."

∽

Approval is one response to what is observed; but there are others, which vary depending on one's vantage point. All such responses may indeed be subsumed under that opening adverb, reducing the events and reactions described to merely the way they appear to the mortal view. Like the victim, the other players in the drama go about their business, while God looks on approvingly—from on high, but with no more "surprise" than that attributed to the lowly Flower. If, in contrast, the author and her readers are moved, it is precisely because everything else is emotionally *un*moved, playing their assigned roles as *in* a "play." For some teleological readers, ranging from unsentimental naturalists to the hopefully religious, the "play" of Frost and Flower may seem a single scene excerpted from a larger trajectory— part of a seasonal drama that may be interpreted as but one aspect of an annual, and perhaps divine, comedy. To quote the sentence with

---

8. *Emily Dickinson's Poetry: Stairway to Surprise,* 177; my emphasis.

which Charles Anderson concludes his discussion of the poem: "What seems to man like a tragic event in time is but another aspect of nature's automatic process—'apparently.'"[9]

By closing with the poem's opening and governing word, Anderson honestly registers—despite his "*merely,*" "*what seems to man,*" and "*but another aspect*"—the *full* range of perspectives, from detached observation of the seasonal cycle to the presentation of moments in time that *do* seem "tragic." In mythology of the sort elaborated in Frazer's *Golden Bough,* sacrifice is part of the ritual of seasonal transition, often (as in Celtic myth, the story of Gawain and the Green Knight, or Yeats's late dance plays) in the barbaric form of a beheading of the old to make way for the new. The sacrificial victim in this poem is the Flower; and the Frost "beheads it at its *play.*" Since the antecedent of the pronoun *its* is ambiguous, it would appear that *both* Flower and Frost are "at" their "play" when the sudden beheading occurs.[10] And since Frost is the instrument of God, God himself is "playing." As earlier suggested, Gloucester's famous observation in *King Lear,* "As flies to wanton boys, are we to th'gods; / They kill us for their sport," seems to have been applied by Dickinson to what she sees as Jehovah's bullying, sadistic treatment of "Old Moses," a "wrong" for which the poet's own sense of "justice bleeds." (In poems 168 and 1201, God's treatment of Moses, "'Canaan' denied," is also denounced as not "fair.") Allowing Moses a glimpse of the Promised Land from Mount Pisgah but denying him "the entering" seems to her,

---

9. Ibid., 179.

10. Applied to the Frost, *play* evokes a mythical dimension, archaic-vegetative and "Yeatsian." Violent death as *play,* both as part of a theatrical-mythical-cycle and as nonchalant behavior, is a motif in two Yeats poems and plays, all adopting, as the Dickinson speaker does in part, an impersonal perspective. In the first, one of "Two Songs" accompanying the unfolding and folding of the curtain for his Dionysian-Christian play *The Resurrection,* Yeats places the sacrifice of the specific victim in the cyclical context of seasonal and divine displacement and rebirth. In response to the crucifixion of Jesus and the dismemberment of his Frazerian brother Dionysus, "all the Muses sing / Of Magnus Annus at the spring, / As though God's death were but a play." In the second poem, from Yeats's 1923 sequence *Meditations in Time of Civil War,* an IRA officer comes to the door of the poet's tower cracking jokes about the ongoing Irish Civil War, "As though to die by gunshot were / The finest play under the sun." Wielding figurative sword rather than gun, Dickinson's "blonde Assassin" similarly engages in lethal "play," as though beheading were the most amusing thing under the sun—as it almost *is* in Yeats's alternately grisly and comic Salome-variation, *A Full Moon in March.*

"In point of injury," to surpass the cruelty inflicted on the Christian Testament's Stephen or Paul,

> For these—were only put to death
> While God's adroiter will
> On Moses—seemed to fasten
> With *tantalizing Play*
> *As Boy—should deal with lesser Boy—*
> To prove ability. (597; italics added)

The comparison of Jehovah's cruel, "tantalizing Play" with the Frost's playful beheading, under divine auspices, of a "happy" Flower "at its play," suggests a further comparison. The situation in "Apparently with no surprise" might be illuminated by applying Blake's famous Contraries from *The Songs of Innocence and of Experience*.[11] At *its* play, the "happy Flower" is a representative of Edenic, primal *Innocence*, struck down in the midst of its joyous existence. The decapitating Frost, at *its* play, would seem to represent the world of grim *Experience*, amusing itself, as Dickinson thought Jehovah had in the case of Moses, at the expense of its victim, at the very least "playing" in a careless or indifferent manner. But there is, in Blake's version of Hegelian dialectic, a higher, *Organized Innocence*, analogous to the Christian and Dionysian cycle in its incorporation and transcendence of painful Experience. Thus perceived, the Frost in this poem *may* be doubly "innocent." Not only does it *not* act intentionally, let alone malevolently; it may also be an "accidental" agent of blind chance serving, perhaps, to promote seasonal change.

That would be both an archetypal theme and a practical concern for a woman who was a poet *and* a cultivator of a garden consisting largely of perennials. Acutely conscious of seasonal transition, Dickinson was perhaps also familiar with Shelley's "Ode to the West Wind," which she seems to have in mind in her own poem "The duties

---

11. Dickinson is presumed to have had no knowledge of Blake, though her gnomic poetry has often been compared with his *Songs of Innocence and of Experience*. Here, as in earlier citations of Blake, I am primarily interested in analogy and mutual illumination; but it is perhaps worth mentioning that Blake's *Songs* were available in New England in the Wilkinson edition the remarkable Elizabeth Palmer Peabody began to sell in 1837.

of the Wind are few." In the Ode, Shelley presents the West Wind as dialectical: in autumnal form, a male "Destroyer and Preserver"; as the vernal West Wind, "thine azure sister of the Spring," a female Creator who "shall blow / Her clarion o'er the dreaming earth." It is she who will resurrect the "buried" (sleeping, not dead) seeds and so green the earth with renewed life. In the final stanza, Shelley invokes the wind to "Drive my dead thoughts over the universe / Like withered leaves to quicken a new birth!" and concludes with a question that is *rhetorical* on the level of Nature, *desperate* in terms of human depression and the longed-for revival of personal and political hope: "O Wind, / If Winter comes, can Spring be far behind?" He hopes for the wind said by Emily Dickinson, in "The duties of the Wind are few," to "Establish March . . . / And usher Liberty" (1137).

Though the Dickinson family library included the 1853 Philadelphia edition of Shelley's *Poetical Works,* we hardly need "Ode to the West Wind" (or, for that matter, Blake's *Songs of Innocence and of Experience*) to confirm what is implicit in "Apparently with no surprise": that life and death are not only natural but human issues. In Dickinson's poem this bond is dramatically emphasized by the violent nature of the central act. So while it is true that the gap between Nature and Man accounts in part for the apparent tonal and perspectival detachment in Dickinson's poem, an empathetic bond is also reaffirmed. However nonchalant and detached the poem seems, its dramatic crux is the brutal beheading of a happy Flower by a sudden, stealthy killer, an "Assassin, hid" (670). Lulled by the dependent clause and the depiction of the Flower as "happy," we, unlike the flower, *are* "surprised," as we are meant to be, by that violent act. The impact of the pivotal moment is reinforced by a technique characteristic of Dickinson: the use of emphatic alliteration and familiar words in an utterly unexpected context (*beheads . . . / blonde Assassin*) in order to shock us into surprised attention. Similarly, the use of personification and pathetic fallacy humanizes the scene, so that we cannot help but respond to what happens from a mortal and engaged rather than a distanced and omniscient—God's-eye—perspective.

From that mortal vantage point, not merely registering what is "apparently" happening, we feel a shared sense of mutability. Flowers seem to be, for Dickinson as for Wordsworth, the one natural form from which we can never be estranged. The freezing of a flower, a form of murder in Emily Dickinson's world, is made to seem to *us* not only

automatic and "natural" but also touching and even tragic. The
poem's central action, a decapitation by Frost, evokes not only the
death and decapitation of Orpheus, which his mother, the "Muse herself," is helpless to prevent (Calliope could do nothing for her enchant-
ing son "Whom universal nature did lament, / When by the rout that
made the hideous roar / His gory visage down the stream was sent"
["Lycidas," 57–62]), but also the sudden death of short-lived "Man."
Born of woman and "of few days . . . He cometh forth *like a flower, and
is cut down*" (Job 14:1–2). And the biblical author doubtless has frost in
mind; as Cynthia Griffin Wolff has noted,

> The Book of Job had taught Dickinson that God resides in the North
> and rejoices in ruination . . . God's frigidity can even become per-
> versely intermingled with the generative force that moves creation.
> "Out of whose womb came the ice? And the hoary frost of heaven,
> who hath gendered it? . . ." (Job 38:29). Divinity seems to applaud
> nothing so much as a devastation by cold, for "By the breath of God
> frost is given" (Job 37:10); and this lesson was reenacted with invari-
> able regularity in Emily Dickinson's own garden.[12]

Wolff then quotes in full (and this is her single reference to the poem)
"Apparently with no surprise." There, emphasizing this floral-human
analogy, as well as the role of an "approving" if not quite "applaud-
ing" God, Dickinson endows the "happy" victim with human feelings
and gives more detached but still human attributes to Frost and Sun,
actors in an eternal recurrence that explains why the Flower's destruction comes as "no surprise." To quote again the Hebrew text closest to
Job, "There is no new thing under the sun," including "the evil work
that is done under" it (Eccles. 1:9, 4:3). Dickinson also presents an
anthropomorphic God, depicted as "Approving" this recurrent
process. In glossing the engendered frost in Job, Wolff remarks that
"God's frigidity can even become perversely intermingled with the
generative force that moves creation," and we know that frost can revi-
talize as well as kill. But despite the possibility of an ultimately benign
interpretation, divine "approval" of the whole trajectory of the natural cycle, there is certainly no overt emphasis here, as there is in Shelley's "Ode to the West Wind," on future rebirth.

---

12. *Emily Dickinson*, 314. See also Paula Bennett, *My Life a Loaded Gun*, 91–94.

Indeed, in making the argument that in this poem there is "not even any indication of an ordered plan," Charles Anderson adds: "For frost can come prematurely, *as here*, killing flowers before the seed stage has been reached and a cyclical purpose served."[13] This seems to me the only plausible reading, making "Apparently with no surprise" a less hopeful poem than many readers, and perhaps most who consider themselves religious, would seem to prefer: that is to say, a poem resistant to any facile conception of either a painless natural teleology or a providential Design. The Flower may be resigned or indifferent to its fate, or simply unconscious of it; the human speaker in the poem, and we its human readers, respond to that decapitation with the *recognition* that, whatever the differences between the natural and the human orders, we *all* perish, we all come forth and are cut down, often prematurely. In the case of Emily Dickinson, that poignant connection between the flowers she cherished and the people she loved was instinctive.

In lesser hands, this botanical/human analogy could deteriorate into maudlin and didactic allegory. As Anderson notes, Dickinson is not exploiting "untimely death in nature *solely* for its human analogy, the sentimental shock when a person is cut off in the full flower of his days."[14] Emily Dickinson is not Robert Burns, who, in his elegy for "Highland Mary," lamented "fell death's untimely frost, / That nipt my flower sae early." Yet, in Dickinson as in Milton and in Wordsworth, the analogy is there—not didactic or sentimental, but poignant. In a letter to Elizabeth Holland, whose son (her "little Byron") had suffered a crippled foot, she wrote: "To assault so minute a creature seems to me malign, unworthy of Nature—but the frost is no respecter of persons" (*L* 369). Though he cites this letter, Anderson undercuts its incipient sentimental shock value, noting that "even there she modified her emotional reaction by 'seems' and by the frost image, which translate nature's apparent cruelty into indifference: it is hostile to man and flower *only* in not being designed wholly to accommodate their flourishing."[15]

This is a salutary antidote to Romantic indulgence, applicable, as we are meant to infer, to any full reading of "Apparently with no sur-

---

13. *Emily Dickinson's Poetry*, 178; my emphasis.
14. Ibid.; my emphasis.
15. Ibid.

prise." But in his anxiousness to clear Dickinson of any taint of didacticism or sentimentality, Anderson may go too far—as he seems to acknowledge himself by inserting *solely, only,* and *wholly.* Anderson's caveats modify only slightly what paleontologist Stephen Jay Gould later referred to as his own "cold bath" theory:

> that nature can be truly "cruel" and "indifferent" [only] in the utterly inappropriate terms of our ethical discourse—because nature does not exist for us, didn't know we were coming (we are, after all, interlopers of the latest geological moment), and doesn't give a damn about us (speaking metaphorically). I regard such a position as liberating, not depressing, because we then gain the capacity to conduct moral discourse—and nothing could be more important—in our own terms, free from the delusion that we might read moral truth passively from nature's factuality.[16]

But Emily Dickinson is not a paleontologist. Her letter simultaneously expresses and modifies her emotional reaction, but it does not *obliterate* it. Thus, the letter may illuminate more than the "absolute detachment" Anderson claims the poet achieves in "Apparently with no surprise." Though a gardener and keen-eyed observer of nature's cycles, Emily Dickinson is neither a scientist nor a detached philosopher, and so not above insisting, repeatedly, on the moral link between botanical and human life. Ironically enough, that bond is reaffirmed by Anderson himself in the very act of diminishing it. For "man *and* flower" are, paradoxically, *allied;* Nature, *not* "designed wholly to accommodate their *flourishing,*" *does* seem designed to bring about their shared *destruction.*

16. Gould, *Leonardo's Mountain of Clams and the Diet of Worms,* in *The Richness of Life,* 602.

Chapter 8

Frost, the Blonde Assassin

That destruction by Nature is accomplished in the first quatrain of "Apparently with no surprise." In the second, we encounter all three of the poem's dramatically described agents: "the blonde Assassin," that "Approving God," and the Sun that "proceeds unmoved." While I personally detect no ambiguity in this *particular* poem, the sun is a bad actor in other Dickinson poems; and there is, I quickly discovered, some dispute among readers as to which of the two natural actors— Frost or Sun—is here personified as "the blonde Assassin." Some, equating "blonde" with yellow, identify the Sun as the Assassin, sometimes reinforcing their case with a naturalistic explanation. One of my respondents suggested that, in nature, while frost stuns flowers, it is the action of the sun that snaps and finishes them off, thus strengthening the argument for the Sun as assassin.

Sun is the second most frequent noun in Dickinson's poetry, and, to be sure, "the sun" often plays a less than nourishing, patriarchal, even destructive role, especially when it comes to flowers. In "the early morning," Angels may "be seen the Dews among," smiling amid "the Buds"; but "when the sun is hottest," those angels are seen "sighing" rather than smiling, the dews replaced by "sands," and "Parched the flowers they bear along" (94). For a delicate bud to flourish, to "obtain its right of Dew," it is necessary that Nature, among other tasks, "Adjust the Heat" (1058). In a remarkable 1852 letter to Susan Gilbert regarding marriage and wifely subordination, Dickinson depicts the woman as a flower and the sun as an irresistible male oppressor. They have "often touched upon," but "been strangely silent upon this subject," she tells Susie, repressing it "as children shut their eyes when the sun is too bright for them."

> You have seen flowers at morning, *satisfied* with the dew, and those same sweet flowers at noon with their heads bowed in anguish before the mighty sun; think you these thirsty blossoms will *now* need naught but—*dew*? No, they will cry for sunlight, and pine for the burning noon, tho' it scorches them, scathes them; they have got through with peace—they know that the man of noon, is *mightier* than the morning and their life is henceforth to him. Oh Susie it is dangerous. (*L* 210)[1]

Contextualizing, too, can be dangerous. Readers, especially those familiar with this dramatic and much discussed letter, may find a similar solar destructiveness in this particular poem. If so, it seems to me inadvertent, as "accidental" as the Frost's destructive power. Even if we grant *some* uncertainty in the case of "Apparently with no surprise," consider the rhetorical obstacles that must be overcome or evaded by those who argue for a solar assassin. Such advocates would, first, have to explain away what would seem to be the obvious connection between the Frost's violent act of beheading and the murderous personification, "Assassin." Second, they would have to explain, or justify, the *repetition*, especially in a poem as economical as this one. For it would be redundant for the poet, having *personified* the Sun in line 5, to then *name it explicitly* in line 6. Those interpreting the sun as a killer, even though they will find, as just noted, support in the larger context of the Dickinsonian canon, will look in vain for any juxtaposition of the sun and violent death by means of anything resembling assassination. My own search yielded only one occurrence, a work-sheet fragment (1127) jotted down on a small piece of paper around 1868. Though it featured the kind of sharp-edged instrument required to behead, its two-line simile—"Soft as the

---

1. See Wendy Barker, "Emily Dickinson and Poetic Strategy," in Martin, ed., *The Cambridge Companion to Emily Dickinson*, 81–82. Dickinson associates the sun, Barker observes, with prose, patriarchal religious sermons, and restraint: the antifloral, one might say.

massacres of Suns / By evening's Sabres slain"—depicts suns not as wielders of murderous instruments but as victims, sunlit days slain by the swords of evening.

Still, for some readers "blonde" seems inescapably color-associated with the Sun, to whose "Yellow Plan" Dickinson refers in one poem (591). But surely "blonde" runs the color chart from gold to silver (pale, ash, platinum), adequately accounting for this striking personification. In a poem delineating the face of the moon, while her forehead is of "Amplest *Blonde*," she has a "*Silver* Will" (737; the moon's "Lips of Amber" may also remind us that, in 337, dew stiffens quietly on summer's newly frosted "Amber Shoe"). In short, the crucial association seems less with precise color than with iridescent light and beauty. Dickinson's personified Frost is not dark-complexioned (despite the etymological origins of the word *assassin* in reference to a Muslim inspired by hashish and religion to kill the infidel). As invisible as Blake's cankerworm in "The Sick Rose," this Frost, though a cold killer, is *not* a "dark" destroyer. Instead, this "blonde Assassin" is a pale rider, an agent of the destruction of beauty that is itself luminously beautiful—pure, prismatic, pristine, glistening.

It is the fusion of beauty with lethality that is most stressed in Dickinson's poems about frost, poems that typically associate frost with death, natural and human. In one poem, in which living beauty becomes petrified, the speaker knows a place

> where Summer strives
> With such a practiced Frost—
> She—each year—leads her Daisies back—
> Recording—briefly—"Lost"—

But the promise of vernal rebirth implicit in the hopeful adverb *briefly* is not always fulfilled, as suggested by the opening line's strenuous and perhaps impotent *striving*. When spring's South wind is more turbulent than usual (echoing "strives," it "stirs" the ponds and "struggles" in the lanes), Summer's "Heart misgives her for her Vow," and she "pours" soft elegiac "Refrains"

> Into the lap of Adamant—
> And spices—and the Dew—

That stiffens quietly to Quartz
Upon her Amber Shoe— (337)

In another poem, Frost's caress is intimate yet fatal. This "Visitor in Marl" (normally, fertilizing loam, but here, as Judith Farr has suggested, a possible play on the contraction for "marble," or gravestone) "influences Flowers— / Till they are orderly as Busts— / And elegant—as Glass—." But the price of this crystallization of flowers into aesthetic artifacts goes beyond abandonment by a bold but transient lover. In this garden version of an *aubade*, the male Frost

> visits in the Night—
> And just before the Sun—
> Concludes his glistening interview—
> Caresses—and is gone—
>
> But whom his fingers touched—
> And where his feet have run
> And whatsoever Mouth he kissed—
> Is as it had not been. (391)

The "sexual dimension" my initial respondents detected in "Apparently with no surprise" is here overt. In both poems, the Frost's "influence," before his "glistening interview" is concluded by the melting rays of the sun, is death, indeed nullification. Any flower caressed and sensuously kissed by this *homme fatale* is "*as if it had not been*": a finality paralleling the more brutal eradication by the beheading Assassin. Natural mutability, the destruction of beauty in nature, is always a human theme as well, repeatedly expressed by Dickinson in terms of frost's assault on flowers. Poems such as "A Visitor in Marl" and "Apparently with no surprise" describe, as Judith Farr says, "the killing of her flowers, an event that always seemed to her like murder."[2] One poem presents a sinister version of what Coleridge (in "Frost at Midnight") beautifully describes as the "secret ministry of frost." In Dickinson's poem, "The Frost was never seen— / If met, too rapid past"; still, the "Flowers" are the first to notice a "Stranger hovering round,"

---

2. Farr, *Gardens of Emily Dickinson*, 10.

A Symptom of alarm
In Villages remotely set
But search effaces him

Till some retrieveless Night
Our Vigilance at ease
The Garden gets the only shot
That never could be traced.

This alien Frost, a kind of sniper haunting the outskirts armed with lethal force, is "never seen" until it is too late, and then becomes emblematic of all the mysterious forces of earth and air:

Unproved is much we know—
Unknown the worst we fear—
Of Strangers is the Earth the Inn
Of Secrets is the Air—

To analyze perhaps
A Philip would prefer
But Labor vaster than myself
I find it to infer. (1202)

The apostle Philip might seek demonstrable evidence of the invisible God ("Lord, show us the Father"), even though Jesus had just said, "If ye had known me, ye should have known my Father also" (John 14:7–9). But Emily Dickinson knows that ultimate mysteries are insoluble. God working through frost in the garden induces not faith but fear, and terrifying inferences of inscrutable, destructive power rather than comforting religious revelation.

In "The Frost of Death was on the Pane," our efforts to fight "Mortality" are futile, defeated by a frigid force at once lethal, serpentine, and satanic. Despite our struggle to protect the feminine "passive Flower," the aggressive Frost, an insidious intruder, began "to crawl":

We pried him back
Ourselves we wedged
Himself and her between,
Yet easy as the narrow Snake
He forked his way along.

Till all her helpless beauty bent
And then our wrath begun—
We hunted him to his Ravine
We chased him to his Den—

We hated Death and hated Life
And nowhere was to go—
Than Sea and continent there is
A larger—it is Woe. (1136)

The passionate intensity of the poem, which Alfred Habegger considers Dickinson's "most wrathful lyric," may in part be attributable to her reaction to the serious illness and death at this time (1866) of a young woman friend. The inexorable frost that "bends" and destroys "helpless beauty" in the form of a flower evokes a tragic version of the romance motif. To that motif, in which a "helpless" maiden cannot be saved, the final stanza, stressing "Woe" (a *human sorrow* more immense than "Sea and continent"), adds a vision from Revelation: "Woe to the inhabiters of the earth and of the sea! For the devil has come down to you in great wrath" (Rev. 12:12). Though she does not cite this biblical passage, Paula Bennett perceptively depicts the forces at work not only in *this* poem but, I would add, also in "Apparently with no surprise" and "Like Time's insidious wrinkle" (neither of which she discusses). "Like a Satanic trinity," she writes,

> the snake is death, frost, and (presumably) the devil in one. As such, it epitomizes the destructive potential which Dickinson seems to have believed was latent in all forms of masculine power, including God's. It is God, after all, who ordains frost, death, and snake. They are the instruments of His will, the means through which His ordination comes to pass.[3]

The other poem I mentioned, though "Shakespearean" in motif, may also be covertly Miltonic. Here Frost "dishevels" rather than "beheads," though mutability merges with mortality:

---

3. Bennett, *Emily Dickinson: Woman Poet,* 73–74. The young woman was Susan D. Phelps. See Alfred Habegger, *My Wars Are Laid Away in Books: The Life of Emily Dickinson,* 509–10.

Like Time's insidious wrinkle
On a beloved's Face
We clutch the Grace the tighter
Though we resent the crease.

The *Frost himself so comely*
Dishevels every prime
Asserting from his Prism
That none can punish him. (1236; italics added)

Though a resented and self-proclaimed indestructible destroyer, Frost is "comely," a male terrible beauty that "dishevels" every physical perfection. The unexpected word may echo Milton's description of unfallen Eve, who her "unadorned golden tresses wore / *Disheveled*, but in *wanton ringlets* waved / As the *vine* curls her tendrils." The vine image is apt, but that disheveled hair, however innocent in immediate context, has clear erotic implications suggesting the tangles in which she will eventually snare Adam. In Dickinson's poem, the male force, the Frost, "dishevels" beauty, beauty which—whatever its human implications—is in the first place a *flower*. This again evokes the Eve of John Milton (whom she dubbed "the great florist"), the Eve with whom Dickinson repeatedly identified herself. That queen of fecund Eden goes forth to tend her "fruits and flowers, / To visit how they prospered, bud and bloom, / Her nursery." She is the first to succumb to the seduction of comely Satan-as-serpent, "never since of serpent kind / Lovelier." Displaying his circling spires, he "*Curl'd* many a *wanton wreath* in sight of Eve, / To lure her eye," just as *she* had lured Adam's eye with her *hair* "disheveled," but in "*wanton ringlets*" curled (*Paradise Lost* 4.305–7, 8.44–46, 9.504–5, 515). Since Eve falls along with Adam, it may be that Frost—in this poem as in "The Frost of Death was on the Pane"—has a satanic aspect. If so, like Satan, who (in the biblical text already cited, Rev. 12:12) is wrathful "because he knoweth that he hath but a short time," Frost is *not* invulnerable. Despite the boastful assertion in this poem, made from the apparent safety of his crystalline "prism," that solidity is subject to the effects of the sun.

And that is what happens in "Apparently with no surprise." Leaving the execution scene, the Frost "passes on," evaporated by the Sun—which, in turn, passes on. Oxymoronically enough, the Sun "proceeds unmoved," with *"proceeds"* picking up the dominant *p*-sound and echoing the sibilance attending the *"Assassin"* that *"passes on."* Together with "unm*o*ved," it also anticipates the sound and stance of an "Appr*o*ving God." Most notably, the poem is dramatically decelerated in its final three lines by that long *e* (proc*ee*ds) and the two long *u*'s (unm*o*ved, appr*o*ving) that drag their slow length along to produce a solemn cadence. Especially heavy weight falls on "proceeds unmoved," a gravitas protracted by the terminal caesura, with no dash needed to mark the vocal pause demanded by sound and sense, and deliberately extended by the repeated *m*-sound: "unm*o*ved / To *m*easure."

But how does the Sun move forward in an orderly manner yet remain "unmoved"? In Dickinson's vocabulary, "unmoved" has to do not with any lack of movement but with the absence of overt emotion. This stoic and stately stance is often approved. A man, standing up to the onslaught of a female Fate, "unmoved regarded Her" (1031). She praises the "little Blue-Bird" who arrives in earliest spring and is the last to leave at summer's end and whose voice "soar[s] unmoved / Above ostensible Vicissitude" (1395). The word occurs twice in the middle stanza of one of her best-known poems, which ends with her closing "the valves of her Attention— / Like Stone." Dickinson is less likely to be echoing Aristotle's Unmoved Mover than Shakespeare's praise of those "Who, moving others, are themselves as stone, / Unmoved, cold, and to temptation slow" (Sonnet 94). Having selected "her own Society" (consisting of a single chosen "One"), the Dickinsonian Soul "shuts the door," rejecting even the most imperious "suitors":

> Unmoved—She notes the Chariots—pausing—
> At her low Gate—
> Unmoved—an Emperor be kneeling
> Upon her Mat— (303)

Sometimes, however, the word is clearly negative: "I cannot meet the Spring unmoved— / I feel the old desire" (1051); were we not insensitive to the point of blindness, "We could not look upon the Earth— / So utterly unmoved" (1284). This is the negative connotation of *unmoved* in "Apparently with no surprise." Making a more-than-astronomical point, Dickinson presents the warm Sun as a cold calculator, utterly unmoved, a detached, indifferent geometer measuring off—in a kind of parody of the merely quantitative measurement to which science is limited, according to Cardinal Schönborn—"another Day" for an approving Supervisor.

We understand how the Sun, appearing to travel through its diurnal round, from dawn to meridian to sunset, marks off the stages of the day. But what are the implications of the modifier in the phrase "*another* Day"? Here, *another* implies, beyond "additional," just one more instance among many—different from the first, but of the same character. It could be "any" day, suggesting a tonal as well as a sonic echo of the earlier phrase, "*any* happy Flower"—*any* meaning one, no matter which, from a number of many such instances. We are being presented with an emblematic scene, a particular instance of a recurrent pattern of change within a changeless paradigm. As she put it in a letter contemporaneous with this poem: "Changelessness is Nature's change" (*L* 848). There is no new thing under the sun; this is the way things are, always have been, and always will be.

The cycle is self-regulating, but is it a cycle with or without *ultimate* purpose? Is it an example of genuine dialectical change? Of Kantian or Darwinian purposivenesss without purpose? Or of that dreary cyclical recurrence Blake condemned as "the same dull round," what Wallace Stevens, in "The Man Whose Pharynx Was Bad," called "the malady of the quotidian"? Stevens opened his great sequence "The Auroras of Autumn" with the repeated declaration, "This is where the serpent lives," with the serpent at once Ananke, emblem of necessity, and, as "form gulping after formlessness," the self-devouring Ouroboros. Stevens stresses *both* the world's beautiful lavishing of itself in change *and* that ultimate change, death. Writing in 1800, the philosopher Johann Gottlieb Fichte briefly projected a devouring vision of inexorable change and asked: "What is the point of this continual, self-contained and ever-returning circle, this repetitive game that always starts again in the same way, in which everything is, in order to fade away, and fades away, only in order to return again as it was—this monster, continually devouring itself in order to reproduce itself, and reproduce itself, in order to devour itself?"[4]

It would take Nietzsche to accept, in terror and life-affirming joy, this ever-returning circle by embracing eternal recurrence, appropriately symbolized by Zarathustra's biting off of the serpent's head.

4. *The Vocation of Man,* book 3, part 2: "Faith."

Fichte's glimpse into this psychologically unbearable abyss was momentary; as an Idealist philosopher, he quickly rejected the devouring vision of a meaningless universe, reverting to an image of nature and of human existence as purposive, with everything progressing toward a harmonious and moral end, no matter how distant.

To refocus these questions in terms of the Frost's beheading of the Flower in "Apparently with no surprise": is it emblematic of a pattern essentially tragic or providential, an illustration of meaningless destruction or of purposive "Design"? And if it *is* "designed," what does that tell us about the Designer? The killing Frost, the lethal headsman in this memorable scene, exemplifies what Yeats called (in "A Prayer for My Daughter") "the murderous innocence" of nature. It destroys in "accidental power," but it is acting, presumably, as the agent of the *Supreme* Power, by whose divine "breath," according to Job 37:10, "frost is given." But if frost is ambiguous in Job and one of the glories of a providential God in Psalms (147:16), it seems a sign of his ruthlessness in "Apparently with no surprise." As an ambassador of death, Frost is an assassin sent forth at the behest, or with the acquiescence, of God, who is himself described as an "Assassin" in poem 1102. The unmoved Sun also performs its measurement "for" this "*Approving* God." Echoing the initial "*Apparently*," this "*Approving*" Deity ("apparently") sanctions the whole of the drama we have just witnessed—a garden scene that at first seems as limited as the garden scene in "The Sick Rose" or as "small" as the tableau in Robert Frost's "Design," but which, as in those poems, confronts us with the human and even cosmic mysteries presented earlier.

All the players in Dickinson's drama—ascending hierarchically from unsurprised Flower to powerful Frost to measuring Sun to approving God—take the beheading casually and in stride. Some readers do as well. Others find the poem disturbing, even shocking. Some may detect in the poem's measured tone and metrical regularity support for an argument that Dickinson herself observes the process she describes with the same equanimity exhibited, in their different ways, by Flower, Frost, Sun, and God. For such readers, the poem conveys an archetypal sense, ranging from the botanical through the psychological to the spiritual, that destruction necessarily precedes new creation; that out of death comes life, out of evil, good. For other readers, myself included, there is the unmistakable sense that—beneath its calm, "detached" surface—the poem's tone and central act reveal Dickinson (or the poem's dramatic speaker) to be *disturbed* by what is described, and that she chooses her subject, language, and dramatic treatment with the deliberate intention of disturbing *us*.

Whichever way readers lean, the central question raised by "Apparently with no surprise" is whether the accidental beheading in the poem is a *merely* destructive act or part of a more inclusive plan, vegetative and theistic. In the world of natural process, frost is not necessarily divorced from rebirth; it can be either lethal, as it certainly seems to be in the case of a beheading Assassin, or a damaging visitation from which renewed life springs—a precursor of cyclical revival. A revitalizing frost—wrote one of my respondents, who happens to be, like Dickinson, a poet *and* an experienced gardener—can also appear in a "decapitating" role, since it "moves forward the maturation of the seed heads on the plants. Even in my own garden I keep an eye on the prettiest flower and wait for the frost; and then after a few days I can go out and collect the seeds from the seed head, with the hope of seeding the same delight in the spring."

Emily Dickinson knew that frost can either cut "back" or cut "down" and can be either vernal or autumnal. She celebrates, and unmistakably *identifies with,* one late-blooming flower: "a little Gentian" that "tried" to be a Rose and "failed." Summer "laughed" until, when autumn came, "There rose a Purple Creature— / That ravished all the Hill," silencing mockery:

> The Frosts were her condition—
> The Tyrian would not come
> Until the North—invoke it—
> "Creator—shall I bloom?" (442)

At times, frost is *overtly* Dickinson's *own* "condition." In "Ourselves were wed," the beloved's (Susan's) cottage faces the sun and her garden blooms first, "For mine—in Frosts—was sown" (631); in another poem, she declares that the season she actually "prefers" is "diversified / With Prospect, and with Frost" (930).

Nevertheless, on both the natural and the human level, frost was for Dickinson a predominantly negative, deadly force—unsurprisingly for a New England gardener used to weather changeable and often cold, one also deeply affected by the many deaths she saw all around her. In the famous "After great pain, a formal feeling comes," the "Hour of Lead" is remembered, if "outlived," as a form of death: "As Freezing persons recollect the Snow— / First—Chill—then Stupor—then the letting go—" (341). But in her poems and letters, it is not snow but, specifically, *frost* that is obsessively equated with death—often as graphically if seldom as dramatically as in the decapitation by the blonde Assassin.

In "I cannot live with you" (640), Dickinson asks how she could stand by and watch her beloved "freeze" without her own "Right of Frost— / Death's privilege." In an earlier poem, she refers to those long dead as "The bosoms where the frost has lain / Ages beneath the mould—" (132). In an 1865 letter, she describes the grave in which Susan's sister had just buried her second child as an "ice nest" (L 444). In an attempt to re-collect the dead, she tries to recall recently deceased friends once pleased by something one said: "You try to touch the smile, / And dip your fingers in the frost—" (509). A poem responding to the death of a fallen soldier begins: "Victory comes late— / And is held low to freezing lips— / Too rapt with frost / To take it—" (690). Searching for metaphors to express "Despair," she initially remarks, "It was not Frost," only to concede that, while it is "most, like Chaos," despair also resembles "Grisly frosts" that on autumn mornings "Repeal the Beating Ground" (510). This repeal of the pulsating life of summer allies human death and despair with floral death-by-frost.

We might end this chilly obituary with the "Darwinian" poem referred to in my Introduction. "There is a flower that Bees prefer" (380) praises the purple clover, a flower both early blooming ("She doth not wait for June") and heroically "sturdy," yet doomed:

The Bravest—of the Host—
Surrendering—the Last—
Not even of Defeat—aware—
When cancelled by the Frost—

Here, as in our main poem, where a happy Flower is beheaded by a canceling Frost, it is, by clear implication, *we* who are "aware" of this sure obliteration. In both cases, especially in "Apparently with no surprise," the inexorable yet sudden, dramatic death by frost with divine approval seems, especially if "design govern in a thing so small," calculated to make our own blood run cold.

Chapter 9

Dickinson's Death-Haunted Earthly Paradise

Emily Dickinson's "awareness" of sure obliteration is reflected in both poems and letters, many of the latter not only accompanied by poems but occasionally themselves poetic. A number of such letters written in the 1850s contextualize the human implications of the death-by-frost of the Flower in "Apparently with no surprise." They also provide examples of Romantic natural supernaturalism. In a letter to Elizabeth Holland, written in August 1856, the human/floral analogy is explicit, with a fortunate exception: "I'm so glad *you* are not a blossom, for those in my garden fade, and then 'a reaper whose name is Death' has come to get a few to help him make a bouquet for himself." The preceding paragraph assumes the analogy and claims this earth would be Paradise enough were it not for frost and that Grim Reaper. Poet Jack Spicer is hardly alone in remarking how often Dickinson's letters are "experiments in a heightened prose combined with poetry."[1] The passage just referred to begins in modified ballad meter: "If roses had not faded, and frosts had never come and one had not fallen here and there whom I could not awaken, there were no need of other Heaven than the one below, and if God had been here this summer, and seen the things that *I* have seen—I guess he would think His Paradise superfluous" (*L* 329).

---

1. *The House That Jack Built,* 234.

The relatively open-minded Christianity of Elizabeth Holland and her husband may have freed Dickinson to confide such thoughts. A few years later, she would put this fusion of nature and heaven, of the physical and spiritual senses, into poetry. What we see, hear, and know is nature: a harmonious heaven whose simplicity is superior to our supposed wisdom:

> "Nature" is what we see—
> The Hill—the Afternoon—
> Squirrel—Eclipse—the Bumble bee—
> Nay—Nature is Heaven—
> Nature is what we hear—
> The Bobolink—the Sea—
> Thunder—the Cricket—
> Nay—Nature is Harmony—
> Nature is what we know—
> Yet have no art to say—
> So impotent Our Wisdom is
> To her Simplicity. (668)

Dickinson's Romantic vision of an Earthly Paradise, its minute particulars as cherished as its sublime manifestations and all the more beautiful because it is under the shadow of death, is reminiscent of Wordsworth, before he froze over, and of Dickinson's beloved Keats, who never froze over. Keats told a religiously conservative friend that his own "favorite Speculation" was that "we shall enjoy ourselves hereafter by having what we called happiness on Earth repeated in a finer tone, and so repeated."[2] In one of the most beautiful passages ever written by Emily Brontë, Catherine Earnshaw's daughter (the second "Cathy" in *Wuthering Heights*) describes *her* "most perfect idea of heaven's happiness." She would be "rocking" at the heart of the natural world, "in a rustling green tree, with a west wind blowing, and bright, white clouds flitting rapidly above; and not only larks, but throstles, and blackbirds, and linnets, and cuckoos pouring out music on every side, . . . grass undulating in waves to the breeze; and woods

---

2. Keats was writing to a pious friend, Benjamin Bailey. *Letters of John Keats*, 1:184–86.

and sounding water, and the whole world awake and wild with joy. . . . I wanted all to sparkle and dance, in a golden jubilee."[3]

Such passages explain Dickinson's reverence of "gigantic Emily Brontë" (L 721), one of whose poems, a favorite of Emily Dickinson's, was appropriately read at her funeral service. Wonderful as it is, Brontë's description of a naturalized "heaven" or "paradise"—a world in motion, *natura naturans*, in which the speaker actively and joyfully engages in her surroundings—is both Keatsian and Wordsworthian. The final gathering (waves, breeze, woods, water, the whole world awake and joyous), especially Cathy's wanting "all to sparkle and dance, in a golden jubilee," unmistakably recalls Wordsworth's (and Dorothy's) "host of golden daffodils, / Beside the lake, beneath the trees, / Fluttering and dancing in the breeze." Those flowers, which outdo "the sparkling waves in glee," comprise "a jocund company" in whose presence a "poet could not but be gay," a joy recalled whenever "They flash upon that inward eye / Which is the bliss of solitude; / And then my heart with pleasure fills, / And dances with the daffodils."[4]

⌒

Had God, like that flower girl Ophelia, "seen the things that I have seen" this summer, Dickinson surmises, he would "think His Paradise superfluous." Emerson claimed that the only thing "certain" about a possible heaven was that it must "tally with what was best in nature, . . . must not be inferior in tone, . . . agreeing with flowers, with tides, and the rising and setting of autumnal stars." "Melodious poets" will be inspired "when once the penetrating key-note of nature and spirit is sounded,—the earth-beat, sea-beat, heart-beat, which makes the tune to which the sun rolls, and the globule of blood, and the sap of trees." Like Keats's "a finer tone," Emerson's "not . . . inferior in

---

3. *Wuthering Heights*, 198–99.

4. The Brontë poem ("Last Lines," also known as "No Coward Soul was Mine") celebrates the "God within my breast" but dismisses as "vain" the "thousand creeds," all "worthless as wither'd weeds, / Or idlest froth." Brontë's God seems doubly Romantic, fusing Coleridge on the poetic imagination (which "dissolves, diffuses, dissipates, in order to recreate") with a Shelleyan fluidity: "With wide-embracing love / Thy spirit animates eternal years, / Pervades and broods above, / Changes, sustains, dissolves, creates, and rears." Wordsworth's most famous flower-poem, "I wandered lonely as a cloud," is almost as much the work of his sister (a journal entry of Dorothy provided the seed) and of his wife. In fact, Mary contributed the poem's most "Wordsworthian" lines: "They flash upon that inward eye / Which is the bliss of solitude."

tone," and his emphasis on keynote, melodiousness, and tune, echoes a text familiar to both Keats and Emerson: Wordsworth's *Excursion* and the Solitary's reference (in book 2) to "Music in a finer tone." Even the later Wordsworth, tamed down and religiously orthodox, never entirely ceased to be a lover "of all that we behold / From this green earth," a poet who found his "Paradise, and groves / Elysian"—pro- vided the human intellect was "wedded to this goodly universe / In love and holy passion"—to be a "simple produce of the common day." Even in revising from a more conservative perspective his account of his early enthusiasm for the French Revolution, he never recanted the desire initially expressed to exercise his skill, "Not in Utopia" or some other ideal place, "Heaven knows where! / But in the very world, which is the world / Of all of us,—the place where, in the end, / We find our happiness, or not at all!"[5]

"Oh Matchless Earth," Emily Dickinson exclaimed in a one- sentence letter, "We underrate the chance to dwell in Thee" (L 478). She was borrowing from the "Prologue" to Wordsworth's *Peter Bell.* Having sailed into the heavens in his little boat in the shape of a cres- cent moon, and described the constellations and planets, the speaker asks rhetorically, "What are they to that tiny grain, / That little Earth of ours?" And so he descends: "Then back to Earth, the dear green Earth . . . See! There she is, the matchless Earth!"[6] Dickinson herself might be "glad" that others believed they were, in the opening excla- mation of her early poem, "Going to Heaven!" But, for herself,

> I'm glad I don't believe it
> For it would stop my breath—
> And I'd like to look a little more
> At such a curious Earth! (79)

5. See *The Excursion* 2:710; "Tintern Abbey," lines 104–5; the "Prospectus" to *The Recluse*, lines 43–55; and *The Prelude* 11:140–44. Emerson is quoted from his Swe- denborg essay in *Representative Men* (*Emerson: Essays and Lectures*, 686–87).

6. *Peter Bell*, lines 49–56. The poem has often been ridiculed—even by Wordsworth's admirers, including Emerson, who despised it, and Shelley, who parodied it. In an interview (reprinted in the *Chicago Tribune*, January 10, 1874), in which Emerson repeated his favorite bon mot about Wordsworth (that in his inspired writing of the Intimations Ode "a way was made through the void by this finer Columbus"), he added, "Wordsworth is *the* great English poet, in spite of Peter Bell." More famously, Shelley mocked the nature lover's sexual timidity in the poem: "He touched the hem of Nature's shift, / Felt faint—and never dared

There is yet another parallel to Emily Dickinson's thought that "Nature is Heaven," or that heaven would be superfluous, if only our earthly paradise were free of frost and death. In a passage familiar to Wordsworth, Keats, Emerson, *and* Dickinson, Milton's archangel Raphael offers a speculative analogy. Explaining to Adam the mysteries of celestial warfare by likening spiritual to corporeal forms, he adds: "Though what if Earth / Be but the shadow of Heaven, and things therein / Each to the other like, more than on earth is thought?" Apparently reversing Raphael's "therein," Dickinson locates love "*Here*in" and concludes this 1852 letter to "Dear Susie" by taking literally the angel's rhetorical but intriguing question: "But *that* was Heaven—*this* is but Earth, Earth so *like* to heaven that I would hesitate should the true one call away."[7]

In a jocoserious, life-affirming poem looking back to Romantic and Emersonian "nature worship" and ahead to the Wallace Stevens of "Sunday Morning," Dickinson rejects religious ritual, a formal "church," and an otherworldly heaven in favor of an earthly paradise, a God immanent rather than transcendent, and salvation as a daily process rather than a static end state:

> Some keep the Sabbath going to Church—
> I keep it, staying at Home—
> With a Bobolink for a Chorister—
> And an Orchard for a Dome—
>
> Some keep the Sabbath in Surplice—
> I just wear my Wings—
> And instead of rolling the Bell, for Church,
> Our little Sexton—sings.

---

uplift / The closest, all-concealing tunic" ("Peter Bell the Third," lines 314–17, in *Shelley's Poetry and Prose,* 335).

7. *L* 195; italics in original. The editors do not catch the Miltonic echo (*Paradise Lost* 5.573–76). Whatever his archangel thought, Milton himself seemed open to the idea of heaven as a projection of earthly happiness. In his fusion of the Classical and the Christian in "Lycidas," he leaves us free to imagine the risen man as either "saint" in heaven or the "genius of the shore," drowned but now, through the power "of him that walked the waves," mounted to a place "Where *other groves* and *other streams* along, / With nectar pure his oozy locks he laves" (172–75; italics added).

God preaches, a noted Clergyman—
And the sermon is never long,
So instead of getting to Heaven, at last—
I'm going, all along. (324)

In an 1863 letter to T. W. Higginson, in which she describes herself as "not reared to prayer," Dickinson pronounces "the 'Supernatural' ... only the Natural, disclosed" (*L* 423–24). In a poem written that year or the year before (Johnson dates it 1862, Franklin 1863), dawn and noon seem symbols of what she *calls* "Heaven." The skepticism implicit in the setting of *Heaven* in quotation marks seems confirmed in the final two stanzas:

The Rapture of a finished Day—
Returning to the West—
All these—remind us of the place
That Men call "Paradise"—

Itself be fairer—we suppose—
But how Ourself, shall be
Adorned, for a Superior Grace—
Not yet, our eyes can see— (575)

In two letters of 1873, Dickinson subverts Paul's text ("For this corruptible must put on incorruption, and this mortal must put on immortality") about the dead being raised and changed as a consequence of Christ's Resurrection (1 Cor. 15:52–53). In the first letter (April 1873), she pronounces the novelist George Eliot (revealed by the *Springfield Republican* in 1859 to be a woman, Marian Evans) a "mortal" who "has already put on immortality," adding that "the mysteries of human nature surpass the 'mysteries of redemption,' for the infinite we only suppose, while we see the finite" (*L* 506). Later that year, in a letter to Elizabeth Holland, she notes that her sister Lavinia, just back from a visit to the Hollands, had said her hosts "dwell in paradise." Emily declares: "I have never believed the latter to be a supernatural site"; instead, "Eden, always eligible," is present in the intimacy of "Meadows" and the noonday "Sun." If, as Blake said, "Everything that lives is holy," it is a this-worldly truth of which believers like her sister and father are cheated: "While the Clergyman tells Father and Vinnie that 'this Corruptible shall put on Incorruption'—it has already done so and they go defrauded" (*L* 508).

Paul, the perpetrator of the "fraud," insists, most dramatically in 1 Corinthians 15, that the resurrection of Jesus heralds the imminent coming of the imperishable Kingdom of God in which pain and suffering will be no more and death will be swallowed up in victory (1 Cor. 15:54–55). For Emily Dickinson, paradise remains an earthly rather than a "supernatural site." In a notably legalistic affirmation of earth, included in an 1877 letter *to* a lawyer, her increasingly skeptical brother Austin, she goes even further:

> The Fact that Earth is Heaven—
> Whether Heaven is Heaven or not
> If not an Affidavit
> Of that specific Spot
> Not only must confirm us
> That it is not for us
> But that it would affront us
> To dwell in such a place— (1408)

Wallace Stevens, who imagines his female persona asking if she shall not "find in comforts of the sun," in any "balm or beauty of the earth / Things to be cherished like the thought of heaven?" insists elsewhere that "poetry / Exceeding music must take the place / Of empty heaven and its hymns"; that we must live in "a physical world," the very air "swarming" with the "metaphysical changes that occur, / Merely in living as and where we live."[8] Stevens seems to be recalling Wordsworth, Emerson, and Nietzsche; he might as well have been thinking of Emily Dickinson and her audacious, even blasphemous preference for the tangible things of this earth, to be cherished above thoughts of an otherworldly heaven, an abstract place offensive to our nature. Dickinson never accepted the Death of God, which is the Nietzschean premise for Zarathustra's imperative that, instead, we must love, and remain faithful to, the earth. Still, when she was only fifteen, Emily confided in her friend Abiah Root that the main reason she was "continually putting off

---

8. Stevens, "Sunday Morning" (19–22); "The Man with the Blue Guitar," section 5; "Esthetique du Mal," section 15. Compare Wordsworth's "Prospectus" to *The Recluse* (42–55) and much of Emerson's *Nature*.

becoming a Christian," despite the "aching void in my heart," was her inability to conceive of an existence beyond this earth as anything but horrible: "Does not Eternity appear dreadful to you? . . . it seems so dark to me that I almost wish there was no Eternity" (L 27, 28). Two years later she told Abby that, while she regretted that she did not seize a past opportunity to "give up and become a Christian," she won't: "it is hard for me to give up the world" (L 67).

The problem, of course, is that this earth, however "matchless," is *not* free of frost and death, so often almost indistinguishable in Dickinson. The invasive force in her Earthly Paradise was less the worm than the frost. The link between the fading and freezing-by-frost of her flowers on the one hand, and the death of those she cannot waken on the other, becomes a dominant motif. Her cherishing of a heavenlike earth is sometimes connected with the pain inflicted from above. In one poem, while noting the "firmest proof" of "Heaven above," she significantly adds, "Except for its marauding Hand / It had been heaven below" (1205). In another letter to Elizabeth Holland and her husband, heaven's "marauding Hand" seems both a grim reaper and a cruel leveler. Writing during autumn 1858, when an epidemic of typhoid fever had struck Amherst, she cries out, not in concluding but in opening the letter: "Good-night! I can't stay any longer in a world of death. Austin is ill of fever. I buried my garden last week—our man, Dick, lost a little girl through scarlet fever. . . . Ah! Democratic Death! Grasping the proudest zinnia from my purple garden,—then deep to his bosom calling the serf's child" (L 341).

This letter has become controversial. The admittedly jarring reference to the "*serf's* child," which happens to be not only "politically" but factually incorrect, has been described as insensitive, shocking, an indication of casual snobbishness at best and class-conscious callousness at worst, compounded by her "equating 'the serf's child' with her frost-killed flowers."[9] We may be reminded of Virginia Woolf's Clarissa Dalloway, who imagines people saying of her, "she cared much more for

9. Habegger, *My Wars Are Laid Away in Books,* 363. With only slightly more justification than critics who have attacked Wordsworth for omitting from "Tintern Abbey" any details about upstream pollution in the River Wye, Domhnall Mitchell is disturbed that Dickinson's letter reveals her insensitivity to "poor standards of health and housing," which she could hardly have known at the time contributed to the ravages of fever. The title of Mitchell's paper—"A Little Taste, Time, and Means"—indicates his emphasis on Dickinson's leisured elitism.

her roses than for" such human but distant "victims of cruelty and injustice" as those who perished in the Armenian genocide. But the best response, it seems to me, is that by Judith Farr. After acknowledging the "insensitivity it projects," she reminds us that "Austin's [serious] illness and the coming of winter are also equated" in the letter. She then makes her central point, one I have been making all along in regard to "Apparently with no surprise," and make again in the Appendix, discussing Derek Mahon's humanizing of a colony of neglected mushrooms in an extraordinarily empathetic poem expressing precisely what Farr calls the "communion and equality of all living forms":

> To begin with, it is simply the case that Emily Dickinson loved flowers quite as much and as if they were human; her implicit comparison was . . . not intended to diminish the "little girl," as she is rather tenderly called. . . . With the cadences of Ecclesiastes and the Elizabethans always vivid in her ear, it was only natural that Dickinson should express the communion and equality of all living forms in death. Indeed, her letter's zinnia and child commingling in Death's grasp calls up such lines as *Cymbeline's* "Golden Lads, and Girles all must, / As Chimney-sweepers come to dust." . . . Not snobbery, but the power of the aesthetic impulse to which she was subject is chiefly manifested in Dickinson's much-discussed letter.[10]

I would add only that Dickinson's equation, not limited to the influence of Ecclesiastes and Shakespeare, also had Romantic auspices. Between Death's "grasp" on a proud flower in her royally purple garden and the death of the little child of a servant there is no more gap than we find in "Threnody," Emerson's elegy for *his* little boy, Waldo. Also a victim of scarlet fever, dead at the age of five, that "hyacinthine boy" and "budding man" was never to blossom, though his father prepares for him, in the conclusion of the elegy, an appropriate heaven: not "adamant . . . stark and cold," but a rather Wordsworthian or Keatsian "nest of bending reeds, / Flowering grass and scented weeds" ("Threnody," lines 15, 26, 272–75).

A less discussed but similar letter to Elizabeth Holland, whose child had suffered a crippling injury, is, as we have seen, mentioned, and dismissed, by Charles Anderson in connection with "Apparently

---

10. Farr, *Gardens of Emily Dickinson*, 126–27. Virginia Woolf, *Mrs. Dalloway*, 88.

with no surprise." Dickinson had commented that "to assault so minute a creature seems to me malign, unworthy of Nature—but the frost is no respecter of persons." In other letters, starting in the 1850s, Dickinson assumes this floral/frost/human analogue, making explicit what is implicit in "Apparently with no surprise": namely, her pervasive connection of flowers and frost with human life and death—and, at times, a vision of transcendence for believers, the hope of spiritual resurrection.

Even when "the frost has been severe," killing off flowers and plants that try in vain "to shield them from the chilly north-east wind," there can be an imperishable garden. I am quoting from a touching letter of October 1851, anticipating the arrival of Austin. She had "tried to delay the frosts," detaining the "fading flowers" until he came. But the flowers, like the poor "bewildered" flies trying to warm themselves in the kitchen, "do not understand that there are no summer mornings remaining to them and to me." But no matter the effect on her flowers and plants of the severe frost brought by the "chilly north-east wind," she can offer her brother "another" garden impervious to frost.

The theme kindles her prose into poetry, minus the line breaks (in fact, this portion of the letter is printed by Johnson as a poem, his number 2). She offers a bright, ever-green garden, "where not a frost has been, in its unfading flowers I hear the bright bee hum; prithee, my Brother, into *my* garden come!" (*L* 149). As Judith Farr remarks, such a garden—which "could never exist, except in metaphor"—is "the garden of herself: her imagination, her love, each of which, she says, will outlast time." As much as any poem in her canon, this early letter-poem, probably written when Dickinson was twenty-one, "discloses the rapt identification she made between herself, her creativity, and her flowers." The passage describing her brighter garden "instinctively focuses on the garden of her mind, with its loving thoughts that transcend the 'frost' of death."[11]

In a remarkably similar letter, written a third of a century later, there is, at least for her beloved brother, an autumnal harbinger of a spiritual as well as a natural spring to come. In this late letter of autumn 1884, the same year she wrote "Apparently with no surprise," she tells a family friend, Maria Whitney:

11. Farr, *Gardens of Emily Dickinson*, 56.

Changelessness is Nature's change. The plants went into camp last night, their tender armor insufficient for the crafty nights.

That is one of the parting acts of the year, and has an emerald pathos—and Austin hangs bouquets of corn in the piazza's ceiling, also an omen, for Austin believes.

The golden bowl breaks soundlessly, but it will not be whole again till another year. (*L* 848)

Anthropomorphizing (as in the 1851 letter, where the flowers try to shield "them[selves]" from the autumn wind), she presents the "tender armor" of her plants as inadequate to protect them against the autumnal frost. So, alert to their needs, she brings them indoors, into the "camp" of her conservatory. She ends by quoting the admonition from Ecclesiastes, that we are to remember God *before* the body disintegrates, before "the silver cord be loosed or the golden bowl be broken" (12:6). But Emily differentiates herself from her brother Austin, a closet skeptic who, for the purposes of this letter, "believes"—has faith, that is, not only in the seasonal rebirth of corn from seeds but also in the spiritual resurrection of the body. His sister confines her hope to a *natural* spring; *her* "golden bowl" will "not be whole again till another year."

Two of her most beautiful, and most Keatsian poems, mark her major seasonal transition, from summer to autumn. In "As imperceptibly as Grief," summer has "lapsed away," a beloved season that can't quite be accused of "Perfidy" since she was always a "Guest, that would be gone." The poem ends with summer having "made her light escape / Into the Beautiful," a Platonic realm beyond us, leaving behind only the cherished memory (1540). In "Further in Summer than the Birds," which has been described as "her finest poem on the theme of the year going down to death and the relation of this to a belief in immortality,"[12] Dickinson employs liturgical language to commemorate, as in Keats's "To Autumn," the insects' dirge for the dying year. "Pathetic from the Grass," that "minor Nation celebrates / Its unobtrusive Mass," the barely noticeable requiem nevertheless "Enlarging Loneliness." The music of the crickets, coming later in summer than the song of the birds, is a "spectral Canticle." Their hymn typifies— in the transition from summer to autumn, with "August burning

12. Anderson, *Emily Dickinson's Poetry*, 169.

low"—the winter sleep to come, a "Repose" perhaps implying eternal rest on another level. In the final stanza, Christian and Hebraic vocabulary yields to pagan. At this moment of seasonal transition, there is, "as yet," no "Furrow on the Glow" of sunlit, burning August, "Yet a Druidic difference / Enhances Nature now" (1068).

That final religious image, whether we take the Druidic reference as stressing primarily the sacrificial or the animistic element in Celtic nature worship, powerfully reinforces Dickinson's *own* reverence for Nature, its beauty enriched and intensified less, perhaps, by what Anderson calls a "belief in immortality" than—again, as in the ode "To Autumn"—by time's evanescence and the pathos of mutability, the deeply moving contrast between seasonal return and human transience. That transience extends to all animal life. This poem, written in late 1865 or early 1866, was enclosed in a laconic January 1866 note to Higginson, with whom she had not corresponded for eighteen months. Referring to her beloved dog and constant companion, Emily Dickinson restricted herself to a single statement, and a wry question, less pleading than ironic, perhaps bitter: "Carlo died. . . . Would you instruct me now?" (*L* 449).

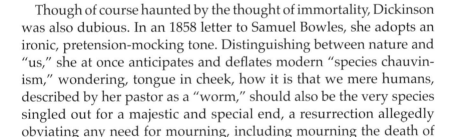

Though of course haunted by the thought of immortality, Dickinson was also dubious. In an 1858 letter to Samuel Bowles, she adopts an ironic, pretension-mocking tone. Distinguishing between nature and "us," she at once anticipates and deflates modern "species chauvinism," wondering, tongue in cheek, how it is that we mere humans, described by her pastor as a "worm," should also be the very species singled out for a majestic and special end, a resurrection allegedly obviating any need for mourning, including mourning the death of what would seem to be paradise enough for us: summer with its cherished fields, its bumblebees and birds:

> Summer stopped since you were here. Nobody noticed her—that is, no men and women. Doubtless, the fields are rent by petite anguish, and "mourners go about" [Eccles. 12:5] the Woods. But this is not for us. Business enough indeed, our stately Resurrection! A special Courtesy, I judge, from what the Clergy say! To the "natural man," Bumblebees would seem an improvement, and a spicing of Birds, but far be it from me, to impugn such majestic tastes! Our pastor says we are a "Worm." How is that reconciled? "Vain, sinful Worm" is possibly of another species. (*L* 338–39)

By this time, the 1730s thunderings of Jonathan Edwards against the moral ills of New England's sinners in the hands of an angry God had lost some of their resonance, even in Calvinist Amherst. But in his debasement of man as a "worm," Dickinson's pastor may (the trope is hardly restricted to Edwards) have been echoing the great Puritan's description of man as "a little, wretched, despicable creature; a worm, a mere nothing, and less than nothing; a vile insect that has risen up in contempt against the majesty of Heaven and earth." Edwards himself—whose "Martial Hand" of "Conscience" threatens "wincing" sinners with hellfire, the "Phosphorus of God" (1598)—was echoing Bildad, the second of Job's false comforters. From the outset, he had advised the innocent sufferer to abase himself. In his final discourse, Bildad wonders if it is even *possible* for man to "be righteous before God." To this fear-instilling God of "dominion," even the moon and stars are unclean; "how much less man, that is a worm? and the son of man, which is a worm!"[13] How *is* that abject status reconcilable with our potential for "stately resurrection"?

Man's biblical genesis itself seemed to put that glorious end in doubt, even before the Fall. Prior to ejecting guilty Adam and Eve from Eden, the "Lord God" tells them, "dust thou art, and unto dust shalt thou return" (Gen 3:19). For Hamlet, man is "the paragon of animals . . . , how like a god," and yet, to him, "what is this quintessence of dust?" (2.2.305–7). Wordsworth, in the opening book of *The Prelude,* "reconciles" the contradiction between "discordant elements." In the 1805 version, the passage had begun, "The mind of man is framed even like the breath / And harmony of music" (1.351–53). The 1850 version reflects the poet's movement from celebrations of the human *mind* to triumphs of the deathless *spirit* over its abject origin: "*Dust* as we are, the *immortal Spirit* grows / Like harmony in music" (1.340–41; italics added).

Emily Dickinson can engage this tension in the grand tradition, observing that "Death is a Dialogue between / The Spirit and the Dust," with Spirit triumphant, "Just laying off for evidence / An Overcoat of Clay" (976). But she takes a different tack in a couplet-poem she opens by ironically addressing God as "Heavenly Father":

---

13. Job 25:2–6. Edwards, *The Justice of God in the Damnation of Sinners* (1734), "Application," pt. I, p. 2.

"Heavenly Father"—take to thee
The supreme iniquity
Fashioned by thy candid Hand
In a moment contraband—
Though to trust us—seem to us
More respectful—"We are Dust"—
We apologize to thee
For thine own Duplicity— (1461)

So much for Bildad-like groveling! Like the image of the *worm*, that of *dust* reflects the Calvinist estimate of human worthlessness. But here the "worm" turns, with the "sinful" creature finding fault with the Creator. Despite his seeming straightforwardness, God committed a dubious act (an inconsistency emphasized by the alliterated *candid* and *contraband*). In fashioning us as he did, he set up, between dust and immortal spirit, not so much a creative tension as a radical contradiction. He thus stands accused of double-dealing, and any "apology" we make to so duplicitous a God will be less an acknowledgment of our own guilt, or a seeking of pardon, than a self-justifying defense—an *apologia* in the form of *j'accuse* directed against a divine adversary. That vindictive God himself supplied the right word. "For I the Lord thy God am a jealous God, visiting the *iniquity* of the fathers upon the children" (Exod. 20:5). Dickinson, who often relishes the role of lawyer for the plaintiff when it comes to amassing evidence against God's providence, has the children of Dust visit the charge of injustice upon an anything-but-paternal Heavenly Father, accusing him—blasphemously, though appropriately, given his supreme power—of "the *supreme* iniquity."

Our apology to God for his "own Duplicity" allies the poem with the most blasphemous of Omar Khayyám's quatrains addressed to God, at least as adapted by Edward Fitzgerald in a translation the Victorian world accepted with a shock of recognition:

Oh Thou, who Man of baser Earth didst make,
And ev'n with Paradise devise the Snake:
      For all the sin wherewith the face of Man
Is blackened—Man's forgiveness give—and take!

The work of such writers as Carlyle, Tennyson, and Arnold and, later, Hardy and Housman, all responding in their different ways to

Darwinian and other scientific and rationalist challenges to religious belief (including biblical Higher Criticism), places an imprimatur on the judgment that Fitzgerald's version of the *Rubáiyát* "reads like the latest and freshest expression of the perplexity and of the doubt of the generation to which we ourselves belong." That acute observation was made, however, not by a British Victorian but by an American—the scholar and man of letters Charles Eliot Norton, writing in 1869, a decade before Dickinson wrote "'Heavenly Father'—take to thee."

Not only the "doubt," but the "perplexity" as well, is reflected in Dickinson's poem, for the syntax of her opening lines suggests petition even more than protest. James McIntosh, identifying "humankind" as "the supreme iniquity," takes these lines to mean: "Father, take humans, who are the supreme iniquity, to thee." Perhaps; but what, then, of the poem's ironic final lines in which, as Jane Donahue Eberwein has said, a duplicitous "God rather than man is to blame for the natural finitude that prevents man from satisfying his creator"?[14] My own reading is closer to Eberwein's than to McIntosh's, and closer still to that of Magdalena Zapedowska, who believes that, in this poem, Dickinson focuses not on the Fall as original sin,

> but on the subsequent expulsion from Paradise, which she blasphemously construes as the original wrong done to humankind by a God who first offered people happiness, then distrustfully put them to the test, and finally doomed them to suffering. Undermining the dogma of God's benevolence, Dickinson contemplates the terrifying possibility that the metaphysical order is different from Calvinist teaching and that the human individual is left wholly to him/herself, unable to rely on the hostile Deity against the chaos of the universe.[15]

∿

For all our immortal longings, we are haunted, and angered, by the death implicit in our originating dust—in the case of Emily Dickinson,

14. McIntosh, *Nimble Believing*, 47; and in correspondence, January 16, 2008; Eberwein, *Dickinson: Strategies of Limitation*, 82.

15. Zapedowska, "Wrestling with Silence," 385. Dickinson's poem would have found favor with another major American writer. In a late notebook (June–July 1896), Mark Twain proposed a deity to "take the place of the present one." Twain's "improved" God "would recognize in himself the Author & Inventor of Sin, & Author & Inventor of the vehicle for its commission; & would place the whole responsibility where it would of right belong: upon Himself, the only Sinner" (quoted in Ray B. Browne, *Mark Twain's Quarrel with God*, 13).

what Byron called "fiery dust." And if the "Heavenly Father" who presides over this beautiful but doomed world really *is* "an Approving God," Dickinson seems to care less for him and for a posthumous, perhaps empty heaven than for this earthly paradise—the perishable beauty that must die, everything she wishes *could* "transcend the 'frost' of death." When she *does* project an earthly eternity, it is, characteristically, in the form of a blossoming season. "No fear of frost to come" would "Haunt the perennial bloom— / But certain June!" (195).

Chapter 10

Flowers, and Thoughts Too Deep for Tears

As her Scripture-riddled poems and letters illustrate, Emily Dickinson is a poet whose dialogues between Spirit and Dust, between belief and disbelief, straddled heaven and earth. She drew repeatedly on the analogy between the natural and the human, on the connection between the familiar and the sublime, the "ordinary" and the "amazing" (448). Flowers, as the poem just cited demonstrates, are often at the heart of it, which helps explain how, as a gardener who happens also to be a great poet, she could distill so much of the pathos of mutability from, say, our poem's short-lived "happy Flower." In fact, her garden-knowledge was sometimes fused with her discipline as an artist. Not only did she seldom utter "a discouraging word about flowers"; her "Flowers helped to create Dickinson's literary imagination, for she thought of them as poems, and vice versa."[1]

The very word *fascicle*, first applied by Mabel Loomis Todd to Dickinson's hand-sewn packets of poems, is a botanical term referring to clustered leaves or flowers, a term Dickinson would have been familiar with from her early study of botany. Her detailed botanical knowl-

---

1. Richard Brantley, *Experience and Faith: The Late-Romantic Imagination of Emily Dickinson*, 90, 91. The "unjustly neglected" poem he focuses on, "There is a flower that Bees prefer" (380), has since (as noted in my Introduction) received a Darwinian reading from James Guthrie, who adds that she uses this poem to "justify her practice of competing with other women authors while simultaneously shunning the publicity she feared fame would entail" ("Darwinian Dickinson," 91).

edge was precisely recorded in her herbarium: a still extant collection (a facsimile edition was published in 2007) of pressed and meticulously labeled stems, flowers, and leaves demonstrating that her love of flowers was matched by her scientific acumen. As Dickinson "matured," Wendy Martin has noted, "the boundaries between plants and pages blurred more and more; she wrote poems about flowers, wrapped flowers in poems, and carefully observed and nurtured words and plants alike." In one poem (675), she identifies poetry with the quintessence of flowers. "Essential Oils—are wrung— / The Attar from the Rose," a fragrant perfume expressed not through the inspiring power of "Suns—alone" but through intense effort, the excruciating "gift of Screws." A year before she wrote this poem, Higginson had remarked in a letter to her: "Literature is attar of roses, one distilled drop from a million blossoms." Lundin, who cites the letter, thinks Dickinson's poem "equated the poet's anguish with the suffering of Christ."[2]

In "This was a Poet," Dickinson, again employing the image of the quintessence obtained from the petals of a flower, reveals herself as a "Discloser" (in the Wordsworthian tradition) of the poetry to be found in the ordinary and familiar, the hitherto overlooked. Such a poet "distills," not amazing Grace, but

> amazing sense
> From ordinary Meanings—
> And Attar so immense
>
> From the familiar species
> That perished by the Door—
> We wonder it was not Ourselves
> Arrested it—before— (448)

This is what Emerson meant in *Nature* by the imaginative "transfiguration all material objects undergo through the passion of the poet."[3] And, as Emerson would have been the first to point out, this attarlike "amazing sense"—imagination drawn from but transforming the ordinary and familiar—*had* been "arrested . . . before" Dickinson distilled

2. Martin, *Cambridge Introduction to Emily Dickinson*, 6–7; Lundin, *Emily Dickinson and the Art of Belief*, 112.
3. *Emerson: Essays and Lectures*, ed. Porte, 34.

it. Noting, in 1866, the seasonal change from February to March, she tells Elizabeth Holland: "Here is the 'light' the Stranger said 'was not on sea or land.' Myself could arrest it, but we'll not chagrin him" (*L* 449). Why she calls him the Stranger I don't know, but here Dickinson is alluding to Wordsworth's description of the creative imagination as "the gleam, / The light that never was, on sea or land" ("Elegiac Stanzas," lines 13–14). Seven years later she would summon up the phrase again, this time quoting the famous second line accurately (*L* 510). But in 1866, she not only alluded to Wordsworth on the imagination as "light" but also claimed equal power, even a paradoxically belated precedence. In the poem, she may "wonder it was not Ourselves / Arrested it—before"; in the letter, she claims she ("Ourselves") "*could* arrest it, but we'll not chagrin" Wordsworth, embarrassing him by playing one-upsmanship with him. It is another reminder that, though Dickinson "is recognizably a post-Wordsworthian poet," the "American difference is as strong in her as it is in Whitman or Melville."[4]

While she never cites him as a precursor, it is Wordsworth more than any other poet who in his approach to nature complements Emily Dickinson's own love of actual flowers. As Judith Farr observes, "Like Wordsworth, she chooses spring flowers, often woodland flowers, the first growth of hillsides and meadows to praise." Quoting Dickinson's early poem, "I robbed the Woods" (41), Farr accurately identifies it as "a distinctly Wordsworthian poem," with "echoes" of the poet's "guilt" in "stealing the little boat" in the famous episode in the opening book of *The Prelude*. Perhaps; though I would propose Wordsworth's poem "Nutting," originally intended to appear in that opening book but published separately and never incorporated in the seasonal episodes of the epic. (In the Dickinson poem, the speaker "robbed" trees described as "trusting" and "unsuspecting." She wonders what hemlock and oak might "say" once she "grasped" and "bore away" what she chose to steal. In "Nutting," the Wordsworthian speaker, "forcing" his way into a virginal nook in the woods, suddenly ravages and mutilates the calm bower. At first exultant, he is finally

---

4. Bloom, *Genius,* 345. We "still," he adds (349), "have not worked out her complex relation to Wordsworth, Shelley, and Keats." By an odd coincidence, the unusual word Dickinson uses as a verb, *chagrin,* was once employed by Emerson as a noun to express the inner disturbance he sometimes felt in reading a man he also acknowledged to be the major poet of the age: "I never," he exaggerated, "read Wordsworth without chagrin" (*Journals and Miscellaneous Notebooks,* 4:63).

remorseful. Despite the violation, in both poems there is a final union with nature: "For," to quote the last line of "Nutting," "there is a spirit in the woods.")

Farr also associates Dickinson's flower poems with William Cullen Bryant's "To the Fringed Gentian," Emerson's "Rhodora," and Tennyson's much anthologized "Flower in the crannied wall." But her central point is the comparison with Wordsworth. It is in "her approach to wildflowers and to their personal and transcendental significance that Dickinson exhibits a vision of nature related to but distinct from Wordsworth's. Like his, her fondness for small flowers like the primrose, daisy, and violet is aroused by their smallness and ubiquity. . . . Small flowers attracted Wordsworth's affection and interest throughout his writing life."[5]

By focusing on familiar, ordinary things—notably, flowers—in a revolutionary way, as an emotionally and intellectually evocative subject of poetry, Wordsworth initiated a revolution that illuminates the human dimension of that doomed Flower in "Apparently with no surprise." The crucial text, unmentioned by Farr, may be Wordsworth's Intimations Ode, the poem that more than any other haunted literary New England. Though she never cites the ode directly, Dickinson occasionally echoes it—as in the famous letter of consolation sent to Susan following the death of her son Gilbert (discussed below) and in the poem beginning "A loss of something ever felt I." Among his "intimations of immortality from recollections of early childhood," Wordsworth refers to a numinous sense of "something that is gone" and of the loss of "that imperial palace whence we came." Dickinson's loss of "something" was "The first that I could recollect / Bereft I was—of what I knew not." Though she was too "young" for any to "suspect / A Mourner walked among the children," she describes herself as an outcast Prince; and even now, "Elder" and "wiser," she still finds herself "bemoaning" a lost "Dominion," still "softly searching / For my delinquent Palaces—" (959). She here "appropriates the *Intimations* ode like a typical reader-poet of her American Romantic age, drawing in her own way on the age's belief in the poetic child's closeness to Eden and eternity."[6]

---

5. Farr, *Gardens of Emily Dickinson*, 110–11.
6. McIntosh, *Nimble Believing*, 55.

The appeal of Wordsworth's ode to Dickinson would have been enhanced by its focus on flowers. The "pansy at my feet" in the fourth stanza speaks to the poet of "something that is gone." That "something," according to the penultimate stanza, has vanished irretrievably, leaving behind what Nietzsche beautifully called, in a December 1885 letter, *Rosengeruch des Unwiederbringlichen,* the faint rose-breath of what can never be brought back. Wordsworth evokes "the radiance which was once so bright," but is "now for ever taken from my sight." Though "nothing can bring back the hour / Of splendour in the grass, of glory in the flower," he asserts, "We will grieve not, rather find / Strength in what remains behind": a compensation for loss based on a bond of "primal sympathy" that can never be obliterated and on "the faith that looks through death, / In years that bring the philosophic mind."

But of course this mature stoicism and rather chilly compensation for loss cannot extinguish the poignancy, power, and beauty of the great lines immediately preceding. The ode's most authentic and haunting music—here, in the lines memorializing the lost "splendor in the grass, the glory in the flower," and in the final stanza, which fuses emotion with cognition—is less philosophic or religious than elegiac. The ode, as much about mortality as immortality, draws to a close with funereal "Clouds that gather round the setting sun," clouds that "take their sober colouring / From an eye that hath kept watch o'er man's mortality." And it concludes (lines 200–203) with a thoughtful *and* "emotional reaction" to a humble rather than a glorious flower:

> Thanks to the human heart by which we live,
> Thanks to its tenderness, its joys, and fears,
> To me the meanest *flower* that blows can give
> *Thoughts* that do often lie *too deep for tears.*

What could be more quintessentially Wordsworthian? Or, given her intense love of flowers, more Dickinsonian? Celebrating Wordsworth as "the most original poet now living," Hazlitt wrote in *The Spirit of the Age:* "No one has shown the same imagination in raising trifles into importance." A youthful (just twenty-three at the time) and *un*-self-reliant Emerson, writing to his remarkable Aunt Mary, wondered rhetorically if it were not "more conformable" to some "golden middle line" to "let what Heaven made small and casual remain the objects of a notice small and casual, and husband our admiration for images of grandeur in matter or in mind?" He was in accord with—perhaps echoing—an anonymous British critic who had complained a decade earlier that all "communion of feeling" between the writer and sophisticated readers of poetry was "necessarily broken off" when "we are called upon to feel *emotions which lie too deep for tears with respect to the meanest flower that blows,* to *cry for nothing . . .* over every ordinary object and every commonplace occurrence."[7]

Of course, the ode, a sublime rather than a maudlin poem, does *not* end with the poet crying but with him experiencing *"Thoughts* that do often lie *too deep for tears."* Writing in that same year, Mary Moody Emerson, who possessed for more than a decade a much deeper appreciation of Wordsworth than did her nephew, repeated and endorsed these lines: "At times a humble flower creates thoughts too deep for tears to use the high language of W," "W" being "the sublime Wordsworth." In time, with the indispensable help of Coleridge, Emerson would come to agree with his aunt, to value in Wordsworth precisely what he had at first denigrated. By the time he wrote *Nature* ten years later, he had learned, as he says in the final chapter, that redemption requires a fusion of "mind" and "affection," and that the "invariable mark of wisdom is to see the miraculous in the common." As in the case of Dickinson's cherished Charles Wadsworth, who between 1857 and 1865 moved from rebuke to approval of the Intimations Ode, the distance Emerson had traveled from conformity to appreciation is one gauge of the triumph of the Wordsworthian Romantic revolution in poetry, marked by the rooting of our most profound experiences in simple, humble things. It was "the peculiar genius of this poet," said Pater in a passage earlier cited, "to open out the soul of apparently little or familiar things."[8]

He might have been speaking of Emily Dickinson as well, a point worth repeating since some astute readers, Wendy Martin among them, see Emily Dickinson's cherishing of the small and apparently

7. Hazlitt, *Complete Works of William Hazlitt,* 11:88. *The Letters of Ralph Waldo Emerson,* 7:148–49. For the comments of the critic (William Gifford?), see anonymous, "Wordsworth's White Doe" (italics in original).

8. Pater, "Wordsworth," 48. Emerson, *Nature* (*Emerson: Essays and Lectures,* ed. Porte, 47). For Mary's comments, see Phyllis Cole, *Mary Moody Emerson and the Origins of Transcendentalism: A Family History,* 151–52. For Wadsworth's change of opinion on the ode, documented in sermons delivered in 1857 and 1865, see Habegger, *My Wars Are Laid Away in Books,* 332–33, 704n.

insignificant as distinctly *un*-Romantic and un-Transcendental. Dedicated to "living a life experienced to its fullest," Dickinson, Martin contends,

> celebrated the marvelous beauties of nature. But unlike the Romantics who cherished nature in its sublime magnitude, its overwhelming grandeur, Dickinson's appreciation for nature includes an appreciation for its details, its minute and often overlooked inhabitants, and its tiny pleasures. Of course, Dickinson also felt nature's sublimity, and recorded it in her poetry, but more often she felt reverence for its subtle processes and intricate details. Thus, much of Dickinson's interest in nature is centered in the small spaces of her garden where she tended her treasured flowers. . . . She saw nature as an end in itself and not merely as a vehicle to philosophic truths. Of course, her observations of nature led her to contemplate the rhythms and meanings of life and to find correspondences between life in her garden and human society, but unlike many Transcendentalists who saw God in and through nature, Dickinson saw nature as godlike, as worthy in itself of worship, attention, devotion.[9]

While there is, of course, considerable truth in these observations, Mary Moody Emerson, Pater, and others have rightly stressed the reciprocity between the sublime and the minute inherent in Wordsworth's peculiar capacity to "open out the soul of *apparently little or familiar things.*" These words were in print before Dickinson wrote "Apparently with no surprise." Whether or not she read them, this is what she did in making us experience, in the destruction of that "happy Flower," precisely the "emotional reaction" judged excessive by Anderson. The humbler, but immensely more significant, flower blowing at the conclusion of Wordsworth's ode evokes elegiac thoughts too deep to be released in tears but expressing the Virgilian "tears that are *in things*" (*Aeneid* 1:462), the pathos of mutability. In its way, Dickinson's beheaded Flower is also one of that "familiar species / That perished by the Door" in "This was a Poet."

We will feel our reaction to the destruction of a mere flower excessively emotional only if we forget that we are *intended* to see in that flower's fate something true throughout nature, including *human*

9. *Cambridge Introduction to Emily Dickinson,* 86.

life—its joys and suffering, either the whole trajectory of life and inevitable death, or, worse, early death, being "cut down" in one's prime. Obviously, for Dickinson as for Wordsworth, it was more than wildflowers, gentians, and zinnias that *perished* by the Door." The flowers she cherished in life were intimately associated by Dickinson with death. In an 1850 letter to Abiah Root, she imagined her own death, anticipating an "early grave; . . . I shall love to call the bird there if it has gentle music, and the meekest-eyed wild flowers" (L 103). When, thirty-six years later, she *did* die it was, appropriately, Susan who prepared her body for burial, choosing both familiar and exotic flowers. She "arranged violets and a pink cypripedium [an orchid, like the flower on the jacket of this book, a "lady's-slipper"] at Emily's throat and covered her white casket with violets and ground pine." And in her obituary ("Miss Emily Dickinson of Amherst"), printed in the *Springfield Republican,* Susan spoke of her friend's "gentle tillage of the rare flowers filling her conservatory, into which, as into the heavenly Paradise, entered nothing that could defile, and which was ever abloom in frost or sunshine, so well she knew her subtle chemistries."

Susan, who knew Emily Dickinson as well or better than anyone, pays tribute to the gardener who loved the flowers she cultivated and preserved from autumn frost in the "camp" of her conservatory. Though her obituary was insightful enough to have served as an introduction to the 1890 edition of Dickinson's poems (Higginson's suggestion was overruled by Mabel Loomis Todd, Austin's mistress), Susan was at times less understanding of the work of the poet who often juxtaposed, while seldom reconciling, flowers and a frost repeatedly associated with that ultimate defilement, death. The blonde Assassin of our poem strikes down its innocent victim "in accidental power"; it may be no "accident" that "Apparently with no surprise" was written at the end of a decade marked by a series of devastating deaths, including those of both her parents, her nephew, and four beloved friends: Samuel Bowles in 1878, J. G. Holland in 1881, Charles Wadsworth in 1882 (the year her mother died), and, in 1884, Otis Phillips Lord, the only man Emily Dickinson may ever have been tempted to marry. The correspondence with Judge Lord became passionate following the death of his wife in 1877 (see L 614–18); after Lord's death, Dickinson wrote to Elizabeth Holland: "Forgive the tears that fell for few, but that few too many, for was not each a World?" (L 816). To call it a "late-blooming" love seems more than metaphorical;

in an 1878 letter in which Dickinson says she will "withhold and not confer" her sexual favor, she employs garden imagery: "for your great sake—not mine—I will not let you cross [the "Stile"], but it is all your's, and when it is right I will lift the Bars, and lay you in the Moss" (*L* 617).

Of all those who meant most to her, only Austin, Vinnie, and Susan were spared. Reporting on her shattered "nerves," she asked rhetorically, "who but Death had wronged them?" "The Dyings have been too deep for me," she confided to an acquaintance, "and before I could raise my Heart from one, another has come" (*L* 843). The letter was written in the fall of 1884, the year she also wrote "Apparently with no surprise."

⟡

Most *potentially* relevant to the untimely cutting down of a "happy Flower," there was, in the preceding autumn, the sudden death by typhoid of her seven-year-old nephew, the charming and gifted Gilbert, Emily's favorite of Austin's and Susan's three children.[10] The sun may proceed "unmoved," but in the case of human beings, even for poets too strong to succumb to merely sentimental analogizing, there are limits to emotional detachment. Nature's frost may be "no respecter of persons," like the poem's indifferent Assassin, whose power is "accidental" rather than deliberately cruel. But the power "to assault" the vulnerable, children in particular, is a different matter and would "seem" to come under the auspices of the Omnipotent: an "Approving God" for whom nothing is accidental and whose approval of such assaults may be interpreted, depending on perspective, as either benign or—as it *seemed* to Emily Dickinson in the letter earlier cited, in which she discreetly transferred the responsibility from God to nature—"malign."

As early as 1859, Dickinson had expressed empathy for doomed children. Innocents "too fragile for winter winds," they are brought to an early and "thoughtful grave," a personified grave depicted as "tenderly tucking them in from frost." But if the grave is tender, God is indifferent to the little ones: "Sparrows unnoticed by the Father— / Lambs for whom time had not a fold" (141). This neglect by a mascu-

---

10. Her niece, Martha Dickinson Bianchi, reports that Emily was impressed by an evening prayer in which Gilbert balanced dependence with the sort of self-sufficiency she admired: "O Lord, you take care of me some tonight, and I'll take care of myself some." Quoted by Zapedowska, "Wrestling with Silence," 391.

line God is in sharp contrast to the maternal care stressed in a related poem, written following the death of her Aunt Lavinia in April 1860. Emily depicts the dead mother looking down "just as tenderly" as when she wove a "little mortal nest" for "her birds," little Louisa and Frances Norcross: "If either of her 'sparrows fall,' / She 'notices' above" (164). In both poems, of course, Dickinson is recalling and altering the comforting words of Jesus. According to Matthew (10:29; compare Luke 12:6) not a single sparrow shall fall without being noticed by "your Father," a text affirmed by Hamlet, for whom "there's a special providence in the fall of a sparrow" (5.2.232). But Dickinson's negligent Father-God simply doesn't notice the children who fall like sparrows, lambs for whom he failed to provide a fold.

If that is the harsh truth in the world of "time," it may not be so in eternity. The untimely death of little Gilbert, if it is relevant to our poem, would tend to support a more benign interpretation of both process and God, rather than, as we might anticipate, the more "malign." For that death—though it affected many neighbors in Amherst, grieved and horrified the family, and felled Emily with "Nervous prostration" (*L* 802)— seems *not* to have embittered or outraged her. The sudden illness and death of Gib, who had reunited Emily and Sue during his short life, also brought the recluse to Sue's house for the first time in two decades. When the bereaved mother went into seclusion, Dickinson sent her the inevitable token of their love and shared grief: "Perhaps the dear, grieved Heart would open to a flower, which blesses unrequested, and serves without a Sound" (*L* 800). But for Dickinson herself, the death seems to have become, instead of yet another occasion to wrestle with God, a parable of "Love and Death" and an anticipation—though, as always, hedged by her sense of ultimate mystery—of a state beyond. Gilbert himself helped. In his final delirium before he died on the afternoon of October 5, 1883, the little boy cried out, "Open the door, open the door, they are waiting for me." What Dickinson called his "sweet command" is recorded in a letter to Elizabeth Holland and in one of the elegies she wrote for the boy.

"*Who* were waiting for him," she wondered, adding that "all we possess we would give to know—Anguish at last opened it, and he ran to the little Grave at his grandparent's feet—All this and more, though *is* there more? More than Love and Death? Then tell me its name!" (*L* 803) "Man is in love, and loves what vanishes, / What more is there to say?" asks Yeats, evoking the Wordsworthian or Nietzschean "irretrievable."

Yeats poses that haunting rhetorical question in one of his greatest poems, "Nineteen Hundred and Nineteen." But in Dickinson, the something "more" and the "name" are supplied in a far more modest poem, a little elegy inspired by the dying boy's petition to "Open the Door":

> The Heart has many Doors—
> I can but knock—
> For any sweet "Come in"
> Impelled to hark—
> Not saddened by repulse,
> Repast to me
> That somewhere there exists,
> Supremacy— (1567)

Despite the knocking at the many-doored Heart, access is denied. This familiar motif in Dickinson is repeatedly associated with the gospel text "ask and it shall be given you; seek, and ye shall find; knock, and it will be opened unto you" (Matt. 7:7).[11] We have encountered this allusion to Matthew in "I meant to have but modest needs" (476) and will discuss it again in connection with a God who cruelly hides himself even from those who most long to know him. In Emily Dickinson's elegy for little Gilbert, an initially repulsed knocking is assuaged by the prospect of a potentially *answered* prayer. The vagueness of "somewhere there exists / Supremacy" (reminiscent of the hidden God who "exists / Somewhere—in Silence" [338]) is made less abstract by the homely, perhaps Eucharistic, "Repast," which apparently satisfies her spiritual hunger. What would *seem* the most painful example of "the Dyings" she lamented in the letter may have provided instead a possible portal to eternity. The boy's sweet command to open the door illustrates one recurrent image in our attempt to make rondural sense of human suffering and mortality. "I am the door," said Jesus (John 10:7–9). In "the hour of death, the visionaries find life and birth. Looked at deeply and unflinchingly enough, death appears as a door, not a hole, and the other side of this darkest door is the purest

---

11. In an 1862 poem probably written with Sue in mind, "Jesus—raps" at the door, seeking access to "the lady's soul." When Jesus retires, chill or weary, there will be "ample time for—me—Patient upon the steps—until then— / Heart! I am knocking—low at thee" (317).

light. . . . Death becomes our birth-canal, our passageway."[12] In the dialectic between faith and doubt, hope and despair, Dickinson stays—to use her own word—"nimble." Even here, she confirms of the door between life and death, "Anguish at last opened it." Usually, it is precisely that *anguish* that she will emphasize. In this elegy for her nephew, she seems to adopt a different, "visionary" perspective.

That visionary perspective is even clearer in another document focused on Gilbert, a letter written to Sue shortly after her son's death. The letter is considered by many the most remarkable Emily Dickinson ever wrote, a work of art in which every rift is loaded with ore. It begins with an emphatic declaration, "The Vision of Immortal Life has been fulfilled," and informs us that "Gilbert rejoiced in Secrets" and "His Life was panting with them."

> With what menace of Light he cried "Don't tell[,] Aunt Emily"! Now my ascended Playmate must instruct *me.* Show us, prattling Preceptor, but the way to thee!
>
> He knew no niggard moment—His Life was full of Boon—The Playthings of the Dervish were not so wild as his—
>
> No crescent was this Creature—He traveled from the Full—
>
> Such soar, but never set—
>
> I see him in the Star, and meet his sweet velocity in everything that flies—His Life was like the Bugle, which winds itself away, his Elegy an echo—his Requiem ecstasy—
>
> Dawn and Meridian in one.
>
> Wherefore would he wait, wronged only of Night, which he left for us—
>
> Without a speculation, our little Ajax spans the whole—
>
> Pass to thy Rendezvous of Light,
> Pangless except for us—
> Who slowly ford the Mystery
> Which thou hast leaped across! (*L* 799)

---

12. Peter Kreeft, *Making Sense Out of Suffering,* 103. A variation, almost fusing door and hole, occurs at the climax of "The Death of Ivan Ilych," where Tolstoy uses the image of a black sack the suffering Ivan finally breaks through into the light.

The letter, prose poetry from the outset, culminates in a quatrain—
later printed as a poem (1564)—confirming the apotheosis of the boy,
a wunderkind all velocity and light. Patricia Thompson Rizzo, in "The
Elegiac Modes of Emily Dickinson," has unpacked the Shakespearean
allusions in this moving and image-laden letter. But given the opening
reference to the "Vision of Immortal Life" and the dominant imagery
of "light," Wordsworth seems present as well, especially the "Ode:
Intimations of Immortality from Recollections of Early Childhood,"
the poem McIntosh suggests helped Dickinson draw "in her own way
on the age's belief in the poetic child's closeness to Eden and eternity."

As noted earlier in this chapter, she had echoed the ode's "imperial
palace whence we came" in lamenting (in "A loss of something ever
felt I") her lost "Dominion." At once determined and puzzled, "bereft
... of what I knew not," she still searches "For my delinquent Palaces"
(959). In an 1873 letter, she seems to recall the ode's palatial imagery as
well as Wordsworth's uncertainty in the ode about the precise nature
of "those shadowy recollections, / Which, *be they what they may,* / Are
yet *the fountain-light of all our Day*" (lines 149–51; italics added). And
she fuses a line earlier quoted from Wordsworth's "Elegiac Stanzas" (*L*
449) with yet another of her many allusions to the knocking-passage
in Matthew 7. Writing to the orphaned Norcross cousins she loved so
dearly, Emily wished that Louisa and Frances were with her, "not precisely here, but in *those sweet mansions* the mind likes to suppose. Do
they exist or nay? We *believe they may,* but *do* they, *how know we*? 'The
light that never was on sea or land' might as soon be had for the knocking" (*L* 510; italics added).

Is she also drawing on the Intimations Ode in her letter of condolence to Susan? Dickinson transforms little Gilbert, appareled in celestial light even on earth, into a luminous phenomenon, an "ascended
Playmate" and "prattling Preceptor" who, as "our little Ajax," nevertheless "spans the whole"—just as Wordsworth had transformed the
little "Child" of the ode, "whose exterior semblance doth belie / Thy
Soul's immensity," into a "Mighty Prophet! Seer blest!" or as Emerson,
remembering his favorite line of the ode, "the fountain-light of all our
Day," had equated *his* dead child with the Christ Child, "Israel's
paragon," transfigured by "the great all-loving Day / [that] Through
smallest chambers takes its way" ("Threnody," lines 217–23). But even
as she imagined Gilbert having entered the radiance of eternity, his
"Rendezvous of Light," Dickinson, like Emerson (whose last words

on earth were "O, that beautiful boy!"), cherished until her own death the lost child as a living presence: "The little boy we laid away never fluctuates, and his dim society is companion still" (*L* 827).

The death of little Gilbert was an emotional loss from which a grief-stricken Emily Dickinson never fully recovered.[13] But, while we have to allow for the fact that Emily is acting as a consoler, ministering to Susan's grieving and to her own, this famous letter suggests that the boy's death was not without spiritual recompense. A few months before that death she had asked a friend: "Are you certain there is another life? When overwhelmed to know, I fear that few are sure" (*L* 779). Even in response to Gilbert's final cry about those "waiting for me" beyond the "door," she wondered "*who* was waiting for him. . . . All we possess we would give to know" (*L* 803). For once, though, there appeared to be light in the darkness, and a possible answer to the problem of suffering. The "Mystery" of death remains a riddle; but in the case of little Gilbert the much-knocked-upon door seemed finally to open. In its visionary ecstasy, this letter-poem, even taking its immediate function to console into consideration, seems antithetical to the bleak, coldly understated vision of "Apparently with no surprise."[14]

13. Several biographers date Dickinson's own final decline as beginning with her response to the death of this much loved child. See, for example, Habegger, *My Wars Are Laid Away in Books*, 621, and Farr, *The Passion of Emily Dickinson*, 4.

14. A more recent letter of consolation comes to mind. In *Letter to a Man in the Fire* (1999), the southern novelist and poet Reynolds Price also employed the "door" as a religious image. In the course of an expanded, public response to a letter from Jim Fox, a young man dying of cancer (Fox died some months prior to the publication of the book dedicated to him), Price, himself a cancer survivor, explored the apparent absence of God in the face of human suffering *and* its converse: occasional healing in answer to prayer. Apologizing that he can do no more, he advises the young man to "go on waiting as long as you can at the one main door, requesting entry from whatever power may lie beyond it" (34). Price's own faith in that power, he tells us, was grounded on childhood "openings" and "intuitions." In his youth, he experienced certain rare, mysterious, luminous "moments," which seemed to him intimations of the soul's immortality and manifestations of a benign divinity. He adds: "Wordsworth's accounts, in *The Prelude* and other poems, of similar findings in his youth are the classic description, as I learned years after my own began" (27–28). Prominent among those "other poems" would be the Intimations Ode, *the* "classic description" of Wordsworth's epiphanic "findings in his youth."

Chapter 11

Questioning Divine Benevolence

We must return, from these intimations of immortality, to the question of perspective and the tension between visionary faith and skepticism, focusing again on the God depicted in "Apparently with no surprise" and the range of responses that God elicits. Our responses as individual readers must be based on what we make of the content and, above all, the *tone* of the *particular* poem before us. But, as we have seen, it is hard to resist the temptation to place this text in the larger *con*text of Dickinson's poetry and religious questioning. Compelled to ask our own questions, let them at least be the right ones: *hers.* Is this "Approving God" benign? calm? indifferent?—a more-than-Aristotelian Unmoved Mover whose "Perturbless Plan / Proceed[s]—inserting Here—a Sun— / There—leaving out a Man—" (724)? God's "approving" stance alone may seem to confirm his ultimate, if distanced, benevolence. But does the approval of a destructive process ally the God of this poem with Dickinson's adamantine "God of Flint" (1076), or her tyrannical "Mastiff" (1317), or the torturing "Inquisitor" (536), or the bully who wronged Moses by subjecting him to "tantalizing Play" (597)? Does *this* poem's tone reveal an underlying voice that seems *primarily* resigned, philosophically and religiously accepting? Or dismayed, indignant, even outraged? Three of Dickinson's many poems engaging God come to mind, all containing violent verbs ("scalps," "gored," "amputated") recalling this poem's "beheads."

In one poem, reminiscent of John Donne's sonnet "Batter my heart, three-personed God," God first "fumbles at your Soul," then "stuns you by degrees," as he "Prepares your brittle Nature / For the ethereal blow," a blow that comes in the celestially savage form of "One— imperial—Thunderbolt— / That scalps your naked Soul" (315). I included "outrage" as one possible description of the speaker's attitude in our poem. In the only other lyric in which a "happy" victim is cut down by an "Assassin," Dickinson is *overtly* "outraged." Alluding to those celebrants of the full-throated nightingale, Milton and Keats, she describes a *dead* songbird, the "joy that in his happy Throat / Was waiting to be poured / Gored through and through with Death." She laments the waste, and mutability itself, but in this 1866 poem directs her fury less against the presumptive assassin, one of Lavinia's troublesome cats, than against the God who approves the wounding and killing of even the most beautiful of his own creatures. The gunfire the rebel angels direct against the Heavenly Host led by Michael, in Milton's account of celestial warfare in *Paradise Lost*, is no more militarily effective than it is poetically persuasive, since the angels are immortal spirits and thus invulnerable. But angels are also winged and so provide an analogy for winged creatures who actually *do* suffer death: a violent ("gored") death permitted, even initiated, by a God deaf to their music. "To be," Dickinson concludes the poem,

> Assassin of a Bird
> Resembles to my outraged mind
> The firing in Heaven,
> On Angels—squandering for *you*
> Their Miracles of Tune— (1102; italics added)

Dickinson was living and writing in an age torn by the tension between Romanticism and Realism, faith and science, belief and skepticism: the Age of Darwin and of Nietzsche. In a poem reminiscent of Matthew Arnold's "Dover Beach" and contemporaneous with Nietzsche's pronouncement of the Death of God, Dickinson graphically dramatizes the ebbing of faith, what she calls in this 1882 poem the modern, increasingly secular, and scientific world's "abdication of Belief." Employing another severing image, she presents the God who scalps and wounds as *himself* mutilated. Those who died in an age of unquestioned faith

Knew where they went—
They went to God's right Hand—
That Hand is amputated now
And God cannot be found— (1551)

A minister's question at a funeral—"Is the arm of the Lord shortened that it cannot save?"—haunted Emily from the time she heard it
as a child. She apparently took as genuine God's *purely rhetorical* question: "Is my hand shortened . . . that it cannot redeem? Or have I no
power to deliver?" (Isa. 50:2). Dickinson wondered, doubted, and settled for something less than full enlightenment. Arnold clung to the
chance of individual fidelity ("Ah, love, let us be true / To one
another") in a world in which "the Sea of Faith," once "at the full,"
had receded, its "melancholy, long, withdrawing roar, / Retreating, to
the breath / Of the night wind, down the vast edges drear / And
naked shingles of the world," leaving us "here," lost and confused,
"as on a darkling plain," where "ignorant armies clash by night."
Nietzsche's response to that loss of faith, to a world in which God
"cannot be found," was at once elegiac and the stimulus to an astrin-
gent, self-redeeming, tragic joy that allowed him, paradoxically, to sur-
mount the very nihilism he more than anyone else forced his readers
to confront. Terrified by the empty darkness of a Godless world, Dickinson, at least in *this* poem, prefers what Nietzsche called a "necessary
fiction." Asserting some vague faith rather than none at all, she
chooses what she knows to be a deceptive and flitting night-light, a
glow possibly rising from decay but still providing *some* illumination
to guide us in the darkness: "Better an ignis fatuus [Medieval Latin for
"foolish fire"] / Than no illume at all—."

This "grotesquely memorable" poem also provides "the inevitable
proof-text" in Jane Donahue Eberwein's 2004 essay on Dickinson's
attempt to salvage a challenged faith. She focuses on four textual features of the poem, the first two of which are immediately germane to
my own concerns. First, whatever its biblical antecedents, the anthropomorphic image of a God subject to mutilation "proves nothing
about the immortal, immutable, unknowable lord of creation as envis-
aged by Calvin." As Eberwein says at the conclusion of her essay,
"even while questioning," Dickinson "continued to hope for immortality," and if the right hand or arm of God "Christians had earlier
relied on for salvation had been amputated, the left one somehow

pulled the sluice to release the flow of grace that sustained Emily Dickinson in 'the Balm of that Religion / That doubts as fervently as it believes' [1144]." In accord with this compensating balance, her second textually based observation expands from a minute, close reading of the poem's metrics to the cosmic. If we "think of this poem as a response to the implosion of the traditional argument for God's existence based on orderly design evident throughout the universe," we have to take into account the poem's

> surprising degree of metrical regularity. There are variants in its iambic beat, of course: trochaic feet at the start of several lines and an opening spondee, all of which could be interpreted as reinforcing the assurance that existed back "then." The iambic smoothness of "They went to God's Right Hand" accords with tone, but equal regularity in the two most devastating lines ("That Hand is amputated now / And God cannot be found") hints that the poet senses more order in the universe than the poem directly acknowledges.[1]

Though this is at once impressive and appealing, I would make two points. First, metrical regularity is obviously not a dependable, let alone a foolproof, guarantee of an analogous order in the universe; to take one striking example—Ezra Pound's line in one of the Hell Cantos (XIV)—"the drift of lice, teething" is *rhythmically* quite beautiful but cosmically appalling. Second, the caveats inserted (the metrical regularity *"hints* that the *poet senses* more order in the universe than the *poem directly acknowledges"*) seem to undermine the critic's own astute textual reading by introducing a divide between what the "poet senses" and what the poem itself "directly acknowledges." While I admire, and even partially concur in, what is being said here, the argument *may* raise once again the question I began with: the degree to which a reader's own religious position may affect his or her interpretation of a text that is either intrinsically ambiguous or that seems, tonally or metrically, to reflect ambivalence on the part of the poet. These issues are obviously germane to our reading of "Apparently with no surprise"—which also happens to be iambically regular. Indeed, I wonder if, to reverse Eberwein's conclusion, in the case of *our*

---

1. Jane Donahue Eberwein, "'Is Immortality True?': Salvaging Faith in an Age of Upheaval," 67, 94, 96.

proof-text, the poet, or the dramatic speaker, "senses *less* order in the universe than the poem directly acknowledges," perhaps "no illume at all."

Of course, religious faith is not the only source of light. Though she was always acutely conscious that Reason alone cannot satisfy our spiritual needs, especially the immortal longings in us, there are occasions when Dickinson endorsed the "illumination" specifically associated with science and the Enlightenment. On such occasions, she displays an appropriately satiric, epigrammatic wit. In his own version of mutilation, Jesus had admonished us that, "if thy right eye offend thee, pluck it out, and cast it from thee" rather than risk the whole body being cast into Hell (Matt. 5:29). Benjamin Franklin had his own sardonic proverb: "The Way to see by Faith is to put out the Eye of Reason." Almost precisely a century after the publication of Franklin's *Poor Richard's Almanac* in 1758, Dickinson seems to recall Franklin's apparent reversal of Jesus in an epigram that honors the rational skepticism of her countryman, a paragon of the Age of Reason who was famed for both worldly wisdom and scientific experimentation:

> "Faith" is a fine invention
> When Gentlemen can *see*—
> But *Microscopes* are prudent
> In an Emergency. (185)

Even when she is being ("apparently") glib, Dickinson is not only witty but also an artist whose thought and poetry thrive on antithetical conflict. After demolishing complacent gentility (note the tongue-in-cheek elegance of *fine* and that ostentatiously formal *Gentlemen*), she makes us realize the paradoxical lack of any *need* for so-called faith when one can actually "see" and focuses our attention on the choice between two very different sorts of "invention." Such poems dramatize the agon between skeptical doubt and religious "faith," certainly when faith is alternately wrestled with and fervently or desperately clung to, and even when it is acknowledged to be an ignis fatuus or an invention. It is that anguished but fruitful tension that produces the power, as well as the wit and mental agility, we find in Emily Dickinson's poems, especially those poems dramatizing the tension between belief and doubt. As a lyric poet and a letter writer, she was, to borrow Irving Howe's description of a skilled political novelist, "a nimble dialectician . . . able to handle several ideas at once," especially, in Dickinson's case, when it came to God. To cite again the draft of her 1882 letter to Judge Lord: "On subjects of which we know nothing, or should I say *Beings,* . . . we both believe and disbelieve a hundred times an Hour, which keeps Believing nimble" (*L* 728).

⟡

Such poems and letters may help us plumb the depths beneath the "apparently" calm depiction of our poem's "Approving God." But if canonical context can provide (to shift metaphors) mutual illumination, it also raises its own question: the extent to which it is legitimate to read a particular poem through the prism of related poems and letters, or what we may know, or think we know, about a poet's own religious stance, whether orthodox, heterodox, agnostic, or, alternately, all of these and more. This is especially so in the case of a poet who doubted and believed with equal fervor, adept at keeping "Believing nimble," whose doubt, "like the Mosquito, buzzes round my faith" (*L* 377). It was a religious doubt that had much to do (as suggested by that famously "uncertain" and irreverent Gothic-comic poem, "I heard a Fly buzz— when I died" [465]) with death—which she refers to in the letter to Samuel Bowles containing "'Faith' is a fine invention" as "that *Bareheaded life,* under the grass," which "worries one like a wasp" (*L* 364).

Yet, though a poem initially (and ultimately) needs to be read intrinsically, in terms of what, and *only* what, is there, "in the text," it is difficult to rule out altogether the extrinsic knowledge we have— especially in the case of a poem depicting God that was written by a poet who, while never doubting God's existence, famously refused, despite immense pressure, to submit (on several occasions, beginning in 1850) to the public confession of faith strenuously urged by her Congregationalist religion. Writing to her friend Abiah Root in May of the critical year, 1850, Dickinson, who had earlier explained to Abby her resistance to becoming a Christian (*L* 27, 67), again raised the great question. She employed Dantean imagery, its slight mawkishness reflecting her infatuation at the time with the rather lush young Abby: "What shall we do, my darling, when trial grows more and more, when the dim, lone light expires, and it's dark, so very dark, and we wander, and know not where, and cannot get out of the forest—whose is the hand to help us, and to lead, and forever guide us; they talk of 'Jesus of Nazareth'—will you tell me if it be he?" (*L* 98). And six months or so later, again to Abby:

You are growing wiser than I am, and nipping in the bud fancies which I let blossom—perchance to bear no fruit, or if plucked, I may find it bitter. The shore is safer, Abiah, but I love to buffet the sea—I can count the bitter wrecks here in these pleasant waters, and hear the murmuring winds, but, oh, I love the danger! You are learning control and firmness. Christ Jesus will love you more. I'm afraid he don't love me *any*! (*L* 104)

"Live dangerously!" Nietzsche advises us, and Nietzsche, by way of Emerson, is not irrelevant at a moment when Dickinson is making a hard, truth-loving choice in favor of a dangerous freedom of thought. She knows the shore is "safer" than the sea and that it might be better to nip in the bud religious doubts than to risk further alienating a Jesus who seems, however, already to have withdrawn his love for *her*. Yet she chooses to "buffet" that sea, to let those thoughts "blossom" and her fruit ripen, even if it should prove "bitter" to the taste. She sounds here like Emerson, specifically a passage in his essay "Intellect" posing a choice between "Truth and Repose." He who simply accepts the comfortable "creed" he has inherited will find rest, "but he shuts the door to truth. He in whom the love of truth predominates will keep aloof from all moorings, and afloat. He will abstain from dogmatism, and recognize all the opposite negations, between which, as a wall, his being is swung. He submits to the inconvenience of suspense and imperfect opinion, but he is a candidate for truth, as the other is not, and respects the highest law of his being."[2]

This passage, which Dickinson seems to have read, may well have had an impact on her life, as it certainly did on the life of Emerson's German disciple, Nietzsche. That great questioner and lover of intellectual danger echoed Emerson's thought, and choice, in a youthful letter to his sister. Anticipating the difficulty and loneliness of the path chosen by dedicated friends of the truth (*philalethes*), Nietzsche struck out on a new path, though one he was perfectly aware had been blazed by Emerson, the author he thought "richest in ideas in this century so far." Should we, Nietzsche asks rhetorically,

arrive at *that* view of God, world, and reconciliation which makes us feel most comfortable? . . . Do we after all seek rest, peace, and pleas-

2. *Emerson: Essays and Lectures*, ed. Porte, 425–26.

ure in our inquiries? No, only truth—even if it be the most abhorrent and ugly. . . . Faith does not offer the least support of objective truth. Here the ways of men part: if you wish to strive for peace of soul and pleasure, then believe; if you wish to be a devotee of truth, then inquire.[3]

It was not only the ways of "men" that parted on this issue. Though Dickinson's "is very much a poetry of the religious imagination," and religion "continues to be a fundamental paradigm through which she interprets her world," this is "*not* to claim that Dickinson is an orthodox religious poet. On the contrary, her work offers a forceful and original critique of traditional metaphysics in ways that recall her near contemporary Friedrich Nietzsche. Religion is in many ways a paradigm that fails Dickinson, and yet she never completely discards it. If she is not devout, she is also not secular."[4] Emily Dickinson never formally joined the church and stopped attending services altogether around 1860, by which time she was a virtual recluse. In an 1862 letter to Higginson, describing her religious position in relation to the rest of her family, Dickinson expressed her rebellious doubt with a clarity and irony, poignancy and pride, worthy of one of Nietzsche's lonely devotees of painful truth: "They are religious—except me—and address an Eclipse, every morning—whom they call their 'Father'" (*L* 404). As Roger Lundin observes in his biographical tracing of her "art of belief," Dickinson "agonizingly approached the threshold of conversion but never passed over it; and throughout her adult life she brilliantly meditated upon the great perennial questions of God, suffering, the problem of evil, death, and her 'Flood subject' [*L* 454] immortality."[5]

Emily Dickinson never relinquished her empathy with the human, crucified divinity, Jesus. And there is sporadic evidence that she became somewhat more prayerful in her final years. What she refused to assent

3. This letter from the twenty-year-old Nietzsche to his sister deserves its place as the first item in *The Portable Nietzsche*, ed. Walter Kaufmann. Nietzsche's later, virtually unreserved praise of Emerson may be found in his *Nachlass*, dating to 1881–1882, when he was writing *The Gay Science*, a book originally dedicated to Emerson.

4. Wolosky, "Public and Private in Dickinson's War Poetry," 115–16.

5. *Emily Dickinson and the Art of Belief*, 4. Lundin's own art of (Christian) belief is manifest in his 2006 *From Nature to Experience: The American Search for Cultural Authority.*

to, what she struggled with and often defiantly rebelled against, was the conventional, "optimistic" depiction of God: that Judeo-Christian Father-God who was traditionally defined—despite the appalling evidence of suffering and disease, death and blight—as omnipotent, omniscient, *and* all-loving. Augustine, Aquinas, and others might argue that God was—*must* be—all three. But how *could* he be simultaneously *all* of these? Epicurus, whose famous riddle I cited earlier from Hume's *Dialogues Concerning Natural Religion,* is only one of many skeptics who have challenged this traditional conception of God.

Whatever philosophy she read, Emily Dickinson certainly read Shakespeare, Pope's *Essay on Man,* and Wordsworth, along, of course, with Wordsworth's principal American disciple, Emerson; and she knew by heart much of Milton and, obviously, Scripture. But where others found (in the Bible, in human life, in Nature, in the Great Chain of Being) evidence of a benevolent Deity whose Design was ultimately providential, Dickinson found an essentially inscrutable God often less compassionate than capricious, even cruel, and often less bountiful than stingy. The latter charge is made in a moving letter written to the Hollands in the autumn of 1859 in which Dickinson manages to bring together cold, poverty, God—and, of course, frost and flowers.

"We have no fires yet," she begins, "and the evenings grow cold. Tomorrow, stoves are set. How many barefoot shiver I trust their Father knows who saw not fit to give them shoes." Like Lear, experiencing "houseless poverty" on the storm-swept heath and pitying all "poor naked wretches" undefended "from seasons such as these," Dickinson too would wish "the heavens more just" (*King Lear* 3.4.26–36). Her tentative and partly ironic "trust" in God's omniscience is inseparable from her direct challenge to his benevolence, a sardonic observation followed by a report that her sister Vinnie was "sick tonight, which gives the world a russet [sober] tinge." Then comes this remarkable sentence, personalizing the charge against a God who allows sickness and a Father who denies shoes to his poorer children, leaving them to shiver barefoot in the cold: "God was penurious with me, which makes me shrewd with Him" (*L* 353).

This miserly God had yielded little to her. (As she put it in an unfinished poem, "the Door" to that "old mansion," Paradise, has been "reversed," for "Bliss is frugal of her Leases / Adam taught her Thrift / Bankrupt once through his excesses—" [1119]). Feeling barren and abandoned, she, in turn, was *shrewd* with him: a word that will appear in altered and intensified form in a poem we have already examined, in which, "grown shrewder" with God, the speaker scans the skies with "a suspicious Air," inferring from the evidence of divine indifference that God is to be found among the "Swindlers" (476). Like *penurious,* the word *shrewd* is multilayered. In her wary, perceptive relationship with God she is discerning, searching, sharp, penetrating; also cunning, approaching God with artful trickery, even, at times, in the guise of a *shrew:* a scolding woman with a fault-finding temperament, at once a "nag" and nagged by her own doubts. It is a *shrewdness* that *we* would attribute to Dickinson, if she hadn't beaten us to it.

"This is September," she continues her letter, and there "has been frost enough. We must have summer now, and 'whole legions' of daisies." She wants the hills to blossom, to be "born again! If we knew how deep the crocus lay, we should never let her go. Still, crocuses stud many mounds whose gardeners till in anguish some tiny, vanished bulb" (*L* 353–54). As a gardener Emily Dickinson knew just "how deep" the crocus lay. "She dwelleth in the Ground," she says of it in a poem (671), aware that the spring-flowering crocus has a floral tube so long that the ovary (the seed-producing part) is belowground, sheltered from climatic change. She may long for spring, when all will be "born again," yet, in autumn, she will "till in anguish some tiny, vanished bulb." God is "penurious" with her, but she will labor at her underground bulbs, not unlike the tiny poems she tilled in anguish, eventually yielding the essential attar distilled from a buried life.

In her mixture of anguish, shrewdness, and nonconformist defiance, Emily Dickinson was wrestling with the traditional God presented by, among many others, Wordsworth. Not the cherisher of flowers we find in so many short lyrics and in the Great Ode, but the later, conservative, and religiously orthodox Wordsworth, who, as much sage as poet, had considerable influence not only on nineteenth-century American literature but also on religious thinking in New England. Along with the Intimations Ode and "Tintern Abbey," the text that meant most to Emerson and his circle (and to Charles Darwin) was *The Excursion,* particularly book 4, "Despondency Corrected." Anticipating Emersonian "optimism," Wordsworth's spokesman, the Wanderer, describes in this book the operations of benign Providence, ever converting "accidents" to "good." The passage in which these lines occur epitomizes Wordsworth's own prose synopsis of the main "Argument" of book 4: "A belief in a superintending Providence the only adequate support under affliction." According to the Wanderer, in a passage excerpted in an anthology widely sold in New England, the sole support for the "calamities of mortal life" is

> an assured belief
> That the procession of our fate, howe'er
> Sad or disturbed, is ordered by a Being
> Of infinite benevolence and power;
> Whose everlasting purposes embrace
> All accidents, converting them to good.
> —The darts of anguish *fix* not where the seat
> Of suffering hath been thoroughly fortified
> By acquiescence in the Will supreme
> For time and for eternity; by faith,
> Faith absolute in God, including hope. (*Excursion* 4.1–22)

By the time he wrote *The Excursion,* the religiously and politically conservative Wordsworth had come a far distance from the 1790s, when he was a political radical and, religiously, close to what Coleridge called him at the time, a "semi-atheist," certainly a pantheist or panentheist. In this passage, though he employs a pious spokesman, Wordsworth essentially presents his *own* late "optimism," stressing a benign reciprocity linking Man, Nature, and a providential Divinity who offers believers consolation in distress. He describes an infinitely powerful and benevolent God whose "purposes" embrace and convert all "accidents" to good. This is the very issue raised by "Apparently with no surprise," in which the Frost wields his weapon "in accidental power," though with lethal results. But in Wordsworth, God's all-embracing "purposes" and our response blunt "the darts of anguish," which fall hurtless, since all our "suffering" is absorbed by "acquiescence in the Will supreme" and by "Faith absolute in God, including hope."

Though she never abandoned "hope," that thing with feathers (254), and sometimes found consolation in spiritual meditation, it was precisely this complacent assessment of an omnipotent, benevolent, "accident"-converting Being that Dickinson rebelled against. Wordsworth's lines, which appeared in a cheaply priced 1846 anthology, provided popular reinforcement of the conviction of many moderate believers in New England, especially but not only Unitarians, that the working poor were to rely on Providence rather than reform.[6] Dickinson, in contrast (and in contradiction, as well, of her "elitism"), was shrewdly critical of the God who did not see "fit" to provide shoes for the poor who shivered barefoot. Since this providential aspect of Romanticism was in accord with a position endorsed by the American Transcendentalists, Unitarians, and Congregationalists, Dickinson would have felt compelled to resist, not only late Wordsworth, but the earlier optimism of Emerson, as well as the conformist pressures of her own church.

Like the second-generation English Romantic poets, and like Emerson and others in America, Dickinson was in part a post-Wordsworthian Romantic. Just as Emerson, the medium between Dickinson and Wordsworth, "enjoins poets in *Nature,* and Wordsworth describes his poet in *The Prelude,*" so the speaker in many Dickinson poems offers herself "in solitude to nature's influence and predicates the sacramental connection between landscape and humanity, between landscape and the divine, which was the hypothesis of the Romantics."[7] Referring to Blake, "young Wordsworth," Shelley, and Keats, poet Louise Bogan noted, in a 1959 lecture at Amherst: "It is surely in the company of these English poets that Emily Dickinson belongs," not least because of "the joy she felt in the natural world—particularly in flowers and in children," a joy recorded in visionary "moments of still and halted perception." Does that make her Emersonian as well? Despite his reputation, Emerson was more than a Transcendental Romantic and serene optimist. But Bogan was of course right to assert that Emily Dickinson's "attitude toward pain and suffering, toward the shocking facts of existence, was far more realistic than Emerson's."[8]

---

6. Joel Pace, who has studied the relation of Wordsworth's poetry to social reform in nineteenth-century America, notes that lines 10–93—excerpted under a title borrowed from Wordsworth's own prose "Argument"—were used by more conservative Unitarians to blunt reform. See Romantic Praxis Circle Series, http//www.rc.umd.edu/praxis/.

7. Farr, *The Passion of Emily Dickinson,* 51. Farr adds that this was a "chief principle of [John] Ruskin," the great art historian who insisted he owed his "eye" to Wordsworth, especially the Wordsworth of *The Excursion.* Another disciple of Wordsworth, the American painter Thomas Cole, is emphasized by Farr as an influence on Dickinson. Cole may have met with Wordsworth in London in 1832, when he was befriended by Coleridge and De Quincey. Cole's 1836 painting *Tintern Abbey* is an obvious homage.

8. Louise Bogan, "A Mystical Poet," 28–31.

Though urged by an Emerson influenced by Wordsworth and, most immediately in her youth, by Congregationalist clergymen to "scrutinize the Book of Nature to find the evidence of God's promises there," Dickinson found, instead of benign purpose, what Cynthia Griffin Wolff characterizes as evidence of "the ambiguity and latent violence that mankind must constantly confront in the course of ordinary existence." Insofar as all three traditions—Romantic, Transcendentalist, and Christian—postulated "some benevolent supernatural force working through nature, Dickinson stood in opposition to them," with her "most general objections . . . raised against the optimistic proclamations that characterized the initial phase of British Romanticism." Wolff has in mind here Wordsworth's claim—in the preface to the second edition (1800) of *Lyrical Ballads*—that the ideal poet "considers man and nature as essentially adapted to each other." Since, like the later Emerson, Dickinson found the bond with Nature violated by painful Experience, her resistance would be, not to what Matthew Arnold called Wordsworth's "healing power," but to the sort of optimism and specifically *religious* consolation-in-distress we find in the despondency-correcting doctrine of the sententious Wanderer.[9]

Dickinson might have encountered that Wordsworth passage directly, through an echoing Emerson, or in that popular 1846 anthology. Or she may not have read it at all. It hardly matters, since it merely confirms traditional belief—held by Isaac Newton no less than Augustine and Aquinas—in a providential ordering of life's "procession," accidents and all, by "a Being / Of infinite benevolence and power." Though Darwin, as he tells us in his *Autobiography*, read, not an excerpt, but the whole of the enormously lengthy *Excursion* "twice through" in 1837–1839, while writing his first notebooks "in relation to the *Origin of Species*,"[10] he could not follow Wordsworth to *this* benignly theistic conclusion, his faith, gradually and with many fluctuations, turning to agnosticism. Nor could Emily Dickinson, who, one suspects, would

9. Wolff, *Emily Dickinson*, 282–83. In "Memorial Verses," written in the very month Wordsworth died, Arnold notes that "since dark days still bring to light / Man's prudence and man's fiery might," time may restore us Goethe's "sage mind" and Byron's "force," "But where will Europe's latter hour / Again find Wordsworth's healing power?"
10. *The Autobiography of Charles Darwin*, 85, 83.

have gone beyond the merely *aesthetic* verdict on these lines that we find in another observation by Arnold on Wordsworth.

In the influential essay introducing his 1879 selection of Wordsworth's poems, Arnold (whose earlier *Essays in Criticism* had been read and marked by Emily Dickinson) quotes skeptic Leslie Stephen's surprising encomium that Wordsworth's "poetry is precious" because his "philosophy is sound," his "ethical system" as "distinctive and capable of exposition as Bishop [Joseph] Butler's." Very well, says Arnold, "let us come direct to the center" of Wordsworth's philosophy as "an ethical system as . . . capable of systematical exposition" as that of the bishop many consider Britain's greatest moral philosopher. He then quotes the opening six lines of this passage from *The Excursion*, ending with that omnipotent and benevolent Being whose "everlasting purposes embrace / All accidents, converting them to good." "That," says Arnold, "is doctrine such as we hear at church, too, religious and philosophic doctrine; and the attached Wordsworthian loves passages of such doctrine, and brings them forward in proof of his poet's excellence. But however true the doctrine may be, it has, as here presented, none of the characters of *poetic* truth, the kind of truth which we require of a poet, and in which Wordsworth is really strong."[11]

At various times and in various moods, that nimble believer Emily Dickinson would feel differently as to how "true the doctrine may be." But she would concur with Matthew Arnold (along with most admirers of this unquestionably "strong" poet) that Wordsworth fails, in such pious and didactic passages, to present "*poetic* truth." One can admire the capacity exhibited here—as in Alexander Pope's philosophic poem and exercise in theodicy, *An Essay on Man*—to synthesize received doctrine. But, as Emerson reminds us, nothing is got for nothing, and to recognize the falling off in terms of "*poetic* truth," one has only to compare these lines from *The Excursion* with those earlier cited from the "sublime" passage of "Tintern Abbey."

It was less the "assured belief" in an omnipotent and benevolent God, placed in the mouth of his Wanderer, than the mysterious sensing of an indefinable "Presence" (in lines encapsulating Spinoza and

---

11. "Wordsworth," in *Poetry and Criticism of Matthew Arnold*, 340–41. Praise of late Wordsworth's "ethical system" is surprising coming from Leslie Stephen, a self-proclaimed skeptic as early as the 1870s and author of the enormously influential *An Agnostic's Apology*.

anticipating Einstein) that made Wordsworth "the paradigm poet for so many in the nineteenth century, across an ontological spectrum ranging from orthodox Christians to atheists."[12]

That range would include, located somewhere near the middle, Emily Dickinson. She had been introduced to the poetry of both Emerson and Wordsworth by Benjamin Franklin Newton, a friend and tutor who died suddenly in 1853, and to whom she pays tribute in an 1854 letter. Writing to Newton's pastor, the distinguished Unitarian minister Edward Everett Hale, Dickinson wondered if her friend—who "often talked of God, but I do not know certainly if he was his Father in Heaven"—was "willing to die, and if you think he is at Home." In life, Newton had become to her "a gentle, yet grave Preceptor, teaching me what to read, what authors to admire," emphasizing "what was most grand or beautiful in nature, and that sublimer lesson, a faith in things unseen, and in a life again, nobler, and much more blessed—" (L 282). Her phrasing is reminiscent of the developmental stages set out in "Tintern Abbey," culminating in the experience of a "presence that disturbs me with the joy / Of elevated thoughts; a sense sublime / Of something far more deeply interfused," resulting in a faith "that all which we behold / Is full of blessings" (lines 93–96, 133–34).

With the passage of years, beginning with the cataclysmic death at sea of his brother John in 1805, Wordsworth moved away from the intuition of a sublime Presence felt in nature and in the mind of man toward a providential, philosophically optimistic theism. In the immediate aftermath of John's death, Wordsworth made his first unambiguous poetic statement of belief in God, petitioning (in a poem he never published) a "gracious God" to "let me be resigned / Beneath thy chastening rod." Writing in anguish to his friend and donor Sir George Beaumont, Wordsworth explicitly addressed the mysterious problem presented by suffering. "Why," he asked, are human beings "moral agents" with "a sense of justice and injustice," with "sympathies that make the best of us so afraid of inflicting pain and sorrow which yet we see dealt about so lavishly by the supreme governor?"

---

12. Here I repeat the observation of Charles Taylor (*A Secular Age*, 607) cited in my Introduction. As an "orthodox Christian," Taylor would be more aligned with the Wordsworth of religious certitude who speaks through the Wanderer than with the poet of mysterious "intimations," of self-contradictory ambiguity and vacillation. It is this Wordsworth (who appealed to less doctrinaire believers, even atheists) with whom I associate Emily Dickinson.

Why should human benevolence "differ so widely from what appears to be his [God's] notion and rule?" He raises two "suppositions," rejecting the first and embracing the second: "Would it be blasphemy to say that upon the supposition of the thinking principle being destroyed by death, however inferior we may be to the great Cause and ruler of things, we have *more of love* in our nature than he has? The thought is monstrous, and yet how to get rid of it except upon the supposition of *another and better world* I do not see."[13]

Emily Dickinson was no stranger to such thoughts—the blasphemous and monstrous, as well as those evoking another and better world. But there are crucial differences in substance and tone. The potentially redemptive suffering of Jesus, which meant so much to her, seems to have meant little to Wordsworth. On the other hand, while immortality was her "Flood subject," Wordsworth's "supposition" of a life to come as consolation in the aftermath of his brother's death remained alien to the restless, inquisitive, skeptical nature of Emily Dickinson. True, she would, in writing to Ben Newton's pastor, seem to allude to "Tintern Abbey" in evoking what Wordsworth called in his own letter to Beaumont "another and better world." But this was hardly the occasion to reveal her more skeptical side. As in the case of her much later and more famous consoling letter to Susan following the death of little Gilbert, Dickinson would not be inclined to express religious doubts in the course of inquiring about the supernatural destination of a recently deceased friend.

As for Wordsworth's Wanderer, with whose dogmatic utterance we began: his religious faith reflects that of Wordsworth himself, a man tested by personal tragedy. Five years after his brother drowned, two of the poet's children died in the one terrible year, 1812, while he was working on *The Excursion*. But even if Wordsworth's own consolation in distress was painfully earned, its expression in *The Excursion* would have been all too conventional for Dickinson, who would have resisted the preachiness of the Wanderer, just as she would any simple acceptance of that final "supposition" of another and better world in the letter to Beaumont.

But Emily Dickinson would have been far more receptive to a second and more celebrated text associated with Beaumont. As its subtitle

13. The unpublished poem and the letter to Beaumont (italics in the original) are cited in Juliet Barker, *Wordsworth,* 242.

indicates, "Elegiac Stanzas" was "Suggested by a Picture of Peele Castle, in a Storm, Painted by Sir George Beaumont." Written in the spring following John's drowning in a storm at sea, "Elegiac Stanzas" poignantly registers the impact of that tragedy on the poet. "A deep distress hath humanized my Soul," he wrote. While "the feeling of my loss will ne'er be old," he now speaks "with mind serene," welcoming "fortitude, and patient cheer." His stoical acceptance, diminishing nothing of his own inextinguishable sense of loss and humanizing grief, is epitomized in the magnificently balanced, all-embracing final line, the utterance of a man no longer "Housed in a dream, at distance from" the rest of humankind: "Not without hope we suffer and we mourn."

The Wanderer also spoke of suffering and hope; but what was there presented as "doctrine" here attains the "*poetic* truth" Matthew Arnold rightly identified as Wordsworth's true strength. With this *poetic* realization of the inevitability and universality of loss and suffering mingled with hope, Emily Dickinson—who twice (*L* 449, 510) summons up this great poem's imaginative "light that never was, on sea or land"—would have had no inclination to quarrel.

Chapter 12

The Final Dialectic

Believing and Disbelieving

Emily Dickinson's quarrel was not with troubled hope but with complacent certitude. Whatever its provenance, and whoever was promoting what Wordsworth's Wanderer called "assured belief" in a Being of "infinite benevolence and power," Emily Dickinson was not buying it. That life was tragic did not make it meaningless; but in the world of circumstances the clear-eyed poet saw all around her—a world of natural violence, of sickness and death—there were "accidents" that could not always be converted into good, let alone accommodated in any grand and benevolent "Design." Dickinson's response to the death of little Gilbert, in which emotional devastation was accompanied by imaginative and spiritual compensation, would seem to be something of an exception to the rule. For the most part, human suffering and death could not be so easily theologized away.

For Emily Dickinson, the Epistle to the Romans notwithstanding, God seemed less often "with us" than "against us" (L 746). In a letter written a year and a half before her own death, she expressed condolences to her Aunt Catharine Sweetser that went well beyond the conventional expression of sympathy after an illness. Again subversively echoing Paul, this time 1 Timothy 1:17, she wrote: "It is very wrong that you were ill, and whom shall I accuse? The enemy, 'eternal, invisible, and full of glory'—But He declares himself a friend!" (L 851). In a poem occasioned by the departure of a friend "never coming back," she contemplates the Great Departure, the thought that "Death is final." She accepts God's assertion that he "is Love" because, as he "tells us certainly," he is a "jealous God," an emotion familiar to lovers. But if he is also omnipotent,

> If "All is possible with" him
> As he besides concedes
> He will refund us finally
> Our confiscated Gods— (1260)

That last line refers to all those lost friends seized by God, laid up in his keeping, but perhaps (in accord with the tongue-in-cheek tone of the preceding stanza) never returned to us. God's promised Heaven offered infinitude, but since God also "stole away the looks and lives of all those one loved," Dickinson "could not support any sweeping attribution to God of every benefit."[1] If he is benevolent ("If God is Love"), if he is omnipotent ("If 'All is possible with' him"), then he ought to be able to "refund" to us those we loved. But God's healing powers, or his compassion, are limited; instead of a refund, we are told that a debt is owed to the celestial treasury! The late poem to which I am alluding raises, and sardonically responds to, two questions based on what "*They* say," what "*They* speak of":

> Is Heaven a Physician?
> They say that He can heal—
> But Medicine Posthumous
> Is unavailable—
> Is Heaven an Exchequer?
> They speak of what we owe—
> But that negotiation
> I'm not a Party to— (1270)

Setting herself apart from the conformist "they," she is adamant in asserting nonparticipation. And whether or not *we* are "party" to a negotiation acknowledging delinquency, *God* may or may not forgive

---

1. Farr, *The Passion of Emily Dickinson*, 67.

the debt, or ultimately "heal." As sickness and death confirm, he certainly afflicts and wounds. According to "There's a certain Slant of light," one of Dickinson's supreme lyrics, it is "Heavenly Hurt" that is given us, "An imperial affliction / Sent us of the Air—." Though the pain might be ennobling as well as excruciating, such wounds are permanent and deep, far beneath the visible surface of the skin: "We can find no scar, / But internal difference, / Where the Meanings, are—" (258). This is the very antithesis of those "darts of anguish" that, the Wordsworthian Wanderer confidently asserts, "*fix* not" in the flesh of the believer fortified by faith. By the time he wrote these lines, the poet was as pious as his Wanderer. As a major modern poet, one of Wordsworth's most perceptive admirers, has put it, as he aged the great Romantic became a poet and a man whose "achieved calm" atrophied into "an implacable complacency."[2] Indeed, those "darts of anguish" the Wanderer is so quick to dismiss sound much less at home in the lexicon of later Wordsworth than in that of such a laureate of "anguish" as Emily Dickinson: dark quiver-companions of her "Bolts of Melody" (505).

Fusing equally piercing poetry and thought, Dickinson pressed to the limits her shrewd and tortured agon with her ancestral God, a Calvinist Deity who veils himself behind the often ruthless processes of nature and human life. If one challenge to the concept of a loving, caring God is the amount of undeserved suffering in the world, another is his intentional, cruel hiding of himself even from those of his creatures who most desire to know him. I earlier cited this opening stanza:

> I know that He exists.
> Somewhere—in Silence—
> He has hid his rare life
> From our gross eyes. (338)

As Fred White observes in his examination of Dickinson's "existential dramas," this speaker suffers "the anguish that comes from the growing fear that the universe may be devoid of God or divine purpose." He notes how her "faith in God's existence," already "compromised by the

---

2. Seamus Heaney, in his introduction to *Essential Wordsworth*, xxviii.

qualifying 'Somewhere—in Silence,'" rapidly "degrades to bitter skepticism," leading "her to wonder if God might just be playing a cruel game of cosmic hide and seek with her."[3] I will return to this poem in a moment, but it may help to briefly place in a larger context this motif: virtual certitude that God exists; anguish that, hidden, he is unresponsive to the petitions of those most in need.

As mentioned earlier, Emily Dickinson almost compulsively associates the hidden or absent God with the gospel text "Ask, and it shall be given you; seek, and ye shall find; knock, and it will be opened unto you" (Matt. 7:7). In an early poem, the speaker says that she has twice "stood a beggar / Before the door of God"; but that "Burglar! Banker—Father!" turns out to be parsimonious, and "I am poor once more!" (49). God is, as she will later put it, "penurious" (L 353). She wrote to absent friends (Dr. and Mrs. Holland) in autumn 1853 that they would be with her that night, "If prayers had any answers to them . . . , but I seek and I don't find, and knock and it is not opened. Wonder if God is just—presume He is, however, and 'twas only a blunder of Matthew's" (L 263–64). Thirty years later, she invoked the same text, again critically, and again in longing for absent friends: "We pray to Him [God], and he answers 'No.' Then we pray to Him to rescind the 'no,' and he don't answer at all, yet 'Seek and ye shall find' is the boon of faith" (L 780). Yet, in a poem written in that same year (1883), she disapproves of those casually arrogant "Cosmopolites" who do not "plea" but simply expect a "compensation fair / Knock and it shall be opened / Is their Theology" (1589).

Whatever the element of play in these allusions, the passage from Matthew comes up in contexts that are unmistakably in earnest. In an 1862 poem, she prays to a distant "Jesus—in the Air," but "I know not which thy chamber is— / I'm knocking everywhere." That raises a crucial question: though he sets

> Earthquake in the South—
> And Maelstrom, in the Sea—
> Say, Jesus Christ of Nazareth—
> Hast thou no Arm for Me? (502).

---

3. "Emily Dickinson's Existential Dramas," 101.

That final image, as we saw, haunted Dickinson from early child-hood. A decade and half after she wrote this poem, she would seek from Higginson clarification of the rhetorical (but, she thought, gen-uine) question posed by a minister at a funeral when she was a small girl: "Is the arm of the Lord shortened that it cannot save?" Since, in Isaiah, God speaks of his "hand" rather than his arm, the connection is most relevant to the earlier discussed poem in which she imagines God's right hand "amputated." As for her own plangent cry to Jesus, "Hast thou no Arm for me?" (compare 564: "Infinitude—Had'st Thou no Face / That I might look on Thee?"), such forsaken cries have a notable precedent. In Gethsemane, Jesus himself prays for the chalice to pass from him and is not heard. His disciples sleep; Heaven remains dumb. The Agony in the Garden culminates in the Psalm-echoing but still shocking cry of abandonment from the cross: *Eli, Eli, lama sabachthani?*—"my God, my God, why hast thou forsaken me?" (Mark 15:34; of the gospel writers, only Matthew [45:46] repeats this anguished cry). "For an annihilating instant," as G. K. Chesterton memorably put it, "an abyss that is not for our thoughts had opened even in the unity of the absolute; and God had been forsaken by God."[4]

Almost as shocking, given her international fame as a nun whose good works (for which she received the Nobel Peace Prize) seemed inextricable from her prayerful holiness, has been the revelation (with the publication in August 2007 of her letters and other private papers) of Mother Teresa's agonized experience, protracted over more than a half century, of being (in her own words) "totally cut off from God." Ironically, these revelations coincided with Charles Taylor's accurate observation that modern secularists, however distanced from religion, "are very moved to know that there are dedicated believers, like Mother Teresa"—who emerges, in his magisterial apologetic, as a prominent example of those "who connect themselves to God." In one of her innumerable dark nights of the soul (more intense versions of Emily Dickinson's seeking and not finding, knocking on a door not opened unto her), Mother Teresa cried out to Jesus: "I call, I cling, I want—and there is no One to answer . . . I am told God loves me—and yet the reality of darkness & coldness & emptiness is so great that

---

4. *The Everlasting Man*, 34–35. As we have seen, in poem 313, Dickinson echoes Jesus's own echo of Psalm 22.

nothing touches my soul." Sustained over half a century, this anguish exceeds the ancient cry of the Psalmist for an answer from the temporarily absent Deity. Cardinal Schönborn, in his chapter on "Suffering in a World Guided by God," proposes Mother Teresa as "a living answer to the challenge of pain and evil in the world" (*CP*, 95). But if, as Mother Teresa often said, "suffering is a gift of God," her God seems to have been remarkably generous.[5]

Mother Teresa's despair is even more excruciating, if less eloquent, than that of Gerard Manley Hopkins. That tormented poet-priest confronted the same emptiness and darkness, suffered the same devastating experience of abandonment by God. The depths of that experience are recorded in the so-called terrible sonnets. They were written (as he said, "in blood") during the bleak period he spent in Dublin—as it happens, in the very year of Emily Dickinson's death. Yet even in those anguished poems, he viscerally testifies to the divine presence. Though bruised by the "lionlimb" of God and trodden upon by that cosmic tyrant and tester of souls, Hopkins ends the most dramatic of these sonnets (which had begun with his refusal to "feast" on the "carrion comfort, Despair") by memorializing "That night, that year / Of now done darkness I lay wrestling with (my God!) my God." Though he is still obsessed by the struggle and the darkness, it is *"now done."* He has come through the ordeal, his anguished prayers apparently answered.[6]

⌒

Emily Dickinson's prayers, which *seemed* answered (for we have to recall their role as documents of condolence) in the poem and apotheosizing letter she wrote in the immediate aftermath of little Gilbert's death, go unanswered in "I know that He exists." In the second of the poem's four stanzas, God's "rare life" is contrasted with the brevity of human existence:

5. Taylor, *A Secular Age*, 727, 684. *Mother Teresa: Come Be My Light*, 187; see also 189, 192–94, 199, 202. Long before she died (in 1997), she had asked that her private papers be destroyed. Given their contents, it is remarkable that church superiors overruled her request. For a harrowingly ambiguous yet redemptive dramatization of God's silence amid unspeakable torture, see the historical novel *Silence* (1966) by the Japanese Christian writer Shusaku Endo (New York: Taplinger, 1980).

6. In this sonnet, "Carrion Comfort," Hopkins insists he will *not* "cry I can no more. I can"; and he will "not choose not to be." Rejecting suicide, he endured and, like Mother Teresa, continued a life of often onerous duties.

'Tis an instant's play.
'Tis a fond Ambush
Just to make Bliss
Earn her own Surprise!

The poem began with God's hiding game, and the word *play*, soon to be repeated, sets up the cruel and lethal joke developed in the remainder of the poem, with the speaker's tone, following the pivotal "But" that divides the poem in two, growing increasingly caustic and accusatory:

But—should the play
Prove piercing earnest—
Should the glee—glaze—
In Death's—stiff—stare—

Would not the fun
Look too expensive!
Would not the jest
Have crawled too far! (338)

In "Apparently with no surprise," a "happy" Flower at its "play" is cut down by a silent killer, an assassinating Frost at *its* "play": all sanctioned by "an Approving God." Here, life, reduced to "an instant's play," is a "fond Ambush" supposedly intended to make eternal "Bliss" earn her own "surprise." However, if (as is all too painfully the case), the "play" proves "piercing," the joke (the "fun," the "jest") will have "crawled too far." In fact, with alliteration reinforcing the change, the "glee" will have been transformed to "glaze," a freezing image equated, as so often in Dickinson, with "Death's—stiff—stare." And, again, this casual petrifaction of brief but happy life into frozen death takes place under the auspices of an inscrutable Calvinist God, hidden and silent, yet somehow expecting his perishable creatures to penetrate, by means of a faith he refuses to nourish, to the spiritually "rare life" presumably revealing the benevolent nature so effectively—and cruelly—concealed from the "gross eyes" of mere mortals.

In a poem written in 1885, Dickinson reprises two bitter parodies of prayer written almost a quarter century earlier. The first we have already looked at, "The Heart asks Pleasure—first." The second— obliquely rhymed *abbacddceec*—portrays a God so unresponsive to prayer that it would have been better—as in Job (3:11–16) and in related poems by A. E. Housman and Thomas Hardy—had the petitioner been left in a state of blissful ignorance, with no consciousness of the acute pain of human existence:

> Of Course—I prayed—
> And did God Care?
> He cared as much as on the Air
> A Bird—had stamped her foot—
> And cried "Give Me"—
> My Reason—Life—
> I had not had—but for Yourself—
> 'Twere better Charity
> To leave me in the Atom's Tomb—
> Merry, and Nought, and gay, and numb—
> Than this smart Misery. (376)

The mental sharpness and stinging pain of consciousness (neatly fused in "smart") recur in the 1885 poem, also unusually rhymed. But in this case, natural happiness is to be condemned, since we are not only incarnate but *incarcerated,* and supposedly guilty from the outset:

> Of God we ask one favor,
> That we may be forgiven—
> For what, he is presumed to know—
> The Crime from us is hidden—
> Immured the whole of Life
> Within a magic Prison
> We reprimand the happiness
> That too competes with heaven. (1601)

Speaking a half century ago, poet Archibald MacLeish cited this poem as an example of "the hot and fearless and wholly human anger" with which Dickinson is able to "face [God] at the end. Other poets have confronted God in anger but few have been able to manage it without rhetoric and posture. There is something about that ultimate face to face which excites an embarrassing self-consciousness in which the smaller of the two opponents seems to strut and 'beat it out even to the edge of doom.' Not so with Emily." MacLeish located the "power" of this "remarkable" poem almost entirely "in its voice, its tone," a level of "laconic constraint" established by the archness of that quietly furious phrase, "He is presumed to know."[7]

Beginning satirically, the poem ends contemplatively, though its tonal shift is partially subsumed by the unusual prolongation of a single oblique rhyme: *forgiven, hidden, Prison, heaven.* As in "I know that He exists," something is hidden from us. In this case, it is the original "Crime" of which we are supposedly guilty. To judge from this and other late poems, notably "'Heavenly Father'—take to thee" (1461), Emily Dickinson rejected the doctrine of original sin. We are, as Eberwein has noted, limited by our radical finitude, but since that is God's doing, the blame is his, not ours. Thus, despite the opening petition that "we may be forgiven," this speaker does not really consider herself party to that primordial, inherited guilt that can cause "us"—subordinating adjective to noun, life's magic to imprisoning constraint—to censure earthly happiness whenever it seems to rival that of the promised heaven. Dickinson here participates, in her unique way, in the familiar secular-Nietzschean critique of a Christianity depicted as scorning "the real, sensual, earthly good for some purely imaginary higher end, the pursuit of which can only lead to the frustration of the real, earthly good, to suffering, mortification, repression."[8]

Yet, beneath the irony and the human anger, some form of faith perseveres, and "we" still ask of God forgiveness. Like "they" in her repeated formulations of what "they say," the plural "we" and "us" (instead of the usual "I") suggest a separation between the religiously orthodox and Dickinson herself—an implication reinforced by the letter accompanying this poem. Writing to her friend and champion Helen Hunt Jackson, who had seriously injured her leg, Dickinson remarks, "Knew I how to pray, to intercede for your Foot were intuitive, but I am but a Pagan" (*L* 867).

In a related but tonally different poem, Dickinson uses botanical imagery to dramatize what *appears to be* (the opening pronoun, "This," is left deliberately ambiguous) the tension between faith found and faith lost. Religious belief or doubt, like the universe itself, seems to be a mysterious process reflecting either divine Design or mere accident.

---

7. "The Private World," 25.

8. Eberwein, *Dickinson*, 185; Taylor, *A Secular Age*, 370 (Taylor, of course, rejects the charge).

The mysterious "This" is first depicted as a flower that grows from a small but special seed sown by purpose or by chance:

> This is a Blossom of the Brain—
> A small—italic Seed
> Lodged by Design or Happening
> The Spirit fructified—
>
> Shy as the Wind of his Chambers
> Swift as a Freshet's Tongue
> So of the Flower of the Soul
> Its process is unknown.

Just as the subtle process of growth and fructification remains mysterious, so we cannot know what we will make of this Flower of the Soul. The second half of the poem presents alternatives. "This," which embraces both poetic inspiration as a spiritual activity and religious faith, may be found and cherished, so that it may take root and increase:

> When it is found, a few rejoice
> The Wise convey it Home
> Carefully cherishing the spot
> If other Flower become—

But faith may be lost, in which case we have, as in Nietzsche, "the death of God." What follows is what Thomas Hardy called, in his 1908–1910 poem of that title, "God's Funeral," with the "man-projected Figure" who once provided "blest assurance he was there" a victim of our own unbelief. In Dickinson's climactic presentation of spiritual loss, God's corpse is adorned with a dying flower marking the withering as well of the sacrifice of Jesus: that crucifixion and resurrection that provided Dickinson with her central example of anguish and possible redemption:

> When it is lost, that Day shall be
> The Funeral of God,
> Upon his Breast, a closing Soul
> The Flower of Our Lord— (945)

One of Dickinson's *most* "nimble" expressions of religious belief, and doubt, is "This World is not Conclusion" (501). The poem begins, paradoxically, on an assertive note (the first line ends with a rare period) regarding an Afterlife, followed by philosophic questioning:

This World is not Conclusion.
A Species stands beyond—
Invisible, as Music—
But positive, as Sound—
It beckons, and it baffles—
Philosophy—don't know—
And through a Riddle, at the last—
Sagacity, must go—

The mystery of Immortality, despite the invisible certitude of a spiritual life "beyond," persists, to beckon but baffle us, as we struggle to penetrate the riddle of death. In the lines that follow, Dickinson expresses respect for the "Men"—the Christian martyrs and others like them—who have endured "Crucifixion" to gain a heavenly reward. But faith, in the quatrain that follows, is treated in a strangely lighthearted, "girlish" way:

Faith slips—and laughs, and rallies—
Blushes, if any see—
Plucks at a twig of Evidence—
And asks a Vane, the way—

This meandering skepticism seems to reduce the Cross to a twig. In addition, instead of addressing the Jesus who described himself as "the way, the truth, and the light" (John 14:6), we ask (presumably and punningly, "in vain") a shifting weather vane, rather than a guidepost or a steeple, "the way." The poem, which had begun on a note of bland confidence, whistling in the dark, ends with portentous and pretentious preaching and strident church music ("Much Gesture, from the Pulpit— / Strong Hallelujahs roll—"). But pious posturing and thundering are inefficacious anodynes unable to dull our gnawing uncertainty about death and what may or may not follow: "Narcotics cannot still the Tooth / That nibbles at the soul."

James McIntosh, who chose this poem to conclude his Introduction to *Nimble Believing*, reads the final image less as the tooth of "doubt" than as Dickinson's "doubt-that-is-also-faith that keeps nibbling comically beyond the borders of the poem. The soul, after all, is not erased but persists (however nibbled at) in the poem's understanding." The speaker's stance is that of what McIntosh, quoting Melville's *Moby-Dick,* describes as "neither believer nor infidel." Though Dickinson adopts "no fixed position toward received belief in the poem," she manages its "vacillations expertly," a "mastery" she shows "in many of her poems that expose her variety, her uncertainty, and her questioning spirit. Thought and tone change and keep pace with one another in her lifelong effort to keep believing nimble."[9] And that's true, too, though in *this* poem, the one McIntosh himself has chosen, that final, pompous "Gesture, from the Pulpit" *does* emphasize Dickinson's visceral disgust at hollow religious platitudes. Indeed, it anticipates a late Dickinson anapestic satire (worthy of Thomas Hardy) on a pontificating, phony minister:

> He preached upon "Breadth" till it argued him narrow—
> The Broad are too broad to define
> And of "Truth" until it proclaimed him a Liar—
> The Truth never flaunted a Sign—
>
> Simplicity fled from his counterfeit presence
> As Gold the Pyrites would shun—
> What confusion would cover the innocent Jesus
> To meet so enabled a Man! (1207)

Whatever the need to distinguish Emily Dickinson the woman from the dramatic speakers in her poems, we see in such poems, along with lyric tension, the existential struggle in Dickinson herself between belief and disbelief. In addition, this particular poem dramatizes the antithesis between pompous pulpit fictions counterfeited as certitude and the simple authenticity of the "innocent Jesus," who emerges in this satire as the moral standard by which to gauge "The Truth" as opposed to the fraudulent religion too often preached in his name and which Dickinson here associates with fool's gold.

Torn between a longing to believe and the intellectual honesty of a theological rebel who refused, even as a teenager at Mt. Holyoke, to count herself among the "saved," Emily Dickinson may have pushed

---

9. *Nimble Believing,* 33–34.

her wrestling with God to the limit. But, in the final analysis, even though "the Brain—is wider than the Sky," "deeper than the Sea," and "just the weight of God" (632), the inquisitive mind *has* its limits. Here, one might say, cosmology, epistemology, and biology converge. Precisely because of our evolutionary history, we have to acknowledge the limits of human understanding—especially of our capacity to achieve complete insight into what may be ultimate metaphysical mysteries. God and his purposes, his hidden "Design," *were*, Dickinson concluded, ultimately inscrutable—as the mystery of the universe would later seem to Einstein, for whom, "behind all the discernible laws and connections, there remains something subtle, intangible, and inexplicable." In "Their Height in Heaven comforts not," Dickinson's vantage point is only apparently more local. Surveying with "my narrow Eyes," and acknowledging "I'm finite—I can't see / The House of Supposition" and "the Acres of Perhaps," she concludes: "This timid life of Evidence / Keeps pleading—'I don't know'" (696).

Her questionings and acknowledgment that some things were ultimately unknowable did not make her a thoroughgoing "agnostic," a term coined by T. H. Huxley. Taking up her own phrase, which supplies the title of his book, McIntosh, as we've seen, defines "nimble believing" as "believing for intense moments in a spiritual life without permanently subscribing to any received system of belief." Writing a third of a century earlier, Denis Donoghue accurately observed that "of her religious faith virtually anything may be said, with some show of evidence. She may be represented as an agnostic, a heretic, a skeptic, a Christian." Christina Rossetti, as earlier noted, judged the Dickinson poems sent her "remarkable" but often "irreligious." And Allen Tate once observed, only half-facetiously, "Cotton Mather would have burnt her for a witch."[10]

One thing *is* certain. Despite the transferred epithet suggesting the "timid life" of the finite "I" in "Their Height in heaven comforts not," we have abundant "evidence" in other poems and letters demonstrating

---

10. McIntosh, *Nimble Believing*, 1. Donoghue, *Emily Dickinson*, 14; Donoghue also quotes (15) the letter in which Dickinson famously says of her family, "They are religious—except me—and address an Eclipse, every morning—whom they call 'Father.'" Rossetti's judgment, earlier cited in Chapter 1, may be found in Lubbers, *Emily Dickinson: The Critical Revolution*, 30. For Tate's remark, see his *Man of Letters in the Modern World: Selected Essays, 1928–1955*, 226.

that the fiercely autonomous self Emily Dickinson refused to relinquish to a God in whom she alternately believed and disbelieved—and, above all, passionately questioned—was anything *but* timid. If "the main irrationality of religion is preferring comfort to truth," and paramount among the "distinctive merits" of "non-religious morality" is its "cultivation of a courageous realism in the face of the less palatable facts of life—and of death," Emily Dickinson would appear to be no less nimble a *non*believer than she was a believer.[11] At the very least, she was entitled to claim—with Emily Brontë, in the religious but heterodox Brontë poem that the other Emily frequently read to her sister Lavinia—"No coward soul was mine." That poem, "Last Lines," recited by Higginson at Emily Dickinson's funeral service, was well chosen.

11. The first statement is from Richard Robinson, *An Atheist's Values*, 117; the second from J. L. Mackie, *The Miracle of Theism: Arguments for and against the Existence of God*, 261.

Conclusion

Multi-Perspectivism in Interpretation

To end where we began, with the questions raised by "Apparently with no surprise" and by those friends whose responses I invited: to what extent does a *reader's own* religious perspective affect interpretation? How "objective," how "subjective," are we being when we conclude that the God of the final line is essentially benevolent, distanced, cruel, unreliable—or simply absent? Some find intolerable the thought of a world without a God to sanction "the meaning" of it all; others find such a thought a "source of great comfort." I am quoting Sir Isaiah Berlin, responding at the age of seventy-five to someone who wrote him for his thoughts on the matter: "As for the meaning of life, I do not believe that it has any," he wrote. "We make of it what we can and that is all there is about it. Those who seek for some cosmic all-embracing libretto or God are, believe me, pathetically mistaken."[1]

One will be reminded, as Berlin doubtless was, of Nietzsche, who has already entered our discussion at several points, and to whom I return in this Conclusion. The pivotal act in "Apparently with no surprise," an exercise of accidental but lethal "power," may, in turn, summon up a worldview dominated not by an "Approving God" but by an amoral Will to Power. Nietzsche's Dionysian vision is one of perpetual creation and destruction, an ever-changing world beyond conventional good and evil. In such a world, the Problem of Suffering is no longer a moral issue since the traditional monotheistic framework,

---

1. Isaiah Berlin to an unknown correspondent, November 20, 1984; quoted in Michael Ignatieff, *Berlin: A Life,* 279.

with its cosmic all-embracing libretto, has been replaced by atheism. Our problem then, says Nietzsche, having recognized that we live in an uncaring, violent, and intrinsically meaningless universe, is to somehow summon the strength to say Yes to so harsh and unpromising an existence. Indeed, as his ultimate test and exercise in the affirmation of life, the Nietzschean hero is to "redeem" this existence by embracing the idea of Eternal Recurrence: the ultimate acknowledgment that the Dionysian power-cycle, this self-propelled wheel of destruction and creation, is "without purpose, unless there is a purpose in the joy of the circle" (*The Will to Power* §1067).

Though she was a seeker who was never comfortable in a world without God, Emily Dickinson often wondered just whose side God was on in this cycle of destructive violence. In defense of her beloved flowers and all they stood for, she was capable, as we saw earlier, of challenging even the great eighth chapter of the Epistle to the Romans. "If God is for us," asked Paul rhetorically, "who can be against us?" (8:31). Looking back at "a fatal season" (fall 1881) in which her flowers were attacked by what she called, remembering the opening scene of *Romeo and Juliet* (1.1.151), an "Envious Worm," Dickinson added, "then in early Autumn we had Midwinter Frost—'when God is with us, who shall be against us,'—but when he is against us, other allies are useless" (*L* 746).

On the other hand, people of steadfast religious conviction, refusing to relinquish their faith, seem able to accommodate horrors far more distressing than the frost's beheading of a flower, horrors others would find proof negative when it comes to belief in an all-embracing libretto and loving Creator. As has been recently and accurately observed by a writer working on "the puzzle of existence," the "doctrine that we are presided over by a loving deity has become so rounded and elastic that no earthly evil or natural disaster, it seems, can come into collision with it." The same is true of many readers of the Bible, who are "far more likely to ignore unpleasant scriptural passages than abandon belief in a benevolent God."[2]

There are others, "those to whom the miseries of the world / Are misery, and will not let them rest." I'm quoting *The Fall of Hyperion* (1.148–49) by Keats, who was one of "those." Others, quoted earlier, include Steven Weinberg, Bart Ehrman, and Darwin, all of whom concur in find-

---

2. Jim Holt, "Beyond Belief," 12; Stenger, *God: The Failed Hypothesis*, 221.

ing "too much misery in the world," too much gratuitous suffering, especially by the innocent, to justify belief in a providential Design and a benign God. Such nonbelievers may either be braced by the detached viewpoint implicit in an understanding of science, the "cold bath" advocated by Stephen Jay Gould, or be inclined to resist the related, tough-minded point Charles Anderson made in regard to "Apparently with no surprise": that we do not live in an anthropocentric universe, that "nature's apparent cruelty . . . is hostile to man and flower *only* in not being designed wholly to accommodate their flourishing."[3]

Such detachment is hard to achieve, let alone maintain. So how is a reader of a poem like "Apparently with no surprise" to deal with his or her own beliefs, perspectives, worldviews, feelings—everything that makes us living, breathing human beings and that necessarily affects *how* we read the texts we read? Surely, however difficult it may be, it is best to make the effort, suspending our own belief or disbelief, to do what we can to temporarily put aside *our own* religious orientation, in order to submit ourselves *to the poem,* allowing it to do *its* aesthetic work *before* we do *it* the Procrustean injustice of imposing on the text our own doctrinal convictions, or lack thereof. Once we have given the poem breathing room, and allowed it to possess us, we are free to bring to bear whatever we believe likely to illuminate the text. But illumination is not the same as resolution. Even after devoting much thought and analysis to a poem as seemingly simple as "Apparently with no surprise," some readers may find *themselves* surprised to discover that, far from plucking out the heart of the poem's mystery, they have generated as many questions as answers. But ending in ambiguity is not what I take to be the result of my own eclectic approach or what may make such an approach potentially useful to other readers, including, but hardly limited to, Dickinson scholars. Instead, I am interested in whatever seems useful in reaching the most plausible interpretation.

In seeking that most plausible reading, and specifically in terms of *approximating,* even if we can never attain, what E. D. Hirsch calls "objective interpretation," our primary Dickinson text summons up one final Wordsworth comparison. I have in mind a poem to which Emily Dickinson would have been, and perhaps *was,* as Richard Gravil has suggested, particularly attracted for reasons both formal and thematic (the

---

3. Anderson, *Emily Dickinson's Poetry,* 178.

tension between Innocence and Experience).[4] Like so many (about two dozen) of Dickinson's poems on this theme, Wordsworth's "A Slumber did my spirit seal" also consists of two quatrains in ballad stanza, alternating iambic tetrameters and trimeters—though here with both odd and even lines rhymed:

> A slumber did my spirit seal;
> I had no human fears:
> She seemed a thing that could not feel
> The touch of earthly years.
>
> No motion has she now, no force;
> She neither hears nor sees;
> Rolled round in earth's diurnal course,
> With rocks, and stones, and trees.

Perhaps the best known and certainly the least susceptible to conclusive interpretation of the so-called Lucy poems, "A slumber did my spirit seal" pitted two distinguished elder critics, Cleanth Brooks and F. W. Bateson, in a celebrated controversy that has continued to divide readers. Even before we get to the point of dispute, we notice many ironies in this little poem. A spiritual or imaginative slumber deludes the speaker into thinking his beloved an inanimate "thing" that "seemed" unable to "feel" the touch of earthly years. That was *Then*. *Now* that beloved's mortality, *her* entrance into the sleep of death, *awakens him* to a belated recognition of the pathos of mutability. Yet, since she died young, he was inadvertently *right*: she *did* "not feel / The touch of earthly years." Now, though she no longer feels at all (bereft of force, hearing, and sight), and has "no motion," she is caught up in a *greater* "motion" (the word epitomizing the Wordsworthian Sublime), in which she is "Rolled round in earth's diurnal course / With rocks, and stones, and trees."

So—and this is the crux of the Brooks-Bateson debate—is the poem a bleak, epitaphic recording of the finality of death, and of the stunned, elegiac anguish of the desolated lover? Or does it—with the final stanza's rolling sublimity, in which everything organic and inorganic is

---

4. Gravil, "Emily Dickinson's Imaginary Conversations," in *Romantic Dialogues: Anglo-American Continuities, 1776–1862*, 203.

swept up in an eternal recurrence—achieve a kind of animistic or pantheistic grandeur in which individual death is subsumed, with the "thing" the girl once "seemed" now revealed as truly elemental, part of a natural and cosmic cycle? Brooks stresses the lover's "agonized shock" at the dead girl's "horrible inertness," a passive state in which, "falling back into the clutter of things," she becomes as static and "inanimate" as they. "Caught up helplessly into the empty whirl of the earth," she is "touched by and held by earthly time in its most powerful and horrible image." At the other extreme, finding in the poem a "single mood" climaxing in the "pantheistic magnificence of the last two lines," Bateson asserts that the "vague living Lucy . . . is opposed to the grander dead-Lucy," even claiming that "Lucy is actually more alive now that she is dead, because she is now part of the life of Nature, and not just a human 'thing.'"[5] Though each interpretation is, perhaps, pushed a bit too far, both, antithetical though they are, seem valid readings of the poem—rather like the general theory of relativity and quantum mechanics, mutually incompatible yet equally valid. As my friends, having arrived at contradictory readings, concluded in the first response to my e-mailed copy of the Dickinson poem: "Go figure."

Though, verbally if not thematically, Wordsworth's is a richer, more complex poem than Dickinson's, it raises closely related, and perhaps equally irresolvable, issues. Some readers see "Apparently with no surprise" as a poem in which Dickinson or the dramatic speaker achieves "absolute detachment." Others see the poem as itself approving of that "Approving God." They may find Dickinson's vision too troubling to equate with that of Robert Browning's Pippa ("God's in his heaven, / All's right with the world"), but they are convinced that the beheading of the flower, and all the suffering and death of which that event may be a symbolic equivalent, are part of a divine Design, one that converts all "accidents" into ultimate "good."

Though I understand the intrinsic and extrinsic grounds for these alternative readings, and do not (any more than Einstein would) expect God to "intervene" in order to thwart the frost, the poem seems to me less a vindication of God than an indictment. But I remain aware that my interpretation may reflect not only what is objectively *there* in the poem, and what illumination may be found in the Dickinsonian

5. The conflict is documented and discussed in E. D. Hirsch's 1960 article "Objective Interpretation."

canon, but also my own experience and subjective beliefs. In retrospect, I am also conscious that I may have been selective in emphasizing *aspects* of that canon in seeking to support my interpretation. Along with poems and letters expressing religious doubt, resentment of her youthful religious instruction, denunciation not only of false preachers but of the hidden God, there are others supporting her assertion of, or at least hope for, a valid faith.

Emily Dickinson remained torn between what she intuited and what she inherited. As it was forcefully put sixty years ago, "all her instincts lead her to believe in the reality of God, and equally induce her to doubt the reality of the preposterous monster proposed to her by conventional religion," an orthodox religion "she finds both morally and intellectually repugnant." Though her God *was* Calvinist, and so more problematic than the benign God of the radical Deists, Dickinson would agree in part with Thomas Jefferson: "I can never join Calvin in addressing *his* God.... If ever a man worshipped a false God, he did.... [His] is not the god whom you and I acknowledge, the creator and benevolent governor of the world; but a daemon of malignant spirit. It would be more pardonable to believe in no God at all, than to blaspheme him by the atrocious attributes of Calvin."[6]

But a tension persists. Though dismissive of all institutional churches and creeds, Dickinson was nevertheless drawn to such preachers as Edward Everett Hale, Washington Gladden, and Wadsworth; and many poems reveal a woman eager for religious experience and, most obviously, haunted by the thought of immortality, her "Flood subject." On rare occasions, she put aside her innate skepticism and the recognition of her own finite limitations and ventured into religious certitudes. It is perhaps not surprising that some of these poems, seldom among her best, remain among her most popular. In one, frequently anthologized, the reclusive poet who "never saw" moor or sea, yet knew "how the Heather looks / And what a Billow be," extrapolates into theology:

> I never spoke with God
> Nor visited in Heaven—

---

6. The first comment is by Henry W. Wells, *Introduction to Emily Dickinson*, 152–56. Jefferson is quoted by Michael Buckley, S.J., *At the Origins of Modern Atheism* (1987); my source is Taylor, *A Secular Age*, 804n59.

> Yet certain am I of the spot
> As if the Checks were given— (1052)

Referring to this poem, Cynthia Griffin Wolff, resistant as always to the pious or at least quasi-orthodox side of Dickinson, concedes, "Clearly the 'wrestle' for faith was always active. Dickinson's best [religious] poetry may denounce God, but the dynamic of hope and despair seems always to have been at work within her." Like most thinking beings, and certainly every dialectical poet, Emily Dickinson was, as Hyatt Waggoner put it many years ago, "capable of entertaining, and taking seriously, various points of view, including even contradictory ones"—a point amplified in much of the critical work on this poet and demonstrated deftly in McIntosh's study of Dickinson's art of nimble believing.[7]

Go figure. *In* figuring, we are free to seek help in external, contextual evidence—not only in a writer's cultural milieu and chosen genre but also in his or her personal preoccupations, given that related poems, letters, and similar documents may reveal authorial intention. But while we can refuse to accept the more stringent restrictions prescribed by the theory of "the intentional fallacy," we must attend, above all, to the ambiguities inherent in the particular poem's perspectives and tonalities. That is what Brooks and Bateson did in reading "A slumber did my spirit seal," and I've tried, however widening the gyre of context in which I found myself turning, not to lose sight of that primary responsibility to the text itself. In doing so, I find it impossible to approve of that "Approving God" and difficult if not quite impossible to believe that Emily Dickinson did. James McIntosh would agree. His insightful study demonstrates that Dickinson, in the words of one reviewer, "was much more than an ever-adolescent angry rebel trying to subvert the religious oppression of benighted Amherst neighbors." Nevertheless, McIntosh cites "Apparently with no surprise" as illustrating "the staying power of her preoccupation" with "God's heartless omnipotence," a source of dismay "into her last years." And since, as the poem emphasizes, the things of nature that attract us have "no capacity for suffering and empathy," and it is only

---

7. Wolff, *Emily Dickinson*, 586n3; Waggoner, *American Poets from the Puritans to the Present*, 204.

humans that "can be shocked at the injustice of a world of death," we are "lonely as well as bereft in the created universe."[8]

Of course, even when we combine the most exhaustive intrinsic scrutiny with the mutual illumination provided by other poems and related letters; even when we try to repossess a poem through an empathetic reexperiencing of the authorial inner life that seems expressed in the text, we may still, in venturing an interpretation, only approximate an absolutely definitive reading. Nevertheless, there is a considerable *difference* between utter verbal indeterminacy (the deconstructionist's free play of *infinitely* diverse readings) and a reasonably determinate meaning—even if, in some instances, the latter will prove to be a meaning *determinately ambiguous.*

It is the difference, we might say (rounding back to our initial discussion), between blind, random chance and reasonable Design. And, unless we succumb to the related theories of the "death of the author" (a demise itself related to the Nietzschean Death of God) and of an infinite and often incompatible play of linguistic signification, there is one final "difference." Though we should always heed D. H. Lawrence's memorable warning to "trust the tale and not the teller," the teller's intention is often achieved *in* the tale. Even such radical linguistic skeptics as Nietzsche and Derrida do not dismiss that point. The latter, founder of deconstruction, refers to authorial intention as an "indispensable guardrail . . . protecting" readings from the wilder excesses associated with his notorious term "freeplay."[9]

Nor would Nietzsche—for whom "there *are* no facts, only interpretations"—equate "freeplay" with anarchy. I am once again quoting *The Will to Power* (§481), a posthumously assembled text, in which he also insists that "Truth" is not something "there" to be discovered, "but something that must be created" (§552), and that, were "optics," or perspectives on the world, to be "deducted," nothing "would remain over" (§567). Such passages are frequently cited by neopragmatist philosophers and postmodern literary critics who find their antifoundationalist roots in Nietzschean perspectivism, with its tonic corrective to attempts to describe things as they "really" were, or are. Yet in *On the*

---

8. McIntosh, *Nimble Believing*, 46–47. The comment of the reviewer (Cynthia L. Hallen, in the *Emily Dickinson Journal*) appears as a blurb on the back cover.
9. Derrida, *Of Grammatology*, 158.

Genealogy of Morals, in one of the pivotal passages in which he advised his fellow philosophers to "guard against" such absolutist "snares," Nietzsche insisted on *two* points. His usual "optical" emphasis—"There is *only* a perspective seeing, *only* a perspective knowing"—was amplified by the following significant addendum, still optical but expansive: "and the *more* affects we allow to speak about this one thing, the *more* eyes, different eyes, we can use to observe one thing, the more complete will our 'concept' of this thing, our 'objectivity', be" (*Genealogy* 3.12). In short, the more points of view we bring to bear, the more integrated and plausible our interpretation will be. Resembling what the physicist Niels Bohr called "complementarity" (discussed in Chapter 2), this Nietzschean "multi-perspectivism" is a cumulative attempt to *approximate* a never fully attainable "objectivity," in the process achieving a genuine advance in understanding, a convergence of different points of view producing a fuller and deeper "seeing."

It should be added that, when it comes to the interpretation of *texts,* Nietzsche can at times turn sternly "objectivist." For then, instead of dealing either with metaphysical "Truth" or with *things,* "natural" objects in the universe, he is dealing with artifacts produced *by* human will, and presumably also accessible *to* it. At such times he calls, as the former philologist he was, *not* for interpretive creativity but for close attention to what is there, actually present in the text. The "art of reading well," he says in *The Antichrist* §52, entails "being able to read off a fact *without* falsifying it by interpretation," or (as he puts it in *The Will to Power* §79) "without interposing an interpretation."

But if it is all a matter of "optics," if there *are* no facts, only interpretations, what can Nietzsche possibly mean in such uncharacteristic passages? What he means, I think, is that, if we are "good" readers, we submit ourselves to the text, permitting what is there, shaped by the human will of the writer, to come through without individual receivers *precipitously* imposing on it an interpretation either arbitrarily subjective or distorted so as to serve one's own agenda. Nietzschean perspectivism does not imply that any interpretation is as good as any other, even in the case of texts as cryptic as many of Emily Dickinson's poems and letters. The fact that there will be, and *should* be, many possible points of view does not by itself make them equally legitimate. We will want to deploy whatever critical approaches seem fruitful and to take into account as many aspects of a text as we can before we settle on (or settle *for*) an interpretation that is both plausible and engaging.

But in even the most adventurous reading, the text should not be reduced to a Lockean tabula rasa on which we merely do our *own* writing. All minds are perspectival; but only the ideological mind—limited to its own perspective, closed off from the claims of others—will forcefully impose itself on a text, even "deforming" it, unconcerned about whether or not one is being "faithful or unfaithful" to the author.[10]

⎯⎯

In the case of an aesthetic artifact such as a poem, then, we are dealing not with a metaphysical hypothesis or a thing of nature but with a work of *art:* something created and essentially if not entirely shaped (for, finally, interpretation *must* play a role) by a demonstrably existent Designer. At times, as every writer can testify, language may exert a will of its own, and the text will escape the "indispensable guardrail" of authorial intention. But, for the most part, the ordered, beautiful thing we call a poem is directed by a Designer who "steers" it—in the Thomistic image earlier noted (*Summa Theologica,* I.2.3)—"as an archer does an arrow." The guiding Intelligence and Celestial Craftsman whom Aquinas says "we call God" we call, in this aesthetic context, by *another* name for a creator. In this case, it is a name proudly claimed by Emily Dickinson herself; and no one who has been pierced by *this* archer's bolts of melody can have any doubt that—in her chosen dramatization of her lifelong wrestling with God, her nimble dialectic between belief and disbelief—"This was a *Poet.*"

10. Michel Foucault, here quoted on how one should read Nietzsche himself: "The only valid tribute to thought such as Nietzsche's is precisely to use it, to deform it, to make it groan and protest. And if commentators then say that I am being faithful or unfaithful to Nietzsche, that is of absolutely no interest" ("Nietzsche, Genealogy, History," in *Power/Knowledge: Selected Interviews and Other Writings, 1972–1977,* 53–54).

Appendix

Derek Mahon's "A Disused Shed in Co. Wexford"

The allusion to the eighth chapter of Paul's Epistle to the Romans, the empathy Emily Dickinson conveys when it comes to the flowers she cherished and tried to protect, as well as the implicitly *human* relevance of what happens to those flowers evoke several texts, most memorably, for me, this celebrated poem by the Northern Irish poet Derek Mahon.

A Disused Shed in Co. Wexford
> Let them not forget us, the weak souls among the asphodels
> *Seferis*—"Mythistorema"

Even now there are places where a thought might grow—
Peruvian mines, worked out and abandoned
To a slow clock of condensation,
An echo trapped for ever, and a flutter
Of wildflowers in the lift-shaft,
Indian compounds where the wind dances
And a door bangs with diminished confidence,
Lime crevices behind rippling rainbarrels,
Dog corners for bone burials;

And, in a disused shed in Co. Wexford,
Deep in the grounds of a burnt-out hotel,
Among the bathtubs and the washbasins
A thousand mushrooms crowd to a keyhole.

This is the one star in their firmament
Or frames a star within a star.
What should they do there but desire?
So many days beyond the rhododendrons
With the world waltzing in its bowl of cloud,
They have learnt patience and silence
Listening to the rooks querulous in the high wood.

They have been waiting for us in a foetor
Of vegetable sweat since civil war days,
Since the gravel-crunching, interminable departure
of the expropriated mycologist.
He never came back, and light since then
Is a keyhole rusting gently after rain.
Spiders have spun, flies dusted to mildew
And once a day, perhaps, they have heard something—
A trickle of masonry, a shout from the blue
Or a lorry changing gear at the end of the lane.

There have been deaths, the pale flesh flaking
Into the earth that nourished it;
And nightmares, born of these and the grim
Dominion of stale air and rank moisture.
Those nearest the door grow strong—
"Elbow room! Elbow room!"
The rest, dim in a twilight of crumbling
Utensils and broken flower-pots, groaning
For their deliverance, have been so long
Expectant that there is left only the posture.

A half century, without visitors, in the dark—
Poor preparation for the cracking lock
And creak of hinges. Magi, moonmen,
Powdery prisoners of the old regime,
Web-throated, stalked like triffids, racked by drought
And insomnia, only the ghost of a scream
At the flash-bulb firing squad we wake them with
Shows there is life yet in their feverish forms.
Grown beyond nature now, soft food for worms,

They lift frail heads in gravity and good faith.

They are begging us, you see, in their wordless way,
To do something, to speak on their behalf
Or at least not to close the door again.
Lost people of Treblinka and Pompeii!
"Save us, save us," they seem to say,
"Let the god not abandon us
Who have come so far in darkness and in pain.
We too had our lives to live.
You with your light meter and relaxed itinerary,
Let not our naive labours have been in vain!"

The poem was written after Bloody Sunday, the day in 1972 when British paratroopers fired into a crowd of Catholic protesters, initiating the most violent stage of the Troubles in the North. Mahon wants his readers to associate that event with the Partition of Ireland back in 1922 and the subsequent Civil War. His deeply humane, obliquely political poem is considered by many (general readers and critics alike) to be the single greatest lyric to have come out of Ireland since the death of Yeats—high praise, considering the quality of the poetry produced over the past three decades by Ireland's preeminent contemporary poet, Seamus Heaney.

Mahon's "disused shed" is found on the grounds of "a burnt-out hotel," burned down during "civil war days." Since then, the mushrooms in that long-abandoned shed "have been waiting for us"—waiting precisely "a half-century, without visitors, in the dark." Registering loss, violence, and suffering in a world groaning for deliverance, Mahon's empathetic heart goes out to these neglected mushrooms: shut-ins he tenderly and persuasively makes emblematic of all those who have suffered and struggled in solitude, abandoned and dispossessed. Surely poet and gardener Emily Dickinson, whose key term *Circumference* incorporated all forms of life, human, natural, and spiritual, and whose empathetic imagination was expressed in poems she struggled with in solitude, albeit self-chosen, would have read Derek Mahon's poem with a shock of recognition.

Mahon begins with various "places" where a "thought might," almost organically, "grow." Those he mentions, before he homes in on the precisely placed disused shed, adumbrate his themes of exploitation, abandonment, and the slow passage of time. "Even now" there are, in his opening example, Peruvian silver mines, once teeming with natives forced to labor in the darkness by exploitative Spanish conquistadores, mines now "worked out and abandoned / To a slow clock of condensation, / An echo trapped for ever." The ticking off of these hard cs is balanced by fluid ls, fricative fs, and short is: "a flutter / Of wildflowers in the lift-shaft"—a haunting delicacy reminiscent of Keats's goddess of Autumn, her "hair soft lifted by the winnowing wind." From these "Indian compounds" the Indians themselves have long since vanished; now only the "wind dances," and a door bangs "with diminished confidence." The challenge (for Mahon as for late summer's oven-bird in Robert Frost's poem of that title) "is what to make of a diminished thing."

The second stanza locates the shed "Deep in the grounds of a burnt-out hotel," where a "thousand mushrooms" crowd to a keyhole: the "one star in their firmament," the "star" of that keyhole framing within it an actual evening star. "What should they do there but desire?" Having survived "so many days" beyond even the evergreen rhododendrons, while the great world waltzes gaily and unconcerned in its amphitheater of cloud, the mushrooms "have learnt patience and silence / Listening to the rooks querulous in the high wood." With the concealed effortlessness of an art great enough to induce the Coleridgean suspension of disbelief that constitutes poetic faith, Mahon has brought us, amazingly enough, into the otherwise inexpressible, unconscious world of abandoned mushrooms, vegetative forms made as hauntingly real as the housed ghosts in Walter de la Mare's "The Listeners."

In fact, they have been "waiting for us"—waiting for those who break into their shed in the penultimate stanza and for those of "us" who read Mahon's poem when it first appeared in 1972—for "a half century," ever since "civil war days." Back then, in 1922, the botanist who tended to them (an "expropriated mycologist") was removed from those chores among the fungi, called to duty in the Irish Civil War. The mushrooms, always listening, mark a "gravel-crunching" departure that proved to be "interminable." Presumably killed in action, he "never came back, and light since then / Is a keyhole rusting gently after rain." Equally gently, and elegiacally, the years are telescoped. Through decades, while "spiders have spun, flies dusted to mildew," the abandoned mushrooms have survived in their constricted shed, isolated and forgotten. Still, clinging tenaciously to their pitiably minimal existence, they listen in the darkness, and "once a day, perhaps, they have heard something— / A trickle of masonry, a shout from the blue / Or a lorry changing gear at the end of the lane."

Not all these auditors have survived the half century they have been patiently waiting. "There have been deaths, the pale flesh flaking / Into the earth," and "nightmares," engendered by that decay and by the nourishing and receiving earth. In this "grim / Dominion of stale air and rank moisture," the mushrooms nearest the door "grow strong," struggling for their own mini-dominion: "Elbow room! Elbow room!"[1] Even in the claustrophobic shed-world there are Darwinian winners and losers, the aggressive and the near-defeated. Those in the mushroom colony nearest the door grow strong;

> The rest, dim in a twilight of crumbling
> Utensils and broken flower-pots, groaning
> For their deliverance, have been so long
> Expectant that there is left only the posture.

In this evocation of diminished but still stubborn hope, and of sheer survival among the crumbling and broken detritus, Mahon combines a question and answer from Paul's Epistle to the Romans. "Who shall deliver me from the body of this death?" the Apostle asks (7:24), adding, in the next chapter, the haunting recognition of sorrow *and* imminent redemption Cardinal Schönborn fell back upon in his Christian resolution of the Problem of Suffering: "For we know that the whole creation groaneth and travaileth in pain until now" (8:22). The mushrooms, less confident than the apostle, or the cardinal, have been "so long / Expectant" that they retain only the *tendency* to believe in their deliverance, only a "posture" or anticipatory attitude. Yet they remain poignantly open to that equilibrium of faith and tragic realization expressed in the

---

1. King John, Shakespeare's poisoned and dying wretch of a monarch, cries out in the final scene of the play, "Now my soul hath elbow-room" (*King John*, 5.7.28). But Mahon's welcome note of jocularity is much likelier an echo of the exuberant exclamation given by Arthur Cuiterman to America's expansive Kentucky frontiersman: "'Elbow room!' cried Daniel Boone."

final line of Wordsworth's "Elegiac Stanzas," a poem Emily Dickinson twice quotes (*L* 449, 510) in her letters. "Not without hope we suffer and we mourn." John Polkinghorne may have had in mind Wordsworth as well as Saint Paul when he observed, in *Science and Providence*, "The mystery of suffering is great, but so is the mystery of persisting hope."[2]

The moment of the mushrooms' partial deliverance comes with a violent cracking of hinges and burst of light. Stunned by the tourists' cameras, by "the flash-bulb firing squad we wake them with," they reveal that "there is life yet in their feverish forms. / Grown beyond nature now, soft food for worms, / They lift frail heads in gravity and good faith." "Tears" are inherent in "things," Virgil tells us, since "mortality touches the heart" (*Aeneid* 1.462). That heartbreakingly vulnerable last line of Mahon's penultimate stanza is at once richly alliterative, paradoxical (frail heads *lifted* in *gravity*), and a tribute to inextinguishable hope: a kind of "Dickinsonian" resilience even in the face of loss.

What more is there to say? Yet Mahon, in the final stanza, chances overreaching by incorporating the marginal life of these forgotten mushrooms, neglected since the days of the Irish Civil War, within a larger moral and historical background of catastrophe: the human tragedy of Treblinka, the natural disaster of Pompeii. The mushrooms, silent auditors till now, are given speech in the final lines—"wordless" speech in the obvious sense that the words are supplied (as in the earlier and amusing cry for "Elbow room!") by the author. Risking all, specifically the danger that his poem's pathos might sink into bathos, Mahon pulls it off, a rhetorical triumph whose glory is humbled by its Wordsworthian attention to the lowly and dispossessed and by an empathy and in-feeling reminiscent of Emily Dickinson and of her favorite Romantic poet, John Keats:

> They are begging us, you see, in their wordless way,
> To do something, to speak on their behalf
> Or at least not to close the door again.

They are begging all of us who read and permit ourselves to be possessed by this uncanny poem to "do" something, *any*thing; or, if we fail

2. Polkinghorne, *Science and Providence: God's Interaction with the World*, 64.

to *act*, to *say* something, to "speak on their behalf." At the very least, they plead with us not to repeat their abandonment, "not to close the door again." For a moment the mushrooms metamorphose into the victims of the modern Holocaust or of ancient Vesuvius, appealing directly to *us*—we mobile tourists and casual recorders of suffering—to bring them salvation, if only in the form of tragic remembrance. Mahon's epigraph is from the Greek poet George Seferis, a Nobel laureate who died the year before this poem was written: "Let them not forget us, the weak souls among the asphodels." Embodying the return of the repressed, those souls, in Mahon's conscience-stricken expansion, include all those who, throughout human history, have struggled and suffered—isolated, abandoned, forgotten, deprived, dispossessed, slaughtered—in a world groaning for deliverance:

> Lost people of Treblinka and Pompeii!
> "Save us, save us," they seem to say,
> "Let the god not abandon us
> Who have come so far in darkness and in pain.
> We too had our lives to live.
> You with your light meter and relaxed itinerary,
> Let not our naive labours have been in vain!"

In *Crediting Poetry*, his 1995 Nobel Prize acceptance speech, Seamus Heaney repeatedly connected the Troubles in Northern Ireland with a poem by his Nobel predecessor W. B. Yeats. The poem was "The Stare's Nest by My Window," Yeats's great invocation, during the original Irish Civil War, for "the honey-bees"—emblematic of natural sweetness, light, and harmony—to "come build in the empty house of the stare [starling]," constructing amid manmade destruction, amid the civil war's embittered "enmities" and desolation. Concluding his lecture, Heaney turns to lyric poetry's "musically satisfying order of sound," a satisfaction he finds in the repetition of Yeats's refrain, "with its tone of supplication, its pivots of strength in the words 'build' and 'house' and its acknowledgement of dissolution in the word 'empty,'" as well as in "the triangle of forces held in equilibrium by the triple rhyme of 'fantasies' and 'enmities' and 'honey-bees.'"

What Heaney says in the peroration of his address, celebrating the "means" by which "Yeats's work does what the necessary poetry always does," applies as well to "A Disused Shed in Co. Wexford," for

Mahon's no less humane and musically satisfying poem also pivots between strength and supplication, with the mushrooms' endurance capped by their petition, "Let not our naive labours have been in vain." This, as Heaney says in conclusion, is to

> touch the base of our sympathetic nature while taking in at the same time the unsympathetic reality of the world to which that nature is constantly exposed. The form of the poem . . . is crucial to poetry's power to do the thing which always is and always will be to poetry's credit: the power to persuade that vulnerable part of our consciousness of its rightness in spite of the evidence of wrongness all around it, the power to remind us that we are hunters and gatherers of values, that our very solitudes and distresses are creditable, in so far as they too are an earnest of our veritable human being.[3]

Wordsworth, an abiding influence in the work of Heaney, informs both these poems, Yeats's and Mahon's, poems that focus on seemingly insignificant processes of nature: plangent labors, *and values*, persisting even amid profound distress. William Hazlitt rightly said of Wordsworth, the "most original" poet of the age, "No one has shown the same imagination in raising trifles to importance." It was his "peculiar genius," Walter Pater added a half century later, "to open out the soul of apparently little or familiar things," especially the small, neglected, humblest details of the natural world. I have already associated that observation with the poetry of Emily Dickinson.[4]

In opening out the soul of these "apparently little or familiar things," poets like Wordsworth, Emily Dickinson, and Derek Mahon are able to move the sympathetic human heart in ways that help account for the emotional impact on us of mother birds and honeybees, of beheaded flowers, even of neglected but persevering mushrooms. The parent text may be Wordsworth's Intimations Ode, a poem of loss and recompense offering, in its final lines, the humanizing consolation attending our empathetic response, emotional and cognitive, to that deeper, truer life surviving beneath, and above, what man has made of man:

---

3. *Crediting Poetry: The Nobel Lecture*, 53–54.
4. Hazlitt, *The Spirit of the Age*, in *Complete Works*, 11:88; Pater, "Wordsworth," 48.

Thanks to the human heart by which we live,
Thanks to its tenderness, its joys and fears,
To me the meanest flower that blows can give
Thoughts that do often lie too deep for tears.[5]

5. "A Disused Shed in Co. Wexford" reprinted by kind permission of the author and The Gallery Press, Loughcrew, Oldcastle, County Meath, Ireland, from *Collected Poems* (1999).

Bibliography

Abrams, M. H. *Natural Supernaturalism: Tradition and Revolution in Romantic Literature.* New York: W. W. Norton, 1984.

Allsop, Thomas. *Letters, Conversations, and Recollections of S. T. Coleridge.* 2 vols. London, 1836.

Anderson, Charles R. *Emily Dickinson's Poetry: Stairway to Surprise.* Garden City, N.Y.: Doubleday Anchor, 1966.

Anonymous [perhaps William Gifford]. "Wordsworth's White Doe." *Quarterly Review* 14 (1815).

Aristotle. *Physics.* Translated with commentary by Hippocrates G. Apostle. Bloomington: Indiana University Press, 1969.

Arnold, Matthew. *The Poems of Matthew Arnold.* Edited by Kenneth Allott. London: Longmans, 1965.

———. *Poetry and Criticism of Matthew Arnold.* Edited by A. Dwight Culler. Boston: Houghton Mifflin, Riverside, 1961.

Augustine, Saint. *Concerning the City of God against the Pagans.* Translated by Henry Bettenson. 1972. Reprint, London: Penguin, 1984.

Baggini, Julian, and Jeremy Stranghorne, eds. *What Philosophers Think.* London: Continuum, 2003.

Baird, Robert M., and Stuart E. Rosenbaum, eds. *Intelligent Design: Science or Religion? Critical Perspectives.* Amherst, N.Y.: Prometheus Books, 2007.

Barker, Juliet. *Wordsworth.* New York: Harper Collins, 2005.

Barrett, Elizabeth. "On Mr. Haydon's Portrait of Mr. Wordsworth on Helvellyn." *Athenaeum* (October 29, 1842): 932.

Baym, Nina. *American Women of Letters and the Nineteenth-Century Sciences: Styles of Affiliation.* New Brunswick: Rutgers University Press, 2002.

Begley, Sharon. "Can God Love Darwin, Too?" *Newsweek,* September 17, 2007, p. 45.

Behe, Michael. *Darwin's Black Box: The Biochemical Challenge to Evolution.* New York: Free Press, 1996.

Bennett, Paula. *Emily Dickinson: Woman Poet.* Iowa City: University of Iowa, 1990.

———. *My Life a Loaded Gun.* Urbana and Chicago: University of Illinois Press, 1990.

Blake, William. *The Poetry and Prose of William Blake.* Edited by David Erdman with commentary by Harold Bloom. Berkeley and Los Angeles: University of California Press, 1965.

Bloom, Harold. *Genius: A Mosaic of One Hundred Exemplary Creative Minds.* New York: Warner, 2002.

———. *Where Shall Wisdom Be Found?* New York: Riverhead Books, 2004.

Boethius. *The Consolation of Philosophy.* London: Penguin Classics, 1999.

Bogan, Louise. "A Mystical Poet." In *Emily Dickinson: Three Views,* 27–34. Amherst: Amherst College Press, 1960.

Brantley, Richard. *Experience and Faith: The Late-Romantic Imagination of Emily Dickinson.* New York: Palgrave, Macmillan, 2004.

Brockman, John, ed. *Intelligent Thought: Science versus the Intelligent Design Movement.* New York: Vintage Books, 2006.

Brontë, Emily. *The Complete Poems of Emily Jane Brontë.* Edited by C. W. Hatfield. New York: Columbia University Press, 1941.

———. *Wuthering Heights.* New York: Norton, 1972.

Brooks, Cleanth; R. W. B. Lewis; and Robert Penn Warren, eds. *American Literature: The Makers and the Making.* New York: St. Martin's, 1973.

Browne, Ray B. *Mark Twain's Quarrel with Heaven.* New York: College and University Press, 1970.

Cameron, Sharon. *Lyric Time: Dickinson and the Limitations of Genre.* Baltimore: Johns Hopkins University Press, 1979.

Chesterton, G. K. *The Everlasting Man.* New York, 1925.

Cole, Phyllis. *Mary Moody Emerson and the Origins of Transcendentalism: A Family History.* New York: Oxford University Press, 1998.

Coleridge, Samuel Taylor. *Aids to Reflection* (1825). *Collected Coleridge,* vol. 9, ed. John Beer. London: Routledge and Kegan Paul, 1993.

Collins, Francis. S. *The Language of God: A Scientist Presents Evidence for Belief.* New York: Free Press, 2007.

Conway, Moncure Daniel. *Emerson at Home and Abroad.* Boston: James R. Osgood, 1882.

Coyne, Jerry A. "The Great Mutator." *New Republic,* June 18, 2007, pp. 38–44.

Darwin, Charles. *The Autobiography of Charles Darwin.* Edited by Nora Barlow. New York: Harcourt Brace and Co, 1958.

———. *The Correspondence of Charles Darwin.* Vol. 6. Edited by Frederick Burckhardt and Sydney Smith. Cambridge: Cambridge University Press, 1990.

———. *Darwin: A Norton Critical Edition,* 3rd ed. Edited by Philip Appleman. New York: Norton, 2001.

———. *The Life and Letters of Charles Darwin.* Edited by Francis Darwin. 2 vols. 1887. Reprint, New York: Basic Books, 1959.

Dawkins, Richard. *The God Delusion.* Boston, New York: Houghton Mifflin, 2006.

Dennett, Daniel C. *Breaking the Spell.* London: Penguin, 2007.

Derrida, Jacques. *Of Grammatology.* Translated by Gayatri Spivak. Baltimore: Johns Hopkins University Press, 1976.

Dickinson, Susan Gilbert. "Miss Emily Dickinson of Amherst." *Springfield Republican* 18 (May 1886). Reprinted in *Emily Dickinson's Reception in the 1890s: A Documentary History,* ed. Willis J. Buckingham, appendix A. Pittsburgh: University of Pittsburgh Press, 1989.

Diehl, Joanne Feit. *Dickinson and Romantic Imagination.* Princeton: Princeton University Press, 1981.

Donoghue, Denis. *Emily Dickinson.* Minneapolis: University of Minnesota Press, 1969.

Dowd, Michael. *Thank God for Evolution! How the Marriage of Science and Religion Will Transform Your Life and Our World.* Tulsa: Council Oaks Books, 2007.

D'Souza, Dinesh. *What's So Great about Christianity.* Washington, D.C.: Regnery, 2007.

Dulles, Avery Cardinal. "God and Evolution." *First Things: A Journal of Religion, Culture, and Public Life,* October 2007.

Dyson, Freeman. "Working for the Revolution." *New York Review of Books,* October 27, 2007, pp. 45–47.

Eberwein, Jane Donahue. *Dickinson: Strategies of Limitation*. Amherst: University of Massachusetts Press, 1985.

———. "'Is Immortality True?': Salvaging Faith in an Age of Upheaval." In Vivian R. Pollak, ed., *A Historical Guide to Emily Dickinson*, 67–102. Oxford: Oxford University Press, 2004.

Edwards, Jonathan. *The Justice of God in the Damnation of Sinners*. 1734. Cornwall: Meadow Books, 2007.

Ehrman, Bart D. *God's Problem: How the Bible Fails to Answer Our Most Important Question—Why We Suffer*. New York: HarperCollins, 2008.

———. *Misquoting Jesus: The Story behind Who Changed the Bible and Why*. New York: HarperCollins, 2005.

Einstein, Albert. "To the Royal Academy on Newton's Bicentennial." Speech, March 1927. www.pbs.org/wgbh/nova/newton/einstein.html.

———. "What I Believe." In *The World As I See It*. New York: Philosophical Library, 1949. Audio version: www.yu.edu/libraries/digital_library/einstein/credo.html.

Emerson, Ralph Waldo. *Emerson: Essays and Lectures*. Edited by Joel Porte. New York: Library of America, 1983.

———. *The Journals and Miscellaneous Notebooks of Ralph Waldo Emerson*. Edited by William H. Gilman et al. 16 vols. Cambridge: Harvard University Press, 1960–1982.

———. *The Letters of Ralph Waldo Emerson*. Edited by Ralph L. Rusk and Eleanor M. Tilton. 10 vols. New York: Columbia University Press, 1939–1995.

———. "Threnody." In *Emerson: Collected Poems and Translations*, ed. Harold Bloom and Paul Kane. New York: Library of America, 1994.

Farr, Judith. *The Gardens of Emily Dickinson*. Cambridge: Harvard University Press, 2004.

———. *The Passion of Emily Dickinson*. Cambridge: Harvard University Press, 1992.

———, ed. *Emily Dickinson: A Collection of Critical Essays*. Upper Saddle River, N.J.: Prentice-Hall, 1996.

Fichte, Johann Gottlieb. *The Vocation of Man*. 1800. Translated by Roderick M. Chisholm. Indianapolis: Bobbs-Merrill, 1956.

Fiddes, Paul. *The Creative Suffering of God*. Oxford: Clarendon Press, 1992.

Foucault, Michel. *Power/Knowledge: Selected Interviews and Other Writings, 1972–1977.* New York: Pantheon, 1980.

Franklin, Benjamin. *Poor Richard's Almanack.* 1758. Reprinted in *Autobiography, Poor Richard, and Later Writings.* . . . New York: Library of America, 1997.

Frost, Robert. *The Poetry of Robert Frost.* New York: Holt, Rinehart, and Winston, 1969.

Gingerich, Owen. *God's Universe.* Cambridge: Harvard University Press, 2007.

———. "Science and Religion: Are They Compatible?" 2001. Reprinted in *Science and Religion: Are They Compatible?* ed. Paul Kurtz, 51–66. Amherst, N.Y.: Prometheus Books, 2003.

Goldberg, Michelle. *Kingdom Coming: The Rise of Christian Nationalism.* New York: Norton, 2006.

Gould, Stephen Jay. *The Richness of Life: The Essential Stephen Jay Gould,* ed. Stephen Rose. New York: Norton, 2007.

Gravil, Richard. *Romantic Dialogues: Anglo-American Continuities 1776–1862.* New York: St. Martin's Press, 2000.

Green, John C. *The Faith Factor: How Religion Influences American Elections.* New York: Praeger, 2007.

Greene, Brian. *The Elegant Universe: Superstrings, Hidden Dimensions, and the Quest for the Ultimate Theory.* New York: Vintage Books, 2000.

Guthrie, James R. "Darwinian Dickinson: The Scandalous Rise and Noble Fall of the Common Clover." *Emily Dickinson Journal* 16 (Spring 2007): 73–91.

Habegger, Alfred. *My Wars Are Laid Away in Books: The Life of Emily Dickinson.* New York: Random House, 2001.

Hardy, Thomas. *Thomas Hardy: The Complete Poems.* London: Macmillan, 1976.

Harris, Sam. *The End of Faith.* New York: Norton, 2005.

———. *Letter to a Christian Nation.* New York: Knopf, 2006.

Haught, John F. *Deeper than Darwin: The Prospect for Religion in an Age of Evolution.* Boulder: Westview Press, 2003.

———. *God after Darwin: A Theology of Evolution.* 2d ed. Boulder: Westview Press, 2007.

———. *God and the New Atheism: A Critical Response to Dawkins, Harris, and Hitchens.* Louisville: Westminster John Knox Press, 2008.

Hawthorne, Nathaniel. *The English Notebooks.* Edited by Randall Stewart. New York: Modern Language Association of America, 1941.

Hazlitt, William. *The Complete Works of William Hazlitt,* ed. P. P. Howe. Vol. 11. London: Dent, 1930–1934.

Heaney, Seamus. *Crediting Poetry: The Nobel Lecture.* New York: Farrar Straus Giroux, 1995.

———. Introduction to *Essential Wordsworth.* New York: HarperCollins, 1988.

Hecht, Jennifer Michael. *Doubt: A History: The Great Doubters and Their Legacy of Innovation from Socrates and Jesus to Thomas Jefferson and Emily Dickinson.* San Francisco: HarperCollins, 2003.

Hedges, Chris. *American Fascists: The Christian Right and the War on America.* New York: Simon and Schuster, 2008.

———. *I Don't Believe in Atheists.* New York and London: Free Press, 2008.

Heisenberg, Werner. *Encounters with Einstein.* Princeton: Princeton University Press, 1989.

Henig, Robin Marantz. "Darwin's God." *New York Times Magazine,* March 4, 2007, pp. 33–43, 58, 62, 77–78, 85.

Hick, John. *Evil and the God of Love.* New York: Harper and Row, 1978.

Hirsch, E. D. "Objective Interpretation." 1960. Reprinted in his *Validity in Interpretation,* 463–79. New Haven: Yale University Press, 1967.

Hitchens, Christopher. "The Boy Who Lived." Review of *Harry Potter and the Deathly Hollows. New York Times Book Review,* August 12, 2007, pp. 1–2, 10–11.

———. *God Is Not Great: How Religion Poisons Everything.* New York: Twelve / Warner, 2007.

Holt, Jim. "Beyond Belief." *New York Times Book Review* (October 22, 2006): 12–13.

Hooker, Joseph. *Life and Letters of Joseph Dalton Hooker.* 2 vols. Edited by Leonard Huxley. London: Murray, 1918.

Hopkins, Gerard Manley. *The Poems of Gerard Manley Hopkins.* 4th ed. Edited by W. H. Gardner and N. H. MacKenzie. Oxford: Oxford Paperbacks, 1967.

Housman, A. E. *The Collected Poems of A. E. Housman.* New York, Chicago, San Francisco: Holt, Rinehart and Winston, 1965.

Huberman, Jack, ed. *The Quotable Atheist.* New York: Nation Books, 2007.

Hume, David. *Dialogues Concerning Natural Religion*. 1789. Reprinted with an introduction by Kenneth A. Richman. New York: Barnes and Noble, 2006.

Huxley, T. H. *Evolution and Ethics*. New York: D. Appleton and Co, 1896.

Ignatieff, Michael. *Berlin: A Life*. New York: Henry Holt and Co., 1998.

Isaacson, Walter. *Einstein: His Life and Universe*. New York: Simon and Schuster, 2007.

John Paul II, Pope. "Truth Cannot Contradict Truth." Address to Pontifical Academy of Sciences, October 22, 1996. www.christusrex.org/www1/pope/vise10–23-96.html.

Johnson, Thomas H. *Emily Dickinson: An Interpretive Biography*. New York: Atheneum, 1967.

Kant, Immanuel. *Critique of Pure Reason*. Translated and edited by Paul Guyer and Allen W. Wood. 1st ed., 1781. 2d ed., 1787. Cambridge: Cambridge University Press, 1998.

Kaufmann, Walter. *Nietzsche: Philosopher, Psychologist, Antichrist*. 4th ed. Princeton: Princeton University Press, 1974.

Keats, John. *Letters of John Keats*. 2 vols. Edited by Hyder E. Rollins. Cambridge: Harvard University Press, 1958.

———. *The Poems of John Keats*. Edited by Jack Stillinger. Cambridge: Harvard University Press, Belknap Press, 1978.

Kessler, Charles, ed. *The Diaries of Count Harry Kessler*. New York: Grove Press, 2002.

Kirkby, Joan. "'We Thought Darwin Had Thrown the Redeemer Away': Evolutionary Theology in Emily Dickinson's New England." March 1999 Darwin Conference, University of Western Sydney. For the Darwin periodical references associated with this lecture, see http://www.ccs.mq.edu.au/dickinson/publications.html.

———. "'Why the Thief Ingredient accompanies all Sweetness Darwin does not tell us': Emily Dickinson and 19th Century Evolutionary Theologians Asa Gray and Minot Savage." Word and Image Conference. Wesleyan Institute. Sydney, 2003.

Krauthammer, Charles. "Phony Theory, Phony Conflict." *Washington Post* (November 16, 2005): A23.

Kreeft, Peter. *Making Sense Out of Suffering*. Ann Arbor: Servant Books, 1986.

Kristof, Nicholas. "Torture by Worms." *New York Times,* February 18, 2007.

Kurtz, Paul, ed. *Science and Religion: Are They Compatible?* Amherst, N.Y.: Prometheus Books, 2003.

Larson, Edward J., and Larry Witham. "Leading Scientists Still Reject God." *Nature* 394 (1998): 313.

Leyda, Jay. *The Years and Hours of Emily Dickinson.* 2 vols. New Haven: Yale University Press, 1960.

Lilla, Mark. *The Stillborn God: Religion, Politics, and the Modern West.* New York: Knopf, 2007.

Lubbers, Klaus. *Emily Dickinson: The Critical Revolution.* Ann Arbor: University of Michigan Press, 1968.

Lundin, Roger. *Emily Dickinson and the Art of Belief.* 2nd ed. Eerdmans Publishing, 2004.

———. *From Nature to Experience: The American Search for Cultural Authority.* Rowman and Littlefield, 2006.

Mackie. J. L. *The Miracle of Theism: Arguments for and against the Existence of God.* Oxford: Oxford University Press, 1982.

MacLeish, Archibald. "The Private World." In *Emily Dickinson: Three Views,* 13–25. Amherst: Amherst College Press, 1960.

Martin, Wendy. *The Cambridge Introduction to Emily Dickinson.* Cambridge: Cambridge University Press, 2007.

———, ed. *The Cambridge Companion to Emily Dickinson.* Cambridge: Cambridge University Press, 2002.

McIntosh, James. *Nimble Believing: Dickinson and the Unknown.* Ann Arbor: University of Michigan Press, 2004.

Mill, John Stuart. *The Collected Works of John Stuart Mill.* 33 vols. Edited by John M. Robson. Toronto: University of Toronto Press; London: Routledge and Kegan Paul, 1963–1991.

Miller, Perry. *The New England Mind: The Seventeenth Century.* New York: Macmillan, 1939.

Milosz, Czeslaw. *The Land of Ulro.* New York: Farrar, Straus, Giroux, 1984.

Milton, John. "Lycidas." In *The Portable Milton,* ed. Douglas Bush, 107–13. New York: Viking Press, 1949.

———. *Paradise Lost.* Edited by Alastair Fowler. London: Longman, 1968.

Mitchell, Domhnall. "A Little Taste, Time, and Means: Dickinson and Flowers." In *Emily Dickinson: Monarch of Perception,* 112–53. Amherst: University of Massachusetts Press, 2000.

Moltmann, Jürgen. *The Crucified God: The Cross of Christ as the Foundation and Criticism of Christian Theology.* 1974. Reprint, London: Fortress Press, 1993.

Morse, Jonathan. "Bibliographical Essay." In Vivian R. Pollak, ed., *A Historical Guide to Emily Dickinson,* 255–83. Oxford: Oxford University Press, 2004.

Newton, Isaac. *Philosophiae Naturalis: Principia Mathematica.* Edited by Alexandre Koyré and I. Bernard Cohen. Cambridge: Harvard University Press, 1972.

Nietzsche, Friedrich. *The Antichrist.* In *The Portable Nietzsche,* ed. and trans. Walter Kaufmann, 565–660. New York: Viking Press, 1968.

———. *Daybreak.* Translated by R. J. Hollingdale. Cambridge: Cambridge University Press, 1982.

———. *Friedrich Nietzsche: Werke in drei Bänden.* 3 vols. Edited by Karl Schlecta. Munich: Carl Hanser Verlag, 1954–1956.

———. Letter to his sister. In *The Portable Nietzsche,* ed. and trans. Walter Kaufmann, 29–30. New York: Viking Press, 1968.

———. *On the Genealogy of Morals.* In *Basic Writings of Nietzsche,* ed. and trans. Walter Kaufmann, 439–599. New York: Modern Library, 1968.

———. *The Will to Power.* Translated by Walter Kaufmann and R. J. Hollingdale. New York: Random House, 1967.

Oberhaus, Dorothy Huff. *Emily Dickinson's Fascicles: Method and Meaning.* University Park: Pennsylvania State University Press, 1995.

———. "'Tender Pioneer': Emily Dickinson's Poems on the Life of Christ." In Judith Farr, *The Gardens of Emily Dickinson,* 105–18. Cambridge: Harvard University Press, 2004.

Onfray, Michel. *Atheist Manifesto: The Case against Christianity, Judaism, and Islam.* New York: Arcade, 2007.

Pace, Joel. Romantic Praxis Circle Series. http://www.rc.umd.edu/praxis/.

Pascal, Blaise. *Pensées.* Edited and translated by Roger Ariew. Indianapolis and Cambridge: Hackett Publishing, 2005.

Pater, Walter. "Wordsworth." 1873. Reprinted in his *Appreciations,* 37–63. New York: Macmillan, 1906.

Plato. *Plato's Cosmology; The Timaeus of Plato.* Translated with commentary by Francis McDonald. New York: Harcourt, Brace, 1937

Polkinghorne, John. *Quantum Physics and Theology: An Unexpected Kinship.* New Haven: Yale University Press, 2007.

———. *Science and Providence: God's Interaction with the World.* Boston: Shambhala, 1989.

Pollak, Vivian R. *Dickinson: The Anxiety of Genre.* Ithaca: Cornell University Press, 1984.

———, ed. *A Historical Guide to Emily Dickinson.* Oxford: Oxford University Press, 2004.

Popkin, Richard H. *The History of Skepticism from Erasmus to Spinoza.* Berkeley: University of California Press, 1979.

Price, Reynolds. *Letter to a Man in the Fire.* New York: Scribner, 1999.

Rizzo, Patricia Thompson. "The Elegiac Modes of Emily Dickinson." *Emily Dickinson Journal* 11 (2002): 104–16.

Robinson, Richard. *An Atheist's Values.* 1964. Reprint, Oxford: Basil Blackford, 1975.

Roughgarden, Joan. *Evolution and Christian Faith.* Washington, D.C.: Island Press, 2006.

Ruse, Michael. *Can a Darwinian Be a Christian? The Relationship between Science and Religion.* Cambridge: Cambridge University Press, 2001.

———. *Darwin and Design: Does Evolution Have a Purpose?* Cambridge: Harvard University Press, 2003.

Schönborn, Christoph, Cardinal. *Chance or Purpose: Creation, Evolution, and a Rational Faith.* San Francisco: Ignatius Press, 2007.

———. "Finding Design in Nature." *New York Times,* July 7, 2005.

———. "Reasonable Science, Reasonable Faith." 2006. Reprinted in *First Things: A Journal of Religion, Culture, and Public Life,* April 2007, pp. 21–26.

Schopenhauer, Arthur. *The World As Will and Representation.* 1819. 2 vols. Translated by E. F. G. Payne. New York: Dover, 1969.

Shelley, Percy Bysshe. *Shelley's Poetry and Prose.* Edited by Donald H. Reiman and Sharon B. Powers. New York: Norton, 1977.

Smolin, Lee. "The Other Einstein." *New York Review of Books,* June 14, 2007, pp. 76–83.

Spencer, Herbert. *Principles of Biology.* London, 1864–1867.

Spicer, Jack. *The House That Jack Built*. Edited by Peter Gizzo. Middleton, Conn.: Wesleyan University Press, 1998.

Spinoza, Baruch. *The Ethics of Spinoza*. Translated by R. H. M. Elwes. 1883. Reprint, New York: Dover, 1951.

———. *A Theologico-Political Treatise*. Translated by R. H. M. Elwes. 1883. Reprint, New York: Dover, 1951.

Steinfels, Peter. "Beliefs; A Catholic Professor on Evolution and Theology: To Understand One, It Helps to Understand the Other." *New York Times*, August 20, 2005.

Stenger, Victor J. *God: The Failed Hypothesis*. Amherst, N.Y.: Prometheus Books, 2007.

Stevens, Wallace. *Collected Poems*. New York: Knopf, 1965.

Tate, Allen. *The Man of Letters in the Modern World: Selected Essays, 1928–1955*. Cleveland: Meridian, 1955.

Taylor, Charles. *A Secular Age*. Cambridge: Belknap Press of Harvard University Press, 2007.

Teresa, Mother [Agnes Bojaxhiu]. *Mother Teresa: Come Be My Light*. Edited by Rev. Brian Kolodiejchuk. New York: Doubleday, 2007.

Thomas Aquinas, Saint. *Summa Theologica*. 3 vols. New York: Benziger Brothers, 1947–1948.

Waggoner, Hyatt. *American Poets from the Puritans to the Present*. New York: Delta, 1968.

Weinberg, Steven. Address to the Conference on Cosmic Design of the American Association for the Advancement of Science. 1999. Reprinted in *Science and Religion: Are They Compatible?* ed. Paul Kurtz, 31–40. Amherst, N.Y.: Prometheus Books, 2003.

———. *The First Three Minutes: A Modern View of the Origin of the Universe*. Rev. ed. New York: Basic Books, 1993.

Weisbuch, Robert. *Emily Dickinson's Poetry*. Chicago: University of Chicago Press, 1975.

Wells, Henry W. *Introduction to Emily Dickinson*. Chicago: Packard and Co., 1947.

White, Fred. D. "Emily Dickinson's Existential Dramas." In *The Cambridge Companion to Emily Dickinson*, ed. Wendy Martin, 91–106. Cambridge: Cambridge University Press, 2002.

Wolff, Cynthia Griffin. *Emily Dickinson*. New York: Knopf, 1986.

Wolosky, Shira. "Emily Dickinson: Being in the Body." In *The Cambridge Companion to Emily Dickinson,* ed. Wendy Martin, 129–41. Cambridge: Cambridge University Press, 2002.

———. *Emily Dickinson: The Voice of War.* New Haven: Yale University Press, 1979.

———. "Public and Private in Dickinson's War Poetry." In *A Historical Guide to Emily Dickinson,* ed. Vivian R. Pollak, 103–31. Oxford: Oxford University Press, 2004.

Woolf, Virginia. *Mrs. Dalloway.* 1925. Reprint, London: Wordsworth Classics, 1996.

Wordsworth, William. *The Poems.* Edited by John O. Hayden. 2 vols. New Haven: Yale University Press, 1981.

———. *The Prelude, 1799, 1805, 1850.* Edited by Jonathan Wordsworth, M. H. Abrams, and Stephen Gill. New York: Norton, 1979.

Yeats, William Butler. *W. B. Yeats: The Poems.* Edited by Richard J. Finneran. New York: Macmillan, 1983.

Zapedowska, Magdalena. "Wrestling with Silence: Emily Dickinson's Calvinist God." *American Transcendental Quarterly* (March 1, 2006): 379–98.

Index of First Lines

Numbers in parentheses designate Johnson's enumeration followed by Franklin's.

General Index

Abrams, M. H., on Wordsworth's influence, 4

Afghanistan, war in, 18–19

Afterlife: death as doorway to eternity, 169–71; in Dickinson's nimble beliefs, 201; Dickinson's skepticism about, 150–51, 155; humans' worthiness or unworthiness for resurrection and, 155–57; Keats on, 145–46; as mystery, 169, 171, 173; as subject of Dickinson's poetry, 40, 99; Wordsworth's faith in, 189. *See also* Heaven; Hell; Immortality

Al-Qaeda, 19

Amherst College, Calvinism and science at, 13–14

Anaxagoras, and Intelligent Design argument, 77

Anaximander, and Intelligent Design argument, 77

Anderson, Charles R., 207; on "Apparently with no surprise," 130–31, 152–53, 166; on "Further in Summer than the Birds," 154–55; on importance of perspective in "Apparently with no surprise," 125–26

"Apparently with no surprise": alliteration in, 125, 139; Anderson on, 125–26, 130–31, 152–53, 166; composition of, 40, 108, 167–68; depiction of God in, 91, 110, 174–75, 209–10; Dickinson's purpose in writing, 32, 141–43, 166, 209–10;

effects of readers' religious beliefs on responses to, 33–36, 205, 207; Frost in, 132–34, 138–39; God and Nature in, 27–28, 43, 91; iambic regularity of supposedly reflecting orderliness of universe, 177–78; importance of perspective in, 122, 124–26, 128; influences on responses to, 33, 113, 141–42, 209–10; McIntosh on, 211–12; as "mini-epic," 31–32; as pastoral elegy, 31–32; polarization over theology and science in responses to, 15, 17; range of responses to, 1, 10, 34–35, 62–63, 107, 179, 209; sexuality and gender in interpretations of, 108, 135; suffering in, 28; Sun in, 31, 132–34, 138–39; text of, 25; use of *unmoved* in, 139–40; violence in, 115–16; Wolff on, 129

Appleman, Philip, editor of Norton *Darwin*, 63n6

Aquinas, Thomas. *See* Thomas Aquinas, Saint

Arguments from Design. *See* Intelligent Design

Aristotle, and Intelligent Design argument, 77, 83

Arnold, Matthew, 157; "Dover Beach" by, 175–76; *Essays in Criticism* by, 187; "Memorial Verses" by, 186n9; on Wordsworth's didacticism in *The Excursion*, 186–87, 190

Atheism: criticism of personal God in, 59–60; Einstein and, 49, 60; Eternal

evolution with, 78–79; evolution *vs.*, 59; God in Arguments from Design, 25, 37–38; history of argument, 77; perfection *vs.* imperfection in, 72; Schönborn on, 56–57, 81

Intimations Ode ("Ode: Intimations of Immortality from Recollections of Early Childhood"). *See* Wordsworth: Intimations Ode

Iran, 19

Iraq, war in, 18–19

Ireland: Civil War in, 217–18, 221; Troubles in, 217, 221

Isaacson, Walter, *Einstein: His Life and Universe* by, 42

Islam: God of, 35–36; in wars in Afghanistan and Iraq, 18–19

Jackson, Helen Hunt, 199

James, William, on compatibility of science and religion, 55

Jarrell, Randall, 101n11

Jesus: abandoned by God, 195; atoning for our sins, 102–3; conquering death, 102–3; crucifixion and resurrection of, 73–74, 92, 95–98, 101, 200; crucifixion and resurrection of, as resolution of suffering, 35, 87, 90; Dickinson on, 91–93; Dickinson's empathy for, 91, 101, 181–82; Dickinson's relationship with, 2, 194; divinity *vs.* humanity of, 93; evil conquered by, 71; love as message of, 99; resurrection of, 92, 97–98, 149–50; as self-revelation of God, 89; suffering of, 91, 95, 161; Words-worth less interested in than Dickinson, 189

Job, Book of: frost in, 2, 3, 89, 109, 111, 141, 156, 198; God's frigidity in, 129; justice in, 28–29; suffering in, 28–30

John, gospel of, 11, 28, 89

John Paul II, Pope, acceptance of evolution, 63–64, 67–68

Johnson, Phillip, 11

Johnson, Thomas H., 27, 74

John Templeton Foundation, survey on purpose of universe by, 7

Jones, John E., III, 6

Justice, 27–28; in Book of Job, 28–29; death lacking, 212; social, 184–85

Kant, Immanuel: *The Critique of Practical Reason* by, 11; *The Critique of Pure Reason* by, 10–11, 53n20; *Failure of All Philosophic Attempts at Theodicy* by, 21n19; Moral Argument of, 82–83; on proof for existence of God, 82; on purposiveness without purpose, 140; separating faith and reason, 10–11, 50–51, 55–56; on things corresponding to thoughts, 125

Kashmir, religion in struggle over, 19n18

Keats, John: on crucifixion and resurrection, 103; Dickinson and, 3, 74, 162n4; "A Disused Shed in Co. Wexford" compared to, 220; *The Fall of Hyperion* by, 206; on life as a "vale of Soul-making," 103; "Ode to Melancholy" by, 115; "Ode to Psyche" by, 115; on opening to love, 115; on Paradise, 145–46; "To Autumn" by, 154

Kempis, Thomas à, *Imitation of Christ* by, 94

Khayyám, Omar, *Rubáiyát* of, 157–58

Kirkby, Joan, on Dickinson and Darwin, 14n13, 65

Kitzmuller v. Dover, 6–7

Krauthammer, Charles, on evolution and religion, 12–13

Kristof, Nicholas, "Torture by Worms" by, 62, 86–87

Leibniz, G. W., on "theodicy," 1, 72

Lemaître, Georges-Henri, proposer of Big Bang Theory, 55

Life affirming: in Dickinson poems, 115–16; Nietzsche on, 92n2, 205–6

Lifton, Robert Jay, 18n17

Lilla, Mark, on Great Separation, 8–9

Lord, Otis Phillips: death of, 167; Dickinson's correspondence with, 14, 38, 67, 179

Love: Dickinson and, 98–100, 167–68; God's, 97–99, 189, 192

Lundin, Roger: on Dickinsonian religious beliefs, 181; on